Build Windows 8 Apps with Microsoft Visual C++ Step by Step

Luca Regnicoli
Paolo Pialorsi
Roberto Brunetti

Published with the authorization of Microsoft Corporation by:
O'Reilly Media, Inc.
1005 Gravenstein Highway North
Sebastopol, California 95472

ISBN: 978-0-7356-6723-5

1 2 3 4 5 6 7 8 9 LSI 8 7 6 5 4 3

Printed and bound in the United States of America.

Microsoft Press books are available through booksellers and distributors worldwide. If you need support related to this book, email Microsoft Press Book Support at *mspinput@microsoft.com*. Please tell us what you think of this book at *http://www.microsoft.com/learning/booksurvey*.

Microsoft and the trademarks listed at *http://www.microsoft.com/about/legal/en/us/IntellectualProperty/ Trademarks/EN-US.aspx* are trademarks of the Microsoft group of companies. All other marks are property of their respective owners.

The example companies, organizations, products, domain names, email addresses, logos, people, places, and events depicted herein are fictitious. No association with any real company, organization, product, domain name, email address, logo, person, place, or event is intended or should be inferred.

This book expresses the author's views and opinions. The information contained in this book is provided without any express, statutory, or implied warranties. Neither the authors, O'Reilly Media, Inc., Microsoft Corporation, nor its resellers, or distributors will be held liable for any damages caused or alleged to be caused either directly or indirectly by this book.

Acquisitions and Developmental Editor: Russell Jones

Production Editor: Christopher Hearse

Editorial Production: Zyg Group, LLC

Technical Reviewer: John Mueller

Copyeditor: Zyg Group, LLC

Indexer: Zyg Group, LLC

Cover Design: Twist Creative • Seattle

Cover Composition: Zyg Group, LLC

Illustrator: Rebecca Demarest

This book is dedicated to Barbara.

—ROBERTO BRUNETTI

This book is dedicated to my parents. Thanks!

—PAOLO PIALORSI

This book is dedicated to my mother, Vanna, the strongest woman I have ever known.

—LUCA REGNICOLI

Contents at a Glance

Contents

Chapter 3   My first Windows 8 app   65

Chapter 4   Application life-cycle management   103

Chapter 5   Introduction to the Windows Runtime   139

Introduction

Windows 8 is Microsoft's newest operating system, intended to let developers fluent in various programming languages—such as C++, C#, or JavaScript—leverage its powerful infrastructure to build applications using a brand-new library called the Windows Runtime API.

This book provides an organized walk-through of the features, APIs, and user experience in Windows 8. The content is *introductory*—it discusses each component from a theoretical viewpoint interspersed with basic but effective code samples, which you can follow to get a jump-start in developing for the Windows 8 platform.

The book provides coverage of almost all the main Windows 8 aspects and features, and it offers essential guidance in learning them using the classic Step by Step approach.

In addition to its coverage of core Windows 8 features using C++, the book discusses some related aspects, such as Windows Communication Foundation (WCF) Data Services, Open Data Protocol (OData), ADO.NET Entity Framework, and applications architecture. Beyond the explanatory content, each chapter includes a rich set of step-by-step examples, as well as downloadable sample projects that you can explore for yourself.

Who should read this book

This goal of this book is to provide experienced C++ developers with the information they need to begin working with the main components of the Windows 8 operating system and the Windows Runtime. Starting with the Windows Runtime APIs, the book moves readers through a comprehensive discussion of the new user experience, including how to design interfaces that work for the keyboard, the mouse, and touch screens. This book does not teach C++; readers need a solid knowledge of the C++ language to fully understand the code presented in the book and to follow along by performing the exercises using Microsoft Visual Studio 2012. This book is also useful for software architects conversant with C++ who need an overview of the components they would plan to include in the overall architecture of a real-world Windows 8 solution.

Who should not read this book

If you have worked with Windows 8 already, this book is probably not for you. It is an introductory guide to developing applications that leverage the platform using C++.

Assumptions

To get the most out of this book, you should have at least a minimal understanding of C++ development and object-oriented programming concepts. Although you can also develop for Windows 8 using any .NET language or JavaScript, this book includes examples in C++ only.

In addition to the C++ language, the examples in Chapter 10, "Architecting a Windows 8 app," assume you have a basic understanding of ASP.NET and WCF, although the code presented for those examples doesn't use any advanced features of either technology.

Organization of this book

This book is divided into 10 chapters, each of which focuses on a different aspect or technology within the Windows 8 operating system and Windows Runtime APIs.

Finding your best starting point in this book

We suggest that you start reading the book from the beginning. By following this path, you will discover all of the aspects of the new look and feel, the new user experience, and the new user interface for touch-based devices required for building successful Windows 8 applications. Chapter 2, "Windows 8 user interface style," is particularly important, because you need to understand the design concepts underlying the Windows 8 UI style. Chapter 3, "My first Windows 8 app," is the fundamental starting point for building your first Windows 8 application. Use the following table to determine how best to proceed through the book.

If you are	Follow these steps
New to Windows 8 development	Start with Chapter 1.
New to Windows 8 UI style	Start with Chapter 2.
Not new to Windows 8 development using the provided templates	Start with Chapter 4.

A XAML developer	Start with Chapter 3 and then skip to Chapter 9 to gain a solid understanding of the controls specific to Windows 8 apps and how to design flexible layouts.

Most of the book's chapters include hands-on procedures and examples that let you try out the concepts discussed in each chapter. No matter which sections you choose to focus on, be sure to download the companion code from the publisher's site (see the "Code samples" section of this introduction), and install them on your system.

Conventions and features in this book

This book presents information using conventions designed to make the information readable and easy to follow.

- Each exercise consists of a series of tasks, presented as numbered steps (1, 2, and so on) listing each action you must take to complete the exercise.

- Boxed elements with labels such as "Note" provide additional information or alternative methods for completing a step successfully.

- Text that you type (apart from code blocks) appears in bold.

- A plus sign (+) between two key names means that you must press those keys at the same time. For example, "Press Alt+Tab" means that you hold down the Alt key while you press the Tab key.

- A vertical bar between two or more menu items (for example, File | Close), means that you should select the first menu or menu item, then the next, and so on.

System Requirements

You will need the following hardware and software to complete the practice exercises in this book:

- Windows 8 installed

- Visual Studio 2012, any edition tailored for Windows 8 (the Express edition for Windows 8 is free)

- Computer with a 1.6 GHz or faster processor

- 1 GB of RAM (1.5 GB if running on a virtual machine)

- 10 GB (NTFS) of available hard disk space

- 5400 RPM (or faster) hard disk drive

- DirectX 9-capable video card running at 1024 × 768 or higher display resolution

Depending on your Windows configuration, you might require Local Administrator rights to install or configure Visual Studio 2012.

Code samples

Most of the chapters in this book include exercises that let you interactively try out new material learned in the main text. All sample projects are available for download from the book's page on the website for Microsoft's publishing partner, O'Reilly Media:

http://aka.ms/BuildW8AppsVCSbS/files

Click the Download the Companion Content link and save the Windows8cplusplusStepbyStep.zip file.

> **Note** In addition to the code samples, your system must have Microsoft Visual Studio 2012 installed.

Installing the code samples

Follow these steps to install the code samples on your computer so that you can use them with the exercises in this book.

1. Unzip the Windows8cplusplus.zip file that you downloaded from the book's website (name a specific directory along with directions to create it, if necessary).

2. If prompted, review the displayed end user license agreement. If you accept the terms, select the accept option, and then click Next.

> **Note** If the license agreement doesn't appear, you can access it from the same webpage from which you downloaded the Windows8cplusplusStepByStep.zip file.

Acknowledgments

We'd like to thank all the people who supported us in writing this book.

Marco Russo has been involved with all of us in the most important phases of writing this book and its twin, *Build Windows 8 Apps with Microsoft Visual C# and Visual Basic Step by Step* (Microsoft Press, 2013).

Vanni Boncinelli tested all the code we wrote.

Errata & book support

We've made every effort to ensure the accuracy of this book and its companion content. Any errors that have been reported since this book was published are listed on our Microsoft Press site at oreilly.com:

http://aka.ms/BuildW8AppsVCSbS/errata

If you find an error that is not already listed, you can report it to us through the same page. If you need additional support, email Microsoft Press Book Support at *mspinput@microsoft.com*.

Please note that product support for Microsoft software is not offered through the addresses above.

We want to hear from you

At Microsoft Press, your satisfaction is our top priority, and your feedback our most valuable asset. Please tell us what you think of this book at:

http://www.microsoft.com/learning/booksurvey

The survey is short, and we read every one of your comments and ideas. Thanks in advance for your input!

Stay in touch

Let's keep the conversation going! We're on Twitter: *http://twitter.com/MicrosoftPress*

CHAPTER 1

Introduction to Windows Store apps

After completing this chapter, you will be able to

- Understand the main features of a Windows Store App.

- Evaluate the key benefits of creating a Windows Store app for Windows 8.

- Recognize the main capabilities and features of the new Windows 8 operating system.

This chapter provides an overall introduction to Microsoft Windows 8 and to the new world of Microsoft Windows Store apps, from a developer's perspective.

The Windows 8 experience

Windows 8 is one of the most innovative and revolutionary investments made by Microsoft in the last decade in the operating systems area. Prior to Windows 8, the operating systems market consisted of three main families: server operating systems, client/desktop operating systems, and mobile/tablet-oriented operating systems.

Windows 8, together with its sibling Microsoft Windows Server 2012, introduces a new paradigm wherein the client/desktop and mobile/tablet-oriented operating systems can be combined, sharing features, capabilities, user interfaces (UIs), and behaviors. In the last few years, the market for tablet devices has exploded, with an increasing number of people working at home and in their offices on a small tablet device. Nevertheless, until the release of Windows 8, it wasn't a simple matter to reconcile the needs of end users using tablet devices with the infrastructural constraints of corporate networks. For example, many tablet end users would like to install software from a trusted and secure online marketplace, regardless the corporate policies of the individual end user's company. Moreover, a common end-user need is to check corporate email accounts as well as any private email accounts using a unique device and unique email client software. Furthermore, the increase in social-media use leads to the sharing of private contacts, agendas, tasks, pictures, and instant messages with business contacts, meetings, and corporate network instant communication and videoconferencing.

However, technology without governance could become a nightmare both for end users and IT professionals. With Windows 8, end users can leverage a corporate-provided tablet device and install software from a safe and secure marketplace (either public or corporate constrained), check multiple email accounts while complying with company security policies, and socialize with friends, colleagues, and business contacts, all within a safe and sandboxed environment.

Moreover, for the sake of backward compatibility, all the software created targeting Windows 7 desktops will still continue to work on Windows 8, using the old-style desktop-oriented approach.

So, let's see the new Windows 8 user interface and the key features of this new operating system. Figure 1-1 shows the new Start screen, one of the revolutionary features introduced with Windows 8.

FIGURE 1-1 The Windows 8 Start screen.

The new Start screen is made up of a set of squares and rectangles called *tiles*, each of which represents a link to a software application. Each tile can also provide an animated feedback to the end user. Tiles can be small (square) or wide (rectangle). Many apps provide both sizes, letting end users choose between them in the main screen according to personal preference. For example, in the top-left corner of Figure 1-1, just under the Main title, you can see a wide tile for the Mail app, which indicates that there are 15 email messages to read in the inbox. The tile also provides a short preview of the messages.

To reduce the size of the tile, you can right-click it or swipe your finger downward on the tile, which both selects it and activates a command bar, called the app bar, which will be discussed later. Figure 1-2 shows the Mail app tile selected.

FIGURE 1-2 The app bar of the Start screen.

The app bar may contain many active commands, which vary according to context. For example, with a tile selected, you can select the Smaller command to change the tile from wide to square, if the tile you selected is wide. You can also turn off dynamic updating of the tile by selecting Turn Live Tile Off. Or you can select Uninstall to remove the app from your device completely. If you select the Smaller command, the tile will become square and the preview of the unread email will disappear. You can see the result in Figure 1-3.

FIGURE 1-3 The small tile of the Mail app.

A user with a tablet device can tap (i.e., touch using a single finger) one of these tiles to start an application instance or to resume an already running instance. Similarly, a user with a desktop PC and a mouse can click the tile and get the same result. The Start screen is based on the idea of the "panoramic view" that has been available in Windows Phone since version 7. In a panoramic view, you can scroll horizontally, using either touch gestures on a tablet/touch screen or the mouse wheel, touchpad, or keyboard if you are using a laptop or desktop. You can also use the traditional scrollbar that appears at the bottom of the screen.

As soon as you tap an app tile, the foreground application becomes the app you selected. When you are starting that app for the first time in a given Windows 8 session, Windows creates the instance and loads it into memory. Otherwise, if the app is already running, Windows promotes it to the foreground application. In both cases, whatever application was previously in the foreground is sent into the background, where it may be *suspended* by the operating system. Suspension means freezing: the app gets no CPU threads and no I/O capability, leaving all the computer resources free to support the main (foreground) application. If the user later returns to a suspended application, the operating system resumes it in its previous state. Later in Chapter 4, "Application life-cycle management," you will learn more about the application life cycle for Windows Store apps. Figure 1-4 shows the Windows Store app Bing Weather running in the foreground.

FIGURE 1-4 The Bing Weather app running in the foreground.

In Figure 1-4, the app takes up the entire screen, which satisfies one of the main ideas of the user experience design for Windows Store apps: "content, not chrome." Chapter 2, "Windows 8 user interface style," will help you more fully understand the meaning of that phrase.

There are some exceptions; not all applications are Windows Store apps. For example, if you launch an old-style desktop application, Windows switches to the classic Windows Desktop, just as if you were in a previous version of Windows. Figure 1-5 shows an older desktop-style application, Microsoft SQL Server Management Studio. Note the absence of the classic Start button.

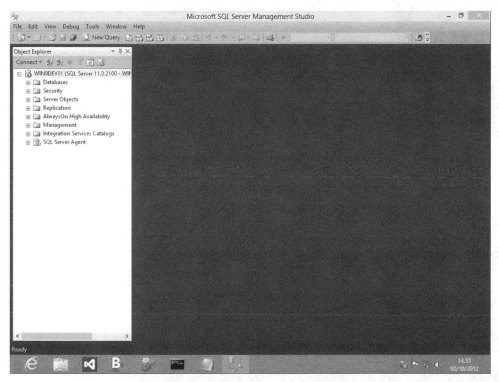

FIGURE 1-5 A standard desktop application in Windows 8.

You aren't limited to one application at a time open. If you have a device with a wide (16:9 or 16:10) screen aspect ratio, you can snap two applications onto the screen at the same time. For example, Figure 1-6 shows the Bing Weather app snapped on the left, with the new Internet Explorer 10 for Windows 8 on the right.

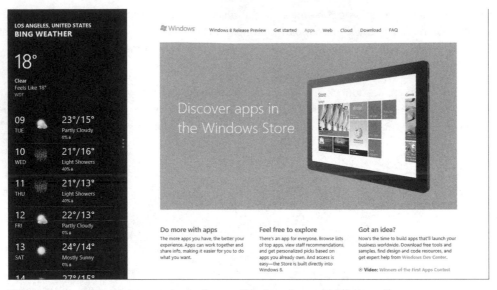

FIGURE 1-6 A couple of apps running in the new Windows 8 snapped view mode.

Of course, you can also switch the sizes of the two snapped apps, as shown in Figure 1-7.

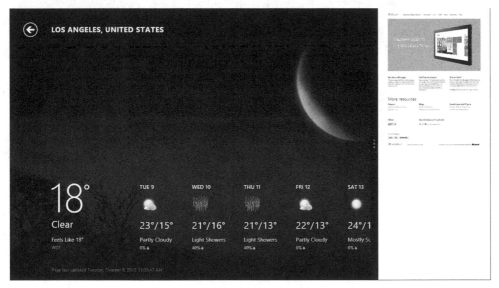

FIGURE 1-7 Another configuration of the new snapped view mode of Windows 8.

From a developer's perspective, the most important thing to understand at this point is that every Windows Store app must support snapping to be certified by the Windows Store. Bing Weather, as you saw in previous figures, supports the snapped view by adapting the layout of the page to present the information in a smaller horizontal portion of the screen. If you create an app that cannot present information in this manner, you must fill the snapped view with a clear message for the user—you would never use the full-screen view for a snapped view because the user would not be able to interact properly with the application.

In fact, whenever you want to publish a Windows Store app, you have to submit it to the Windows Store (or eventually to a corporate Enterprise Store) for approval. From the public, official Windows Store point of view, an app must adhere to a clear set of requirements before it will be certified. Any application that does not adhere to these requirements will be rejected. You can find complete details about the requirements on the official page available on the Windows 8 developer section of Microsoft Developer Network (MSDN): *http://msdn.microsoft.com/library/windows/apps/hh694083.aspx*. For example, one rule states that if your app connects to the Internet for any purpose, you must provide a privacy information page. Thus, if your app invokes a remote web service, which is a common situation, you must provide a privacy page that explains how you manage users' data. Chapter 4 discusses the process of submitting an app to the Windows Store in more detail.

Going back to the Start screen, another useful bit of information is that you can arrange tiles in groups, which helps organize them on the Start screen. To move a tile from one group to another, you simply need to drag and drop it, using either touch gestures or the mouse. To create a new group, you move a tile into the middle region between two existing groups. When you do that, a gray bar appears, representing the frame of the new group. Dropping the tile onto this gray bar creates a new group.

If you zoom out the Start screen, by using a "pinch" gesture (explained in Chapter 2) or by scrolling the mouse wheel backward while pressing Ctrl, the Start screen changes. You can assign a name to a group by clicking it or swiping your finger down on the group to select it and then clicking the Name Group button in the bottom app bar. Figure 1-8 shows the Start screen while zoomed out, with a group of tiles selected and the bottom app bar showing the available commands.

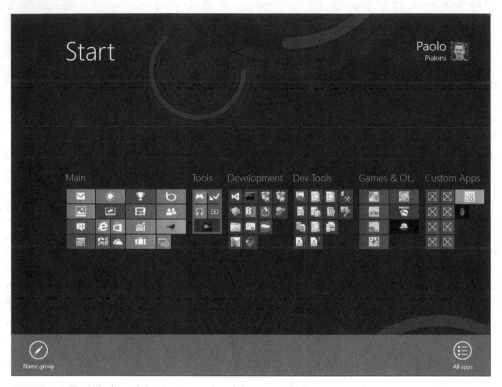

FIGURE 1-8 The Windows 8 Start screen when it is zoomed out.

Charms bar and app bars

Other new and key features of Windows 8 are the app bars and the charms bar. Chapter 2 discusses these in more detail as well as the philosophy behind them. For now, simply consider that these changes arose from the need to support new devices such as tablets and smartphones, where users interact primarily with their hands, through touch. This new touch-oriented perspective necessarily introduced new tools and solutions. Using the bottom app bar, you can manage tasks and actions related to the current context or item. You can see an example in Figure 1-9, where Internet Explorer 10 for Windows 8 displays the bottom app bar so the user can edit the current URL, refresh the page, pin the page on the new Start screen, or change the browser settings.

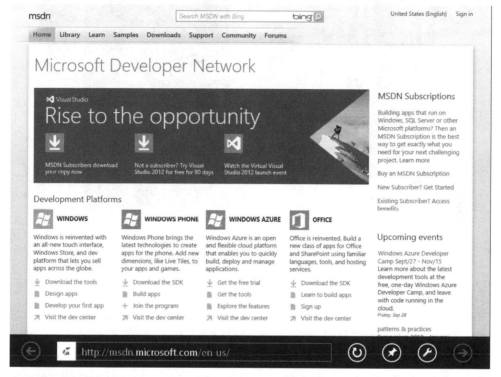

FIGURE 1-9 The new Internet Explorer 10 UI.

The top app bar provides navigation assistance to end users. For example, you might use it to show a top-level menu or a list of main sections available in the current app. Figure 1-10 shows the top app bar of the Windows Store app, which is the app you can use to search, download, buy, and install other apps.

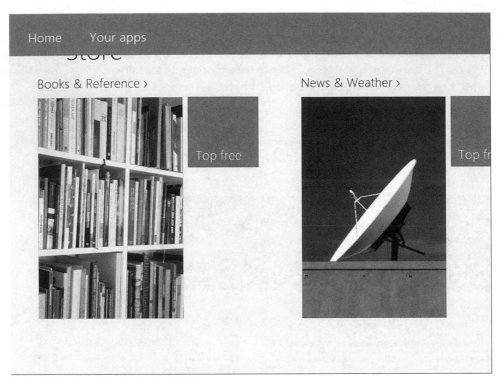

FIGURE 1-10 The top app bar of the Windows Store App.

To show the top and bottom app bars, swipe your finger from the top or bottom border of the screen toward the center of the screen. Alternatively, you can press Windows+Z or right-click the mouse.

Finally, the charms bar allows you to access useful features and actions provided by the operating system, regardless of where you are. For example, you can use the charms bar to access system settings, the local search engine, Sharing features, and so on. Figure 1-11 shows the charms bar in action.

FIGURE 1-11 The Windows 8 charms bar.

To show the charms bar, swipe your finger from the right border of the screen toward the center of the screen. Alternatively, you can press Windows+C on the keyboard. You can also move the mouse pointer to the lower- or upper-right corner of the screen. Finally, you can activate specific charms bar commands directly using keyboard shortcuts. For example, pressing Windows+Q activates a search for installed applications (*Q* = query), while pressing Windows+F (*F* = find files) activates a search for files. To activate the sharing feature, press Windows+H.

Through the charms bar, you can activate specific panels such as the Settings panel, which you can also activate by pressing Windows+I. Figure 1-12 shows the Settings panel in action.

FIGURE 1-12 A flyout configuration panel for managing the settings from the charms bar.

One key feature of the charms bar is that you can also host custom commands and custom panels in it. For example, if you are developing a Windows Store app and you want to provide some custom settings for end users, you can add a command to the charms bar. By pressing the custom command while your app is in foreground, you can activate a flyout panel, which is a custom control that renders within the charms bar (see Figure 1-13).

FIGURE 1-13 Another example of a flyout panel for configuring settings of an app.

The charms bar illustrated in Figure 1-13 provides Support Request and Privacy Policy commands, which are custom commands specific to the app currently in foreground. The Privacy Policy command navigates to the privacy page required for any app that consumes a remote service over the Internet, as you learned earlier in this chapter.

Windows Runtime

A Windows Store app is a software solution that adheres to the UI and technical specifications of the Windows Store. You can create a Windows Store app using any language that supports the new Windows Runtime (WinRT). WinRT is a rich set of application programming interfaces (APIs) built upon the Windows 8 operating system that provides direct and easy access to all the main primitives, devices, and capabilities from any language with which you can develop Windows 8 apps. WinRT is available only to Windows 8 apps. Its main purpose is to unify the development experience of building a Windows 8 app, regardless of the programming language you use to program that app.

For now, saying that you can use "any language supporting the Windows Runtime" means that you can choose to use C++, .NET (C# or VB), or JavaScript. Nevertheless, there are no technical limitations restricting use of WinRT from any other language, as long as it adheres to WinRT specifications. Chapter 5, "Introduction to the Windows Runtime," explains more about this topic as well as the architecture of WinRT.

At this point, you can think of WinRT as an infrastructural framework of libraries that simplify developing Windows Store apps by hiding the inner details of the operating system from the common and everyday developer perspective. For example, you can ask WinRT to open the webcam standard user interface to capture photos or videos without having to know anything about the underlying driver or Win32 API.

Here's a more complete example. The following code excerpt shows how easy and simple it is to capture a picture from your PC's camera using the C++ language.

```cpp
void CaptureWin8::MainPage::TakePhoto_Click(Platform::Object^ sender,
        Windows::UI::Xaml::RoutedEventArgs^ e) {

    CameraCaptureUI^ dialog = ref new CameraCaptureUI();
    concurrency::task<StorageFile^> (
        dialog->CaptureFileAsync(CameraCaptureUIMode::Photo)).then([this] (
            StorageFile^ file) {
        if (nullptr != file) {
            concurrency::task<Streams::IRandomAccessStream^> (
            file->OpenAsync(FileAccessMode::Read)).then([this] (
                Streams::IRandomAccessStream^ stream) {
                    BitmapImage^ bitmapImage = ref new BitmapImage();
                    bitmapImage->SetSource(stream);
                    image->Source = bitmapImage;
            });
        }
    });
}
```

You could define the same action using JavaScript, as shown in the following code excerpt:

```javascript
var dialog = new Windows.Media.Capture.CameraCaptureUI();
dialog.captureFileAsync(Windows.Media.Capture.CameraCaptureUIMode.photo).done(
    function (file) {
    if (file) {
        var photoBlobUrl = URL.createObjectURL(file, { oneTimeOnly: true });
        document.getElementById("capturedPhoto").src = photoBlobUrl;
    }
};
```

Moreover, even using C# you can achieve the same result, as you can see in the following code excerpt:

```csharp
private async void TakePhoto_Click(object sender, RoutedEventArgs e) {

    var camera = new CameraCaptureUI();
    var img = await camera.CaptureFileAsync(CameraCaptureUIMode.Photo);
    if (img != null) {
        var stream = await img.OpenAsync(FileAccessMode.Read);
        var bitmap = new BitmapImage();
        bitmap.SetSource(stream);
        image.Source = bitmap;
    }
}
```

Badges, live tiles, toasts, and lock screen

Another group of new features in Windows Store apps are badges, live tiles, toasts, and the lock screen. Badges and live tiles support showing dynamic information to end users, even when those users may not be directly using your app but are browsing through the Start screen. You can use a badge and/or a live tile to provide information about news, new items to check, new tasks to execute, or whatever else is meaningful and appropriate so users get a better experience with your app from the Start screen without opening the application. For example, the out-of-the-box Mail app uses the badge to show the number of unread mails in the inbox and a live tile to show a rotating list containing excerpts from all the unread emails. Moreover, the Windows Store app uses a badge to notify users about the number of available updates for their installed apps. Figure 1-14 shows some badges and live tiles in action.

FIGURE 1-14 The Start screen with tiles showing badges and live tiles.

Notice the number 4 in the bottom-right corner of the Windows Store app—this is a badge indicating that there are four pending updates. You can also see the badge with number 15 in the bottom-right corner of the Mail app, notifying the user that there are 15 new emails in the inbox. Furthermore, the Mail app uses a live tile to show an excerpt of the most recent unread mails.

A live tile has even more functionality. For example, a live tile can completely change its content to remain dynamic and fresh, and pique the curiosity of the end user. Figure 1-15 shows four different states that can be assumed by the tile of a single app (the Bing Travel app, in this case).

FIGURE 1-15 Some sample layouts for a live tile.

Official guidelines for Windows Store apps (see *http://msdn.microsoft.com/library/windows/apps/ hh465403.aspx*) suggest using a wide tile only when you have live tiles to display. For apps that do not require a live tile, you should use the smaller square tiles. If you need to display only relatively static content for your tiles, you can simply use a badge to provide small and lightweight notifications. Chapter 9, "Rethinking the UI for Windows 8 apps," covers how to create a live tile.

Toasts are another technique for providing asynchronous alerts to an end user. For example, an alert/alarm application can ask the operating system to send to the user a toast at a predefined wake-up time. WinRT will send the toast even if the application that requested the toast is not active at that time.

Toasts are also important for notification purposes because when the user is working with an app in the foreground, background apps cannot interact with the user except through toasts. In fact, as you will learn in Chapter 4, due to the Windows 8 architecture and the application life-cycle management of Windows Store apps, only the foreground app has the focus and is running; all the other background apps can be suspended (or even terminated) by WinRT. A suspended app cannot execute or consume any CPU cycles. However, you can define a background task that will work in the background (more on this topic later in this chapter)—even in a separate process from the owner app—and you can define background actions. When these actions need to alert the user about their outcomes, they can use a toast.

A toast can be a simple text, or an image, or many combinations of the two. Figure 1-16 shows a toast in the upper-right corner of the screen provided by the Windows Store app, informing the user that an app installation task has completed in the background. Chapter 9 shows you how to create a toast for your own Windows 8 apps.

FIGURE 1-16 A toast rendered within a user session in Windows 8.

One last opportunity you have, while developing a Windows Store App, is to provide lightweight information to the end user through the lock screen. The lock screen is the screen that displays when a Windows 8 user session is locked out, which can occur after a period of inactivity or is displayed when the end user presses Windows+L to lock the session.

For example, in Figure 1-17, the lock screen provides some information about the current date and time, the next appointment in the user's agenda, and a set of small icons in the lower part of the screen. Those icons provide information about network connection status, battery status (for a device running on battery power), unread email in the inbox, and some other lightweight information.

FIGURE 1-17 The Windows 8 lock screen.

An end user can choose what to see on the lock screen by using the proper panel in the system configuration. However, users may not display more than seven lock screen items at once that provide such detailed information. All seven apps will be able to show badges and toasts on the Start screen, but only one of those apps will be allowed to show the text of its latest tile notification on the lock screen.

Figure 1-18 shows the configuration panel for the lock screen. To reach it, you need to show the charms bar by, for example, pressing Windows+C and then selecting the Settings command. Finally, click the Change PC Settings command. Under the Personalize section on the Lock Screen tab, you will find the lock screen configuration settings.

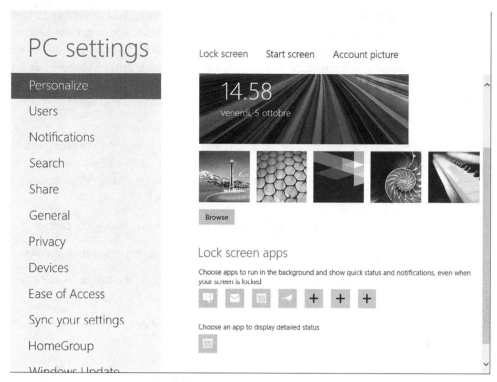

FIGURE 1-18 The PC settings for a Windows 8 system.

As you can see, the lock screen settings page enables users to choose the background image to display on the lock screen and to select which seven apps will execute in the background to provide information through the lock screen icons. Last but not least, users can select which app can display detailed text status. The last app, by default, is configured to be the Calendar app. To be available to function as a lock screen app, your software must declare that capability within an *app manifest file*, which will be explained later starting in Chapter 3, "My first Windows 8 app."

The information shown by a lock screen–enabled app is the same as the information that app shows on the Start screen. In fact, the text shown beside the small icon on the lock screen comes from the app's badge, while the detailed text status is taken from the app's tile text.

Background tasks

As stated earlier in this chapter—and as you will explore further in Chapter 4—a Windows Store app executes code only when it is in the foreground. However, there are situations where you want to be able to execute some code, even if your app is not the one currently in foreground, which nec-essarily means your app is in the background. To do that, you need to create a *background task*. A background task can execute code even when the corresponding app is suspended, but it runs in an environment that is both restricted and resource managed. Moreover, background tasks receive only a limited amount of system resources. Therefore, you should use background tasks only to execute small pieces of code that don't require any user interaction. For example, you should not use a background task to execute complex business logic or calculations, because the amount of system resources available to the background task is very tight and limited. In addition, complex background workloads consume battery power and CPU cycles, reducing the efficiency and responsiveness of the system.

To create a background task, you must define a class and register it with the operating system. A background task is just a class that implements a specific interface (*IBackgroundTask* in C#, for example) defined by WinRT. You register the task using a *BackgroundTaskBuilder* class instance. Many types of background tasks are available that respond to different kinds of triggers:

- **ControlChannelTrigger**   Raised when there are incoming messages on the control channel

- **MaintenanceTrigger**   Happens when it is time to execute system maintenance tasks

- **PushNotificationTrigger**   Raised when a notification arrives on the Windows Notifications Service channel

- **SystemEventTrigger**   Happens when a specific system event occurs

- **TimeTrigger**   Triggered when a time event occurs

In particular, a *SystemTrigger* can occur in response to any of the following system events:

- **InternetAvailable**   The Internet becomes available.

- **LockScreenApplicationAdded**   An app tile is added to the lock screen.

- **LockScreenApplicationRemoved**   An app tile is removed from the lock screen.

- **ControlChannelReset**   A network channel is reset.

- **NetworkStateChange**   A network change such as a change in cost or connectivity occurs.

- **OnlineIdConnectedStateChange**   The online ID associated with the account changes.

- **ServicingComplete**   The system has finished updating an application.

- **SessionConnected**   The session is connected.

- **SessionDisconnected**   The session is disconnected.

- **SmsReceived**   A new SMS message is received by an installed mobile broadband device.

- **TimeZoneChange**   The time zone changes on the device (for example, when the system adjusts the clock for daylight saving time).

- **UserAway**   The user becomes absent.

- **UserPresent**   The user becomes present.

Whenever such an event occurs, you can check a set of conditions to determine whether or not your background task should execute. The conditions you can check are as follows:

- **InternetAvailable**   The Internet must be available.

- **InternetNotAvailable**   The Internet must be unavailable.

- **SessionConnected**   The session must be connected.

- **SessionDisconnected**   The session must be disconnected.

- **UserNotPresent**   The user must be away.

- **UserPresent**   The user must be present.

To optimize resource consumption, some triggers fire only to apps in the lock screen. For example, a *TimeTrigger* can be leveraged only by an app in the lock screen. The same requirement is valid for *PushNotificationTrigger* and *ControlChannelTrigger*. Even some of the *SystemTrigger* events are reserved for apps in the lock screen, such as *SessionConnected*, *UserPresent*, *UserAway*, and *ControlChannelReset*. Because your app should register for these events and triggers only when it's in the lock screen, the *SystemTrigger* events *LockScreenApplicationAdded* and *LockScreenApplicationRemoved* are provided, which let an app register and unregister such triggers appropriately.

Generally speaking, common language runtime (CLR) and C++ apps can execute a background task in the app itself or in a system-provided host (BackgroundTaskHost.exe). Moreover, tasks for triggers of type *PushNotificationTrigger* or *ControlChannelTrigger* can also execute in the app process.

To properly introduce the background tasks, one last topic to cover is resources management. Every background task must execute its code using a constrained amount of CPU and network bandwidth. For example, each app on the lock screen receives 2 seconds of CPU time every 15 minutes, plus 2 more seconds for executing background tasks, just after the previous 2 seconds. In comparison, an app that is not on the lock screen receives 1 second of CPU time every 2 hours.

From a network bandwidth perspective, these constraints are a function of the amount of energy consumed by the network interface. For example, with a throughput of 10 megabits, an app on the lock screen can consume about 450 MB per day, while an app that is not on the lock screen can consume about 75 MB per day.

So the purpose of these constraints is to reduce battery and resource consumption. These rules do not apply for apps that rely on critical background tasks such as *ControlChannelTrigger* and *PushNotificationTrigger*—those kinds of tasks receive guaranteed resources. Finally, there is a global pool of resources (CPU and network) that is shared across apps, and that can be used to provide extra resources to those apps that need them. Of course, an app should not rely on the availability of such resources, because they are shared between all background tasks of any app, so another app could already have consumed them all. The global pool is refilled every 15 minutes, using a refill quota related to whether the device is running on an AC adapter or on battery power.

Contracts and extensions

A powerful set of features available for developing Windows Store apps are called WinRT contracts. WinRT and Windows Store apps can share data, information, features, and behaviors through shared communication contracts. A *contract* is an agreement between an app and the Windows 8 operating system by which an app that follows specific rules can communicate and exchange data with any other app—without directly knowing about the other app—using the operating system and WinRT as a proxy.

For example, start the Bing Travel app from the Start screen and navigate to a target location for a journey, such as Rome in Italy. Then show the charms bar (press Windows+C) and select the Share command. You will be prompted by a panel within the charms bar asking you to decide whether you want to share that location by email, with friends using the People app, or via any other Windows Store app configured as a sharing target for the type of content you want to share. You can see the result in Figure 1-19.

FIGURE 1-19 The share content flyout panel within the Bing Travel app.

As soon as you have made a choice, for example by selecting Mail, Windows launches the sharing target app behind the scenes, so it can handle the shared content. In Windows Mail for example, you can send the information about Rome to someone else via email (see Figure 1-20).

FIGURE 1-20 The UI exposed by the Mail app while sharing some content with it.

In reality, neither app (Bing Travel nor Windows Mail) is aware of the other. WinRT, sitting in the middle, joins them through a contract called a *Share* contract.

These features are shared by all apps, not just custom apps. For example, when you are using the Windows Store app, and you activate the search feature (Windows+Q), the operating system uses a Search contract to query the Windows Store app for apps that satisfy the search criteria provided.

WinRT includes a rich set of contracts, as shown in the following list:

- **Cached File Updater**   You can leverage this contract to keep track of files changes and cache them. For example, the SkyDrive app uses this contract to monitor file changes.

- **File Picker**   This contract enables you to register your app as a target for the file picker UI.

- **Play To**   This contract allows your app to be listed in the list of apps available in the Play To section of the Connect command in the charms bar.

- **Search**   This contract provides search capabilities to your app.

- **Settings**   This contract supports providing a panel where users can enter custom settings for your app.

- **Share**   This contract supports sharing content between apps.

In addition to contracts, there are also *extensions*, which allow an app to adhere to an agreement with the operating system rather than a third-party app. You can use an extension to extend Windows standard features. For the sake of simplicity, consider what happens when you connect a device or insert a disc into the CD/DVD reader. An operating system message informs the end user that he or she can execute/play the new device or media, providing a list of available actions and players. You can register your app as supporting the AutoPlay extension, and your app will then appear in the list of available AutoPlay targets.

The following is a list of available extensions:

- **Account picture provider**   When an end user changes his or her own account picture, you can register your app as an account picture provider.

- **AutoPlay**   This extension enables your app to be included in the list of AutoPlay targets.

- **Background tasks**   The app can run background tasks.

- **Camera settings**   You can provide custom UI for camera settings.

- **Contact picker**   You can register your app as contact picker provider.

- **File activation**   This extension enables you to register an app to execute a specific file type based on the file extension.

- **Game Explorer**   You can register you app as a game, providing a Game Definition File (GDF), and your app will be available as a game only if compliant with the target family safety rules.

- **Print task settings**   You can declare that your app can have a custom printer UI and can print by communicating directly with a printer device.

- **Protocol activation**   This extension allows you to register a protocol moniker for your app. For example, Windows Mail can be activated with a mailto: protocol moniker. Internet Explorer 10 can be activated with an http: protocol moniker. You can register your own moniker and use it to activate your app.

- **SSL/certificates**   This extension enables your app to install a digital certificate onto the target device.

As you will learn in Chapter 3, it is simple to register or consume a contract through WinRT.

Visual Studio 2012 and Windows 8 Simulator

To develop a Windows Store app, you will first need to install a development environment such as Microsoft Visual Studio 2012. To accomplish this task, you can buy and install a regular license for Visual Studio 2012 either directly from Microsoft or from an authorized reseller. However, for evaluation purposes, you can get started with a free edition of Visual Studio 2012, called Visual Studio Express 2012. In particular, one edition of the Visual Studio Express family of products is called Visual Studio Express 2012 for Windows 8. Using this development tool, you can create Windows Store apps either from scratch or by starting with a set of prebuilt application templates and models. You can download Visual Studio Express 2012 for Windows 8 from the Microsoft website at *http://www.microsoft.com/visualstudio/*. Alternatively, you can acquire it through the Windows Store, where it's listed under the Tools category of apps. Figure 1-21 shows the page dedicated to Visual Studio Express 2012 for Windows 8 in the Windows Store.

FIGURE 1-21 The Visual Studio Express 2012 desktop application within the Windows Store.

Perhaps even better, you can download a 90-day evaluation copy of Visual Studio 2012 from *http://www.microsoft.com/visualstudio/eng/downloads*. This 90-day trial version should provide sufficient time for you to complete this book and experience all the exercises and demos using a complete version of the product.

After installing Visual Studio, you will be able to create custom apps and publish them in the Windows Store. Chapter 3 and Chapter 4 discuss how to accomplish these tasks in more detail.

Another possible development track to consider is that you can download and install a retail version of Visual Studio 2012 (Professional, Premium, or Ultimate), even on previous editions of Windows. For example, perhaps you still don't have a Windows 8 PC; instead, you're using a Windows 7 desktop machine. You can still install Visual Studio 2012 and develop software solutions. However, you will not be able to develop Windows Store apps. Moreover, you cannot download and install Visual Studio Express 2012 for Windows 8 on a computer without Windows 8, because that edition requires you to have Windows 8 or later.

A final option for testing and executing your apps is to use the Windows 8 Simulator, which is part of the Windows 8 SDK included with Visual Studio 2012. Figure 1-22 shows the Windows 8 Simulator in action.

FIGURE 1-22 The Windows 8 Simulator in action.

As you can see from Figure 1-22, the Simulator looks like a small tablet PC with Windows 8 on board. On the right side, the Simulator includes a set of commands through which you can simulate all the various scenarios for Windows 8. These commands are as follows, from top to bottom:

- **Always on top** This command puts the Simulator always on top.

- **Mouse mode** When you move and click your mouse, the Simulator will react to mouse interactions as well.

- **Basic touch mode** Your mouse pointer will become like a finger, and when you click the Simulator, it will be handled as a finger touch.

- **Pinch/zoom touch mode** This command is similar to the previous option, but you use it to simulate zoom-in and zoom-out via touch gestures.

- **Rotation touch mode** This command is similar to the previous option, but you use it to simulate touch rotation gestures.

- **Rotate clockwise (90 degrees)** This command rotates the device clockwise 90 degrees.

- **Rotate counterclockwise (90 degrees)** This command rotates the device counterclockwise 90 degrees.

- **Change resolution** This command changes the screen resolution of the simulator device. The available resolutions are as follows:

  10.6", 1024 × 768

  10.6", 1366 × 768

  10.6", 1920 × 1080

  10.6", 2560 × 1440

  12", 1280 × 800

  23", 1920 × 1080

  27", 2560 × 1440

- **Set location** This command allows you to simulate a GPS location, for testing location-based apps.

- **Copy screenshot** Use this command to create a screenshot of the Simulator screen, which is useful for creating promotional pictures of your apps and is required to publish a real app on the Windows Store.

- **Screenshot settings** This command configures the copy screenshot behavior, such as the destination directory of the image files.

- **Help** This command provides a link to the Simulator's help.

Using the Simulator, you can fully test your apps, even without a physical tablet device or touch screen, and without a Windows 8 environment.

One of the most important features of the Simulator is the ability to change the resolution, orientation, and form factor of the screen so you can test your application's behavior in many different "devices" without the need to buy real ones.

Last but not least, remember that you cannot develop a Windows Store app using Microsoft Visual Studio 2010 or any other earlier edition of the product. The only edition of Visual Studio suitable for developing Windows Store apps is Visual Studio 2012 or later.

Summary

This chapter presented an overview of Microsoft Windows 8 and Windows Store apps. You learned about the key new features of Windows 8 as well as the main goals behind the development of a Windows Store app. You learned about apps, the Windows Store, badges, live tiles, toasts, background tasks, the new lock screen, the new Start screen, and more. The chapter also provided information about which development environments you can use to develop Windows Store apps.

Quick reference

To	Do this
Notify a user of an action that happened in the background	Use a toast, a badge, or a live tile. You can also use the lock screen, in case it is suitable for your context.
Execute some code while your app is suspended	Use a background task.
Make the contents managed by your app searchable by the end user	Support the Search contract.
Develop a Windows Store app	Install Microsoft Visual Studio Express 2012 for Windows 8 or Microsoft Visual Studio 2012 on a Windows 8 device.
Simulate the execution of a Windows 8 app in different resolutions, orientations, and form factors	Run the Windows 8 Simulator available within Visual Studio 2012.

CHAPTER 2

Windows 8 user interface style

After completing this chapter, you will be able to

- Understand the design concepts underlying the Windows 8 user interface (UI) style.

- Understand the user experience of a Windows 8 app.

Why devote a chapter of this book to design concepts? Since you are reading this book, you probably want to create great applications for the Microsoft Windows Store, and great apps must be graphically in sync with the Microsoft Windows 8 ecosystem, which means they must be designed according to the Windows 8 design and usability guidelines. Therefore, it is worthwhile to dedicate an entire chapter to exploring the details of the new design language for Windows 8: the Windows 8 UI style.

It is important to understand from the beginning that a design language is not like a programming language. It does not have strictly enforced rules; instead, it is a set of ideas and philosophies related to graphics and—specifically for applications—to the user experience. A design language doesn't have a "compiler" that can help let you know what is right and what is wrong. To discover whether your results are in line with a design language, you have to rely not only on your experience and graphic sense, but also, and even more important, on the study of the basic ideas behind that design language.

Influences

To fully understand the concepts underlying Windows 8, which represents the (for now) culminating point of a long journey, you need to understand where that journey began. This section touches on the historical artistic movements that have inspired the ideas behind the user experience of Windows 8.

The primary source of influence is the school of architecture, art, and design called Bauhaus (its full name was actually Staatliches Bauhaus). Figure 2-1 shows the school's logo.

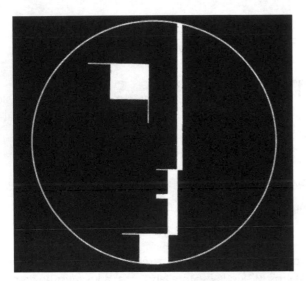

FIGURE 2-1 The logo of the school of architecture, art, and design called Bauhaus.

You could describe this logo in technical terms by specifying the element colors, the thickness of the lines, and so on, but the first thing to notice about this logo is its modernity; even without any knowledge of art history, you have probably assumed that the image is contemporary. Yet the Bauhaus school operated in Germany from 1919 to around 1933! The fundamental principle of the Bauhaus philosophy is the concept of *fair reduction*—that is, removing all the adornments and reducing everything to its essence. It's this very idea, which results in simplicity, that makes the works of this movement, including the previous logo, so modern.

The Bauhaus represented not only a school for learning the art of design, but also a point of reference for the artistic movements generated by rationalism and functionalism, which were part of the modern movement or modern design. Rationalism and functionalism were not confined to architecture and design; they included all forms of art and communication.

Functionalism was originally an architectural movement that held that any building should be functional for its purpose, a school of thought where what is "useful" is opposed to what is "beautiful." The rules dictated by this artistic movement are simple but clear:

- Function comes first.

- Function determines the shape and characteristics of an object.

- Function makes an object beautiful.

- In essence, the function is the object.

These concepts can be easily adapted to the computer world. In fact, saying that "function makes an object beautiful" is the analogue of such common ideas as "an app is beautiful because it is useful, because it offers interesting content and important functionality, not just because it has nice graphics."

At the time of the Bauhaus school, the design works were produced only by skilled craftspeople who made unique pieces for their customers. Bauhaus revolutionized the market by claiming that the design could be industrialized without sacrificing quality. To demonstrate the point, it produced some works of design realized with easy-to-assemble industrial elements. In creating these design elements (chairs, tables, bookcases, and so on), the designer's attention focused on planning and product design, not on the production itself, as was the case with handcrafted design.

Going into further detail about the works of the Bauhaus school is beyond the scope of this chapter, but the Wikipedia page at *http://en.wikipedia.org/wiki/Bauhaus* has good general information. You can find more detailed information on the Bauhaus website at *http://bauhaus-online. de/en/atlas/das-bauhaus*. The influence of the school is apparent; if you just type "Bauhaus furniture" into any search engine you'll find some products that are still on the market today.

In the world of software development, the concept of industrialization introduced by the Bauhaus school of design turns into the idea of software industrialization. Actually, developers have been industrializing software for many years already using object orientation techniques. For example, creating a base class with all the shared functionality needed by subclasses avoids wasting time rewriting the same functionality in different final products. Basically, you invest your time in creating *projects*, not *products*. These concepts also apply to the user interface. According to this principle, indeed, you should invest your time in creating templates for your graphics, not in drawing each graphic object from scratch every time you need it.

The other source of inspiration for the Windows 8 UI style is the International Typographic Style, or Swiss Design, an artistic movement developed in Switzerland in the 1950s whose style was based on a clear typography, symmetry, and the use of few and contrasting colors.

This style has a predilection for photography instead of drawings and places particular emphasis on typography. In fact, Swiss Design gave rise to fonts that are still widely popular, such as Univers and Helvetica, both based on the Akzidenz-Grotesk font, shown in Figure 2-2.

FIGURE 2-2 The Akzidenz-Grotesk font.

Swiss Design devised a framework for organizing the information included on a page in a consistent way. This artistic approach acquired the name *grid system*. The core ideas of the grid system were presented in the book *Grid Systems in Graphic Design* by Josef Müller-Brockmann, a book that was seminal in spreading the knowledge of the grid layout. The success of such a layout system is attested to by daily experience: the newspaper you read every morning and many of the websites that you consult. Moreover, signs in airports, bus and train stations, and throughout cities use grids to separate the various graphic elements and organize information semantically (see Figure 2-3).

FIGURE 2-3 A real-world example of Swiss Design.

In the sign at the top of Figure 2-3, you can see a real-world application of some of the ideas of Swiss Design: the grid layout; the simple, straightforward, and clear typography; the wise use of element symmetry, an essential iconography, and only three major color variations.

One important principle of the International Typographic Style is related to the use of an "international language," so it tried to avoid conventions or styles that could be traced back to specific countries, groups, or companies; instead, it adopted a style that could be understood anywhere in the world. Figure 2-4 shows an example of this concept. Even though the first line of the sign is in Italian, the meaning of the iconography is so clear that the text underneath is almost superfluous.

FIGURE 2-4 A real-world example of "international language."

The use of an international language becomes, in the case of Windows 8 applications, absolutely critical, because if you want to increase the revenue of your apps need to forego concentrating only on what might appeal to your friends, your local customers, or your fellow citizens, and try to imagine how to communicate your ideas, features, and messages to an international audience.

Another suggestion of Swiss Design is to reduce the iconography, leaving only the distinctive features of a graphic message. Figure 2-5 shows a clear example.

FIGURE 2-5 A real-world example of a simple iconography.

In the image above, the directions to get to the departures area are unmistakable. Once you start looking, you'll start noticing the hundreds of road signs, television spots, advertisement signs, and so on that are based on an essential iconography.

To sum up the different ideas and philosophies underlying the Windows 8 UI style, the principles are as follows:

- Enhance the functionality and the content, not the container.

- Industrialize the software and user interface, and create projects, not products.

- Use clear typography.

- Take advantage of the grid system.

- Prefer photos over drawings.

- Select few and contrasting colors.

- Strive for international language.
- Employ essential iconography.

Bauhaus style in the Windows 8 UI

Keeping the principles you learned about in the previous section in mind, try to find the implementation of those principles in Figure 2-6, which shows the Windows 8 Start screen.

FIGURE 2-6 The Windows 8 Start screen.

Enhance the functionality and the content, not the container

Without a doubt, the star of the Windows 8 Start screen is the content. There is no longer an empty desktop with few colorful icons—the old icons have been replaced with tiles. Tiles are personal; they contain important information for the user. Users can customize the appearance of the Start screen to make it uniquely theirs. The focus of customization lies in the content, which is not impersonal but applies directly to the user, such as contacts from various social networks, personal photos, the weather forecast based on the user's current GPS position, interesting news based on user topic selection, and so on. It is clear that PC customization rises to a new level compared to simply arranging icons or the choosing wallpaper as in previous versions of Windows and other operating systems on the market.

As developer, you can customize the content that your app's tiles display, giving you a way to improve the overall quality of your software (see Chapter 9, "Rethinking the UI for Windows 8 apps" for further details). Remember that a tile is not just an icon, it's an extension of your app.

Industrialize the software and user interface, and create projects, not products

Tiles are also a good example of the concept of industrialization of the user interface. The old icons are a case in point. Graphic designers used to spend several hours to complete each single icon, while now with tiles the efforts of Microsoft's graphic designers have been focused on the creation of the "tile projects," or tile templates, if you prefer. As a developer, you need only provide the content for a tile (text and/or images), and the Windows 8 framework will take care of the rest.

Use clear typography

Focusing on typography, Windows 8 uses a brand-new version of the Segoe UI font that has a number of redesigned default characters, new Microsoft OpenType alternates, new weights, and expanded language support. Just open any app in Windows 8 to appreciate the quality of the typography in the new operating system. Notice how on the Start screen the use of fonts with a pronounced difference in size provides a natural semantic organization of information. At first glance, you intuitively understand what represents the title of a tile and what represents the content.

Take advantage of the grid system

The grid system has been used extensively in conceiving the new Windows 8 user experience. The Start screen provides a clear example of a layout grid, but a grid-based layout is also clearly distinguishable in various apps. For example, look at the native Weather app in Windows 8, shown in Figure 2-7.

FIGURE 2-7 The grid system used in the Weather app.

Prefer photos over drawings

The Start screen (like many other apps in the Windows Store) is full of examples of this principle: the People application uses a collage of your friends' pictures, Bing shows the photo of the day, the news reader shows a picture of the most important news of a user-selected category, and so on.

Select few and contrasting colors

If you take a look at the Windows 8 Start screen, or even at the Weather app, you will notice that it has just one foreground color, which stands out clearly against the tile background color. You can customize the foreground of a tile in the Windows 8 app; in fact, you can choose between a dark and a light template to achieve better contrast, and therefore greater legibility, between the background and foreground.

Strive for international language and employ essential iconography

The last two principles, those relating to international language and the reduction of the iconography, can be described together, because one of the ways to make a message more "international" is to simplify the graphics. For example, look at the Windows Store tile in Figure 2-6. Its icon is universally recognized and contains the concept of shopping, but it is not an icon with a complex three-dimensional shape or colorful gradient effects; a simple stroke is sufficient to convey the message. The human mind does not need other information to understand and process the visual input.

> **Note** One piece of advice to improve the international language of your app is to use widely accepted conventions. For example, you do not need to invent a new way to represent navigating to the home page of your app; the classic house-shaped icon is already widely used and accepted. One trick that can help you evaluate whether your app is headed in the right direction for internationalization is if you translate all the text in the app into a language unfamiliar to your testers and then conduct usability tests. If the testers are still able to perform some or most of the app's required tasks without depending (too much) on the text, you have achieved a true international language.

Characteristics of a Windows 8 app

The previous section discussed the basics of the design language called Windows 8 UI style. This section defines the characteristic features of a Windows 8 app.

Silhouette

The most important aspect of an operating system is the ability to create a harmonious, homogeneous user experience. Switching between applications should not be "traumatic" for users; instead, applications should seem linked by a common theme (in terms of user experience, of course). To achieve this goal, it is essential for Windows 8 apps to have the same silhouette, where *silhouette* means the look of the app at a glance, without focusing on specific functionality or context. Therefore, having the same silhouette means that basic elements are always positioned in the same location and have the same characteristics. Take a look at Figure 2-8.

FIGURE 2-8 A collage of different apps for Windows 8.

Figure 2-8 doesn't show a single app—it's a collage of several different apps for Windows 8 (Bing Sports, Bing Finance, Bing Daily, and Bing Travel). Each app has different features, a different purpose, and a different context, but they all share the same silhouette: the title is in the same position, the back button has the same shape and position, the font is identical, and so on. Also, the text is aligned.

Indeed, if you zoom in on the first two apps of the composition, you can see that the text of both is perfectly in line, as shown in Figure 2-9.

FIGURE 2-9 The text of two different apps is perfectly in line.

It is precisely this attention to detail that is the key to creating a harmonic system.

The Microsoft website has many documents that relate to various specific techniques for improving the silhouette of your app, but the simplest and most straightforward is to use the project templates provided by Microsoft Visual Studio 2012. Figure 2-10 shows some of the Visual Studio 2012 project templates.

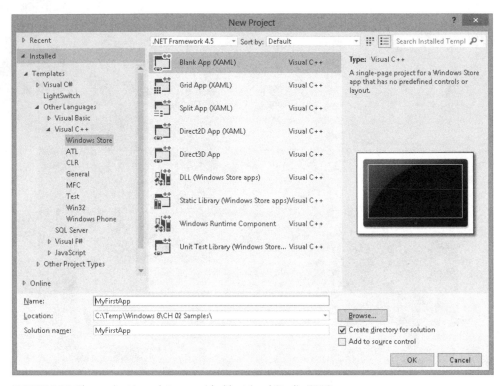

FIGURE 2-10 The project templates provided by Visual Studio 2012.

The Grid App (XAML) template provides a multipage project for navigating multiple layers of content. Users reach details for an item by tapping or clicking the item itself. The details are then displayed on a dedicated page. The Split App (XAML) template is a good starting point for creating a master details list, where items appear in a list on the left side of the page and the details for a selected item appear on the right side of the same page.

 Note Chapter 3, "My first Windows 8 app," provides a more complete description of the various templates.

Selecting the Grid App (XAML) or the Split App (XAML) template results in an app that still needs to be customized and filled with content and functionality, but that already has a silhouette in line with the specifications. Figure 2-11 shows the home page of an app created with the default Grid App (XAML) template.

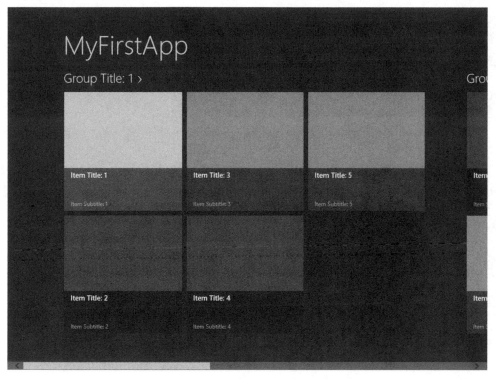

FIGURE 2-11 The default layout of a home page created with a Visual Studio 2012 project template.

If you compare the previous image with Figure 2-12, which shows a custom photo application, you can see how the project templates provided by Visual Studio 2012 can simplify the development of an app. By starting with these project templates, all you have to do to create an app consistent with the operating system is add your own content.

FIGURE 2-12 The home page of a custom application created with a Visual Studio 2012 project template.

The various templates also include the display of the item details. Figure 2-13 shows the layout of the Grid App (XAML) template.

FIGURE 2-13 The default layout of an item details page created with the Grid App (XAML) Visual Studio 2012 project template.

Figure 2-14 shows one of the news items from the Bing Daily app. It uses the same layout as the previous figure, this time filled with real content.

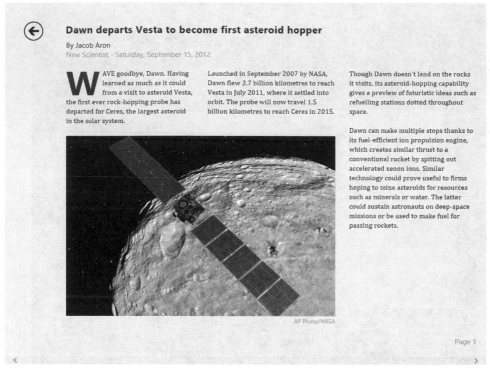

FIGURE 2-14 The Bing Daily app.

Full screen

The fundamental purpose of Windows 8 app design is to emphasize the content, not the container. The motto "content, not chrome" has become a symbol of the Windows 8 UI style philosophy, but—in addition to what has already been explained in the previous section—it's important to add another key concept. In earlier versions of Windows, not only was an application relegated to a window, but also a good portion of that window was filled with bars, widgets, panes, gadgets, and so on. In contrast, in a Windows 8 app, the entire surface of the screen is dedicated to content. Figure 2-15 shows a screen shot of classic Microsoft Internet Explorer running on the desktop. In comparison to the clean Windows 8 design, the application (the website, in this case) seems smothered by the other on-screen elements.

FIGURE 2-15 Internet Explorer running on the desktop.

The user experience in Internet Explorer 10, specifically designed for Windows 8, assumes a decidedly new connotation. Figure 2-16 shows the same website in the Internet Explorer 10. Notice how the entire screen of the app is now available for content, creating a more immersive user environment.

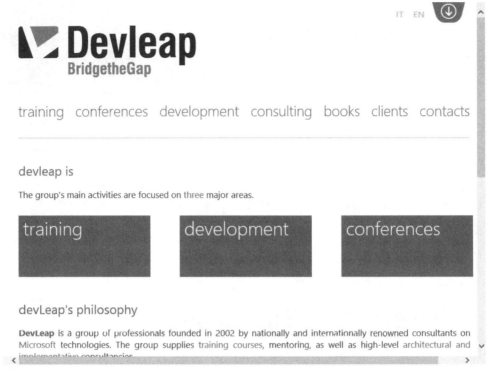

FIGURE 2-16 Every Windows Store app runs in full-screen mode.

Edges

In Windows 8, the edges of the screen assume a very important role. As a matter of fact, the left edge of the screen is entirely dedicated to the "back" functionality. When you swipe repeatedly from left to right (performed on the left side of the screen, typically with the thumb of the left hand), Windows will cycle through all the open applications. You can think of this as the new implementation of the classic Alt+Tab functionality, but now based on a gesture. Swiping from the right side of the screen activates the charms bar, which contains five icons representing operating system functions that provide the following features: Search, Share, Start, Devices, and Settings. Figure 2-17 shows the charms bar after activation by a right-to-left swipe.

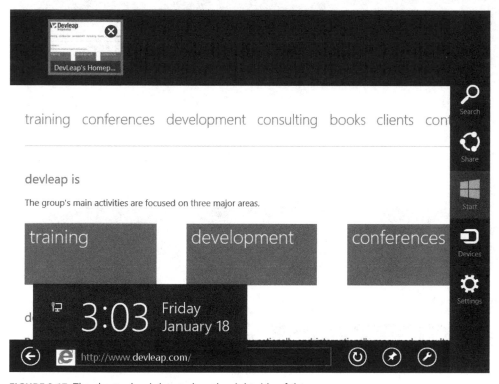

FIGURE 2-17 The charms bar is located on the right side of the screen.

Because both the left and right swipe operations are reserved for the operating system, to prevent user frustration you should avoid placing user interface controls such as buttons in those areas. However, your application can leverage both the top and bottom edges of the screen, so you can insert your own menus and toolbars. A swipe from bottom to top, performed from the bottom edge of the screen, or a swipe from top to bottom, performed from the top edge of the screen, activates a custom app bar control where you can place buttons and custom controls. These features are available to all Windows 8 applications, including most system applications such as Internet Explorer and Microsoft Office. Figure 2-18 shows the app bar for Internet Explorer 10.

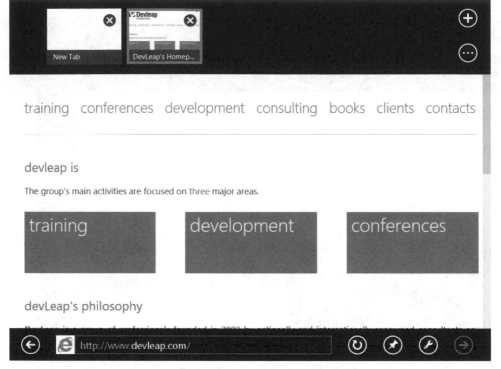

FIGURE 2-18 Internet Explorer 10 with the app bars opened.

It's important to include only the most important and frequently used controls in the main canvas, leaving the less important commands visible only through the edge gestures (typically in the app bar). A Windows 8 user should be able to discover your application's commands in a natural way because nearly all apps on Windows 8 work in exactly the same way.

Comfort and touch

Windows 8 and the innovations concerning the user experience have been developed to satisfy the growing demand for a more touch-friendly operating system. Designing a user interface for tablets, for example, is not just a question of adjusting size and displaying objects in a canvas, but it is mainly a rediscovery of the interaction between human and machine. The main input mechanism is represented by touches and gestures, which required a number of usability studies. Microsoft has performed a lot of usability testing with Windows 8 installed on tablet devices to understand how to improve the usability in these contexts. From the various experiments, some interesting facts have emerged. One of the first findings is that the majority of users hold a tablet with both hands but leave their thumbs free to move on the screen. Thanks to this information, Microsoft engineers have developed a sort of map that identifies which areas of the screen are easiest to reach with thumbs and which are more difficult. The result is shown in Figure 2-19.

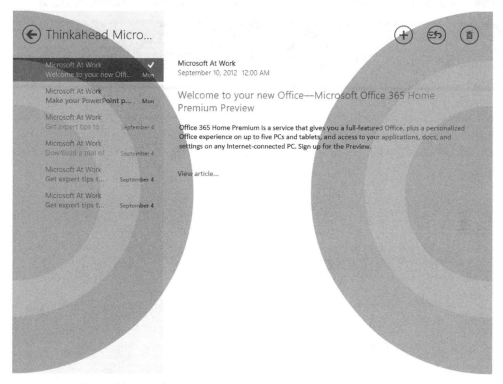

FIGURE 2-19 Microsoft's map of the easiest areas to reach on a tablet device.

This map makes it easy to understand that the green areas are the easiest to reach, while the yellow ones are less comfortable to reach, and the red areas require an even greater effort.

This valuable image is very important for you as a developer or designer, because now you know that you should put the most common controls for your apps in the green area of the image, thus increasing the usability of your application. The map can also help you see when to place controls in the app bar. In fact, according to this scheme, you should place the most frequently used commands on the left or right side of the app bar and lesser used controls toward the center of the app bar. Figure 2-20 illustrates some examples.

FIGURE 2-20 A composition of different app bars.

The commands in Figure 2-20 are arranged on the left and the right side of the screen. Even the Windows 8 touch keyboard presents a nice feature that allows users to split the keyboard into segments so that the most used parts are within the green area of the scheme. Figure 2-21 illustrates this feature.

FIGURE 2-21 The split touch keyboard.

It thus becomes crucial to design applications so that they become fully usable with various input modes (it is important to think about touch and gestures, but don't forget the classic mouse and keyboard). One recommendation is to design your user interface by considering touch input first and, if you use the framework standard controls (which you will become acquainted with in later chapters), you will get support for mouse and keyboard out of the box—that is, without the need to write code to specifically enable those input devices. To clarify these concepts, try the following procedure.

Experiment with touch, mouse, and keyboard support

1. Start Windows 8.

2. From the Start screen, click or touch the Weather app's tile.

   The Weather app appears.

3. If you have a touch screen, swipe your finger from bottom to top in the lower side of the screen.

4. Take a look at the two app bar controls at the top and bottom of the screen.

5. Close the app bars by touching in the middle of the screen.

6. Place your mouse cursor anywhere on the screen and then click the right mouse button. The app bars will appear.

7. Take a look at the app bar controls.

8. Close the app bars by clicking in the middle of the screen.

9. If you have a touch screen, perform a swipe from right to left, starting from the right edge of the screen. The charms bar will appear.

10. Take a look at the charms bar.

11. Touch the screen inside the app to make the charms bar disappear.

12. On your keyboard, press Windows+C.

13. Take another look at the charms bar.

As you can see, all the native objects of the framework fully support all input modes: touch, mouse, keyboard, and digital stylus—definitely a great convenience for developers.

Design the user experience of your apps touch-first, following the same approach that even the designers of complex applications such as Office for Windows 8 have followed. Avoid designing different user interfaces for touch, mouse, and keyboard; use a single layout for all the input modes. If you have a traditional mouse and keyboard setup, you will be able to create and test applications for the touch environment using the Windows 8 Simulator that is included with Visual Studio 2012. In fact, the tool has a command called *basic touch mode*. In this mode, your mouse pointer becomes like a finger; when you click the simulator it will be handled as a finger touch.

It thus becomes vital to understand the new touch language introduced with Windows 8 and use it in your apps, without the need to invent new fancy or special gestures that would only result in confusion for the end user. Fortunately for all the developers, Microsoft designers have simplified the various modes and minimized the number and the types of gestures supported. The ultimate goal of the new Windows is simplicity of use, and a number of complex gestures would certainly decrease the usability of the entire system. Figure 2-22, taken from the Microsoft documentation, summarizes the touch gestures supported by the system and their meanings.

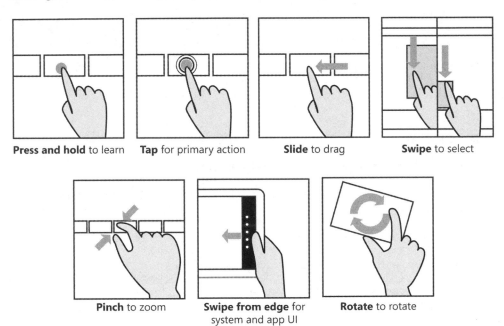

FIGURE 2-22 Touch gestures supported by Windows 8.

Gestures such as tap, slide, pinch (and stretch), slide, and rotate are so frequent in any touch system that there is not much to add here to describe them, but a few of the others deserve some further explanation. The first gesture illustrated in Figure 2-22, press and hold, is associated with the action of "learn," so it should be used to show a tooltip, a help screen, or something that can provide further information and explanation. You should avoid using such a gesture to show a contextual submenu or enable some editing mode. As you can see in the image, there is no double-tap gesture; that was considered to be too difficult to use.

The swipe gesture, typically performed on an element of a collection, allows you to select or deselect an item. If you have a device with touch support, try the following procedure.

1. Start Windows 8.

2. On the Start screen, move your finger from the top toward the bottom of a tile.

3. Look at the tile. It now shows a selected check box in the top-right corner.

4. Perform a swipe gesture on another tile.

   Notice that a selected checkbox appears on that tile.

5. Perform a swipe on the tile you selected at the beginning of this procedure.

   Notice how the current element is now deselected.

6. Swipe again on the second tile.

   Notice how the second tile is now deselected.

7. Perform another swipe on any tile, but this time keep dragging the tile toward the bottom.

   You will notice that the tile becomes "detached" from the rest of the Start screen.

8. Drag the tile where you prefer, and then release it.

The previous procedure, very trivial and at first glance obvious, has brought some interesting considerations about the touch gesture to light. First, the various gestures are reversible—that is, no matter which state you are in, you can always go back to the previous state (as exemplified by the previous procedure). Another important consideration is based on the absence (or, at least, the strong reduction) of the "modes." In the previous procedure, you did not have to choose some other element such as a menu item to enter the element selection mode; a gesture was the only thing you needed. Similarly, you did not have to take multiple actions to get to the tile positioning mode; a natural gesture (drag and move) was sufficient to complete the step.

Semantic Zoom

Another very important feature of the new Windows 8 touch language is represented by an innovative Semantic Zoom. The pinch and stretch gestures are usually associated with an optical zoom feature, and Windows 8 fully respects this principle, though Semantic Zoom extends the concept to allow simple navigation among larger data sets. The next procedure illustrates this feature.

1. Start Windows 8.

2. If you have a touch screen, perform a swipe from right to left on the right side of the screen and touch the Search icon in the charms bar.

    If you don't have a touch screen, press Windows+F. Windows 8 will open the Search page.

3. Click or tap Apps in the list on the right side of the screen. The following image shows the result—the list of applications installed on your PC.

4. If you have a touch screen, perform the pinch gesture in the middle of the screen.

    If you don't have a touch screen, scroll the mouse wheel down while holding the Ctrl button.

5. Notice the new visualization, a set of letters representing the initials of the applications presented in the previous list. The following figure shows the result of this operation.

As you can see, the pinch operation is not just an optical zoom (in this case, it would have rendered the same list shown in the previous image, just with different dimensions). Instead, it's a higher-level semantic visualization of the data.

6. Touch or click a letter. You will get back to the default visualization, but the focus is now on the applications grouped under the letter you selected. In fact, Semantic Zoom's purpose is to simplify navigation through long lists of data on a touch device.

As demonstrated, Semantic Zoom offers two different views of the data: a zoomed-in view (the default view), where the list of data is presented expanded, and a zoomed-out view that typically represents the grouping keys of the underlying data. For a complete example of these concepts and of the use of the *SemanticZoom* control, see Chapter 9.

Discussing touches and gestures also raises some questions about performance. The mouse and keyboard provide "indirect" input to a device, and people are usually inclined to better tolerate slight lags in interface response using these types of input. In contrast, touch, which is by definition a direct input, amplifies any problems associated with an app's performance. In other words, when users select a user interface element through a gesture, they expect a more immediate response from the app than when using a mouse or the keyboard. For developers, this means you should fully test your app's performance, especially on low-end devices.

Animations

To increase the perception of fluidity of the entire system, Windows 8 uses lots of animations. If you pay attention, you will notice that the Microsoft designers have inserted animations in most operations: opening an application, removing an element from a list, tapping a user interface control, navigating from one page to another, closing an application, and so on all include animation. These animations are light, noninvasive, and not tiring in the long run. They give a sense of fluidity to the entire system. So you can take advantage of animations easily, Microsoft has developed the Animation Library, a collection of fluid and natural animations that you can use in your application. Interestingly, the standard framework controls already use the features offered by this library. For example, the *GridView* control uses animations when you select an element (using the same look and feel as the selection of a tile on the Start screen).

Different form factors

Windows 8 is not just for tablet devices; it can be installed on traditional notebooks, desktops, and ultrabooks. Each device may have its own screen size, resolution, and definition, so as a developer or designer, it is your job to make sure that your application can be used by any of these form factors to improve its sales. The good news is that the project templates provided by Visual Studio 2012 and the standard controls of the framework provide excellent scaling support, even though not all that support comes predefined out of the box. You will always need to use the various controls in the most appropriate way and test your code often to ensure that the user interface adapts appropriately to whatever device is in use. In Chapter 7, "Enhance the user experience," you will work with the Windows 8 Simulator installed with Visual Studio 2012. This tool enables you to test your Windows 8 app with varying resolutions.

Figure 2-23 shows a screen shot of an app with a resolution of 1366 × 768 pixels (a tablet device with an 10.6-inch screen). Notice how the list of elements exceeds the screen dimensions on the right side.

FIGURE 2-23 The Bing Travel app running on an 10.6-inch screen.

Figure 2-24 shows the same application running at a resolution of 2560 × 1440 pixels (on a 27-inch screen), where the available space has been wisely used to display more content.

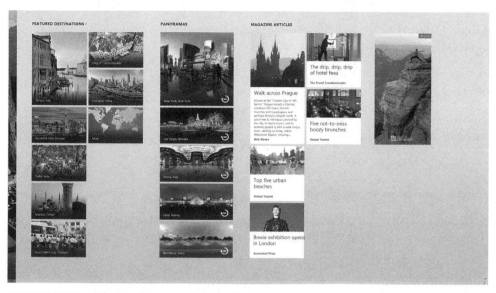

FIGURE 2-24 The Bing Travel app running on a 27-inch screen.

More specifically, this app is based on the Grid App (XAML) project template and uses a unique *GridView* control to display the data, so you don't need to use different forms for different resolutions; a single layout is sufficient.

As far as the graphical assets are concerned, you have two different options. The first involves vector art and thus *Path* objects of the XAML framework. The second option consists of rasterized assets (such as .jpg and .png files). For vector art, scaling support is completely transparent and guaranteed, while for raster access you can address scaling sufficiently by including three distinct versions of the same image in the Visual Studio 2012 project with scales of 100 percent, 140 percent, and 180 percent, respectively. At run time, the platform will analyze the device in use and load the most appropriate asset. Figure 2-25 shows a rasterized graphical asset from a real app with the three different scales.

100%

140%

180%

FIGURE 2-25 Different scales of the same graphical asset.

Don't forget that you must take into account not only the landscape display (the default visualization), but also the portrait display. It's your job to decide which mode is enabled and, if so, what changes to the user interface your app must implement to respond to a change in the orientation (for instance, the back button might be smaller in the portrait version, the left margin of the application could be different, and so on). Chapter 9 contains an example that illustrates these concepts.

Snapped and fill views

The last feature of a Windows 8 app to take into account is related to the snapped state of an app. The following procedure is useful for explaining the idea.

View an app in snapped state

1. Start Windows 8.

2. From the Start screen, launch the Weather app.

3. Press the Window button on the keyboard to go back to the Start screen. If you have a touch device, you can activate the charms bar and touch the Windows icon in the bar.

4. From the Start screen, launch Internet Explorer.

5. Place your mouse cursor in the top-left corner of the screen to open the thumbnail of the previously active application—in this case, that should be the Weather application.

6. Drag the Weather app thumbnail to the center of the screen. You'll see a snapped area on the left outlined. At this point, release the mouse; you'll see a result similar to the one shown in the following image.

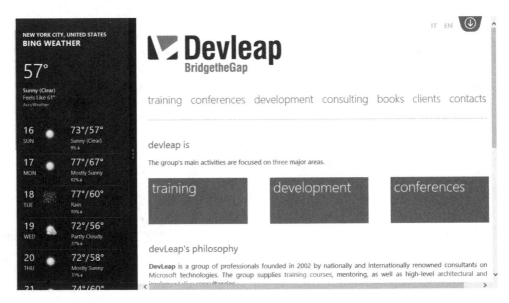

The Weather app is running and is in the snapped state, which offers a "reduced" visualization of its content (the snap view is 320 pixels wide).

7. Move the delimiter of the snapped area to the right and release the mouse button at around two-thirds of the overall screen size. The result should resemble the following image.

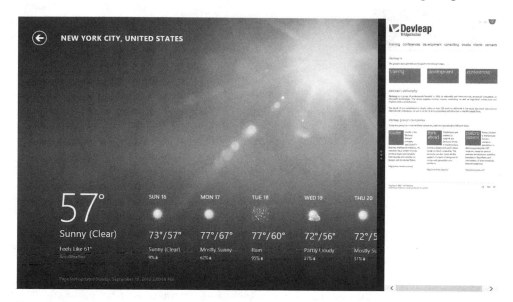

Now the Weather app is currently in the filled state, while Internet Explorer has been reduced to the snapped state.

This exercise demonstrated that an app may be in one of three different states: full screen (default), filled, or snapped. It is a good idea, as developer or designer, to provide a special display for the snapped status; doing so allows users to run your app even while performing other activities with another application. Chapter 9 contains an example of how you can customize your user interface when a change in app state occurs.

Many native Windows 8 applications can inspire you with ideas for handling the snapped state of your application. The following images show side-by-side screen-shots of snapped (on the left) and full-screen (on the right) applications (the full-screen views have been cropped so they'll fit in this book). Figure 2-26 shows the Bing Daily app, and Figure 2-27 shows the Bing Finance app.

FIGURE 2-26 The Bing Daily app running in snapped state (on the left) and in full-screen state (on the right).

FIGURE 2-27 The Bing Finance app running in snapped state (on the left) and in full-screen state (on the right).

Summary

In this chapter, you explored the basics of Microsoft Windows 8 UI style, along with a little history, the influences, and the philosophy underlying the user experience upon which the entire operating system is based. You saw how Windows 8 values contents over the container ("content, not chrome"), a crystal-clear typography, the grid system, and the simplification of iconography. You also covered the basics of how to design the user experience for your own applications so that they are consistent with the operating system principles. These basics include using the Microsoft Visual Studio 2012 templates to create a proper silhouette, designing the interface for "touch-first," using common conventions, creating custom tiles, employing app bars and the charms bar correctly, and making your application aware of snapped and filled states and orientation changes. Also remember that an app in harmony with the ecosystem of Windows 8 is, most likely, an app pleasant to look at and comfortable to use.

Quick reference

To	Do this
Design a great Windows 8 UI style app	Respect the following principles: • Enhance the functionality and the content, not the container. • Industrialize the software and user interface, and create projects, not products. • Use clear typography. • Take advantage of the grid system. • Prefer photos over drawings. • Select few and contrasting colors. • Strive for international language. • Employ essential iconography.
Improve the silhouette of your app	Use the project templates provided by Visual Studio 2012.
Enhance integration with the operating system	Customize the application's tile. Use the app bar controls. Implement the snapped state.
Design the user experience for different input devices	Design "touch-first" and use the standard controls of the framework.
Define the positions of the controls	Position the most important controls in the areas that are easiest to reach, and make the less important commands visible only through the edge gestures (typically in the app bar).

CHAPTER 3

My first Windows 8 app

After completing this chapter, you will be able to

- Install and use the tools to develop a Windows 8 app using Visual Studio 2012.

- Understand and use the project templates.

- Create a simple application using C++.

- Test the application.

- Use the WinRT APIs from a Windows 8 application.

The preceding chapters showed how Microsoft Windows 8 provides a new user interface and a completely new user experience, and exposes a new set of APIs called Windows Runtime (WinRT) APIs. The new user interface and experience is based around the Windows 8 UI style you learned about in Chapter 2, "Windows 8 user interface style."

This chapter translates what you just learned into practice. You will start by creating a simple Windows 8 app from scratch using one of the templates provided in Microsoft Visual Studio 2012 and deploy it to your local machine. Then you will implement a simple call to some WinRT APIs.

Software installation

To start developing Windows 8 applications, you need Visual Studio 2012. This new version of Visual Studio can be installed to run side by side with an existing installation of Visual Studio 2010. Even though you can develop applications using other versions of Windows and deploy them to a Windows 8 box or test them in the provided emulator, it is advisable to install the development environment directly on a machine with Windows 8 in order to speed up the development and testing processes on hardware-related components. For instance, if your apps use the accelerometer, the inclinometer, the camera, the NFC sensor, or any other sensor, the testing and debugging phase will be more accurate as well as quicker on Windows 8.

To download Windows 8, go to *http://msdn.microsoft.com/windows/apps*, the home page for Windows 8 app development. From this page, you can easily reach all the downloadable versions of Windows 8, and in the Getting Started section, you can find useful information for the download and installation process.

 Note Because URLs and component packaging may change after this book is published, start looking for Windows 8 and Visual Studio 2012 on the Windows 8 home page (*http://msdn.microsoft.com/windows/apps*) or search for them on Bing (*http://www.bing.com*).

Microsoft Visual Studio Express 2012 for Windows 8 is a tailored version of Visual Studio that contains just what you need to develop a Windows 8 app. You can use the full version of Visual Studio 2012, installing it on top of the Express version or as a separate installation.

To summarize, you'll need the following components to start developing a Windows 8 app:

- Visual Studio Express 2012 for Windows 8. On top of this version, you can install a more advanced edition of Visual Studio 2012 (for instance, the Ultimate edition).

- The Windows 8 SDK, to obtain the templates and the integration with the Windows 8 environment. This component is packaged together with Visual Studio Express 2012 for Windows 8.

- Windows 8, to test the application in the real environment.

- A developer license. The integrated development environment (IDE) handles this requirement automatically and all you need to do is select Yes when the dialog box pops up.

Windows Store project templates

The easiest way to start developing a Windows 8 application is to use one of the out-of-the-box project templates. Visual Studio 2012 provides a group of templates called Windows Store templates to develop applications for the Windows Store. These templates provide all the files you need in the project to start developing, testing, and deploying the application on the local box and the emulator, and they also provide a procedure to create the application package for the Windows Store.

Every template provides a good starting point to begin developing different kinds of Windows Store applications. The characteristics of the various templates are as follows:

- **Blank App (XAML)** This template provides a minimal skeleton using Windows Store frameworks.

- **Grid App (XAML)** This template provides a multipage project for navigating multiple layers of content. The item details can be reached by tapping or clicking the item itself and are displayed on a dedicated page.

- **Split App (XAML)** This template is a good starting point to create a master detail list of items, with a list on the left side of the page and the details on the right side of the same page.

- **Direct2D App** This template generates a WinRT application that uses Direct2D. It provides a good starting point for developing games or applications with advanced animated graphics in two dimensions.

- **Direct3D App** This template generates a WinRT application that uses Direct3D. It provides a good starting point for developing games or applications with advanced animated graphics in three dimensions.

- **DLL (Windows Store apps)** The resulting project is a native dynamic-link library (DLL) that can be used to centralize the code for Windows Store applications.

- **Static Library (Windows Store apps)** The resulting project is a static library of native code that can be used for Windows Store applications.

- **Windows Runtime Component** With this template, you can develop a component that can be used by Windows Store applications, regardless of the programming languages in which the apps are written.

- **Unit Test Library (Windows Store apps)** The goal for this template is to create a project that contains unit tests to be used with Windows Store apps, WinRT components, or class libraries for Windows Store apps.

As you may remember from Chapter 1, "Introduction to Windows Store apps," the SDK setup process installed some new templates and wizards to facilitate the creation of a Windows Store project. Under the Visual C++ project types is a new section, Windows Store, that represents the entry point for these new kinds of projects. This section exposes all the templates that are tailored to Windows 8.

Create the project

In this procedure, you will create a new application project.

1. To create a new application project, open Visual Studio 2012, and from the File menu, select New Project (the sequence can be File | New | Project for full-featured versions of Visual Studio). Choose Visual C++ in the Templates tree and Windows Store from the list of installed templates. Then choose Blank App (XAML) from the list of available projects.

2. Name the new project **MyFirstApp**, and then choose a location on your file system as well as a solution name.

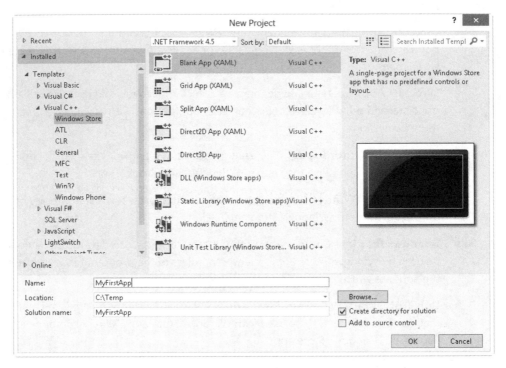

3. If you use a source control system, you can select the Add to Source Control check box. When you've finished, click OK.

At this stage, Visual Studio 2012 normally creates the solution folder, the project folder, and a project related to the chosen template. Because you selected the Blank App project template, Visual Studio uses the simplest project structure to create your new application.

At first glance, the resulting project is very similar to a traditional Microsoft Silverlight application, as shown in Figure 3-1.

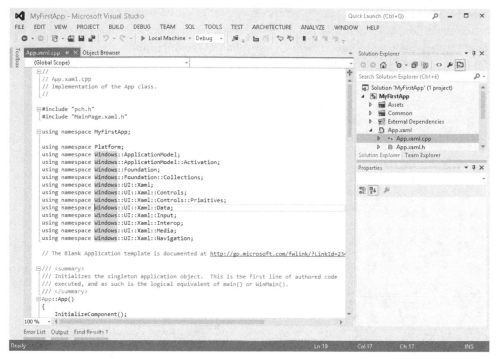

FIGURE 3-1 A blank Windows Store app in Solution Explorer.

In Solution Explorer, you can easily find the files App.xaml and MainPage.xaml. These files contain the XAML definition of the application (application styles) and of the initial page, respectively. The Common folder contains a StandardStyles.xaml file that includes common Extensible Application Markup Language (XAML) styles. The External Dependencies folder contains references to standard include files that are required to compile the project.

There are no local configuration files. Because the runtime system is somewhat sandboxed, the user cannot navigate to the file system where the application will be installed and change some files, since Windows Store apps usually are downloaded and installed from the Windows Store. The exception to this rule is the development environment where Visual Studio, or you with a simple command-line tool, can install the application for testing purposes.

The Package.appxmanifest file contains the description of the application (the icon to be used, the synergy with the operating system) and the operating system features that the application uses, which are called *application capabilities* and *declarations*.

Figure 3-2 shows the Package.appxmanifest designer that Visual Studio provides to simplify the application definition. The Application UI tab enables you to choose the display name of the application (that is, the name for the Start screen), a description of the application, three logos of different sizes for the application, and so on.

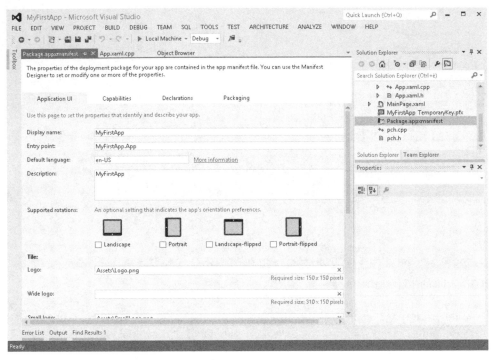

FIGURE 3-2 Visual Studio application Manifest Designer.

The Assets folder contains the images used by the application that are also referenced from the Package.appxmanifest file. The default template uses an image for the application logo that is used for the default application tile (Logo.png), an image for the initial splash screen (SplashScreen.png), a small logo image that is shown in the tile of the application in case the application changes the tile from code (SmallLogo.png), and last but not least, the image used by the Windows Store to represent the application (StoreLogo.png). As you can see in Figure 3-2, there is no default wide logo, and this image is not referenced by Package.appxmanifest.

If you run this application now, accepting all the default files and manifest settings, you will see the splash screen after a short delay during which Visual Studio will deploy the application to the developer system, and a completely blank screen that represents the application. This can sound strange, since Visual Studio traditionally adds some sample text to all the templates; in reality, many things happen during the deployment of the application. The following procedure guides you to discover them.

Explore the deployed app on the system

The first thing to notice is the absence of the classic window with the *X* button, as well as the minimize and maximize buttons—in fact, this is the first version of Windows without windows.

Follow these steps to explore what Visual Studio has asked Windows 8 to do during the deployment of the application.

1. Press the Start button of your tablet or keyboard, or go to the bottom-left corner of the screen using your mouse and click the Start menu item to return to the Start screen.

2. Scroll to the right using your finger, the mouse wheel, or the bottom scroll bar until you reach the end of the applications' tiles.

3. At the very end of the applications' tiles will be your first Windows 8 app, shown by a tile with the name MyFirstApp.

4. Click the MyFirstApp tile to reopen the application. You may see the Start screen again.

5. Return to Visual Studio and stop the debugging session using the Stop button on the debug toolbar.

6. Repeat steps 1 through 3, and then tap and hold your finger or use the right button of the mouse. The command bar will ask you if you want to uninstall or simply unpin the application. "Unpin" means deleting the application tile from the Start menu, while leaving the application on the system.

7. Unpin the application by clicking the Unpin button.

8. Point the mouse in the bottom-right corner to open the charms bar and choose Search, or press Windows+Q on the keyboard. The Search pane will appear on the right of the screen.

9. Type the initial letters of the name of the application—for example, **myfi**—in the text box, and choose Apps from the list of places to search. Your application will appear in the left pane, as shown in the following image. The background and foreground colors might look different in your installation, depending on the theme you have selected for your Windows 8 machine.

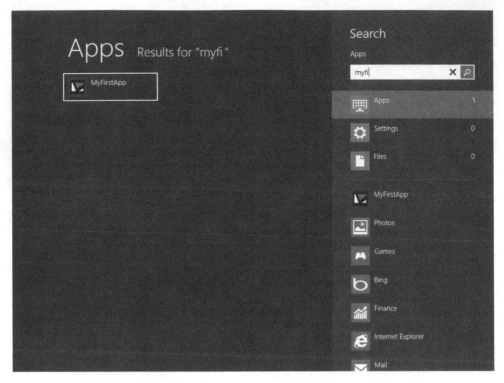

10. You can launch the application by tapping or clicking the application, but don't do that now. Instead, tap and hold or right-click the application to open the command bar.

11. Pin the application using the Pin button. The application is now listed in the Start menu using the default tile. You can verify the tile presence by repeating steps 1 and 2 of this procedure.

Please note that you can also search for files and for settings within the same pane as well as perform a search inside the listed applications. These applications have declared the search capability in their Package.appxmanifest files. You'll try to add this declaration to the simple application you are developing in this chapter.

Before proceeding further, if you have launched the application from the Search pane or the Start screen—that is, if the application was launched outside Visual Studio—you need to close it before you can deploy it again. If you use Visual Studio to start an application, the first operation that the IDE requests to the operating system is the package deployment, and then Visual Studio starts the application and attaches the debugger to it. If you stop the debugging session from Visual Studio, the Windows process is terminated; the same termination happens if the application crashes. If the application was launched outside Visual Studio, you do not have any close button, as you have seen in the previous examples. The application occupies the entire screen and there is nothing but Task Manager to let you manually stop (*kill* is a better word) the process from running indefinitely. You can also press Alt+F4 or use the application closing gesture to close the application in a more graceful way. The application closing gesture allows you to close an application by quickly swiping your finger from the top-center of the screen to the lower-center.

You will learn the details of the life cycle for Windows 8 applications in Chapter 4, "Application life-cycle management." For now, it is important to understand that Windows 8 has a completely new way to manage an application's life cycle: an application is in the running state when the user uses it (the user has chosen the application as the foreground application), and when the user leaves the application by pressing the Start menu button, or going back to the previous application, or starting a new search, and so on, the application can be suspended from the system or also terminated if the system needs more memory. This behavior recalls in some ways the application life-cycle management of Microsoft Windows Phone, as well as other modern operating systems.

To stop a running application or to see the application status, you can start Task Manager, which has been renewed in Windows 8, and enable the display of suspension state by using the Status Values options in the View menu. As you can see in Figure 3-3, Task Manager shows that MyFirstApp is in the suspended state. Save The Planet, a real application ported from Windows Phone 7 to Windows 8, is not in the suspended state, meaning that it still running.

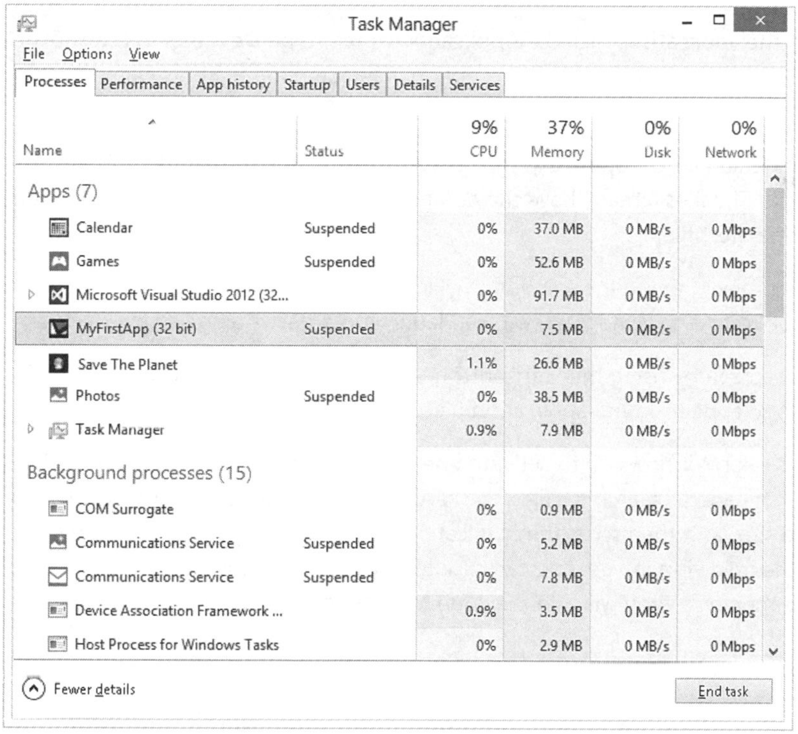

FIGURE 3-3 Task Manager showing the suspended/running state for a Windows Store app.

This mechanism applies only to Windows Store applications and not to classic .NET or Win32 applications. In fact, many other Win32 applications are in the running state.

Add a search declaration

In this procedure, you will enrich the application manifest with the Search declaration to let the user search some text "inside" this application. Follow these simple steps inside the Visual Studio 2012 project you are building.

1. Double-click the Package.appxmanifest file inside the MyFirstApp application to open the designer.

2. Click the Declarations tab to manage the declarations for this application.

3. Choose Search from the Available Declaration list box, and click the Add button. As stated in the Description section, the Search declaration "registers the application as providing search functionality. End users will be able to search the application from anywhere in the system." The term "search the application" means passing the text entered by the user to the application to search inside the application.

4. Before testing the application, click the Application UI tab, type **DevLeap** in the Short Name property, and make sure that the All Logos option is selected in the Show Name drop-down list.

5. To change the default logo, copy the .png files you can find in the Chapter 03 Demo Files into the Logos folder. The files already have the default names, so you do not need to modify the Package.appxmanifest file.

6. Right-click the project item in the solution (MyFirstApp) and choose Deploy. This operation deploys the application to Windows 8 without launching a debugging session.

7. Open the Start screen by using the Start button, and scroll to the right to verify that the name and the new logo appear on the application tile.

8. Press Windows+F or Windows+Q to activate one of the Windows Search interfaces (the first opens the search page to search for files, the second to search for applications), type some text in the text box, and then scroll the applications to verify that your application is shown in the list, as in the following image. You can click to open the application. The application does nothing at the moment—you will add the code to implement the search in the last part of this chapter.

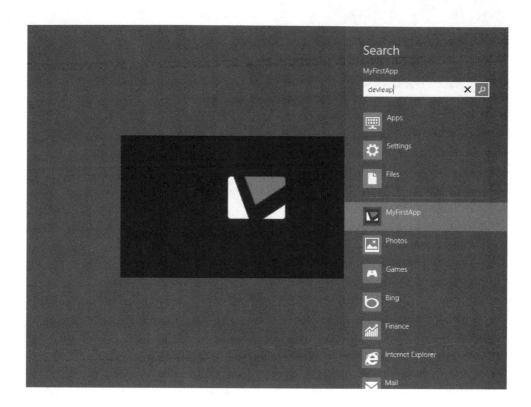

UI elements

In this section, you will analyze the remaining project items and add some code to build a list of people and bind it to the user interface.

Note It is beyond the scope of this chapter to analyze the various binding techniques as well as the user interface patterns such as Model-View-ViewModel (MVVM) or Model-View-Controller (MVC). However, the last chapter of this book is dedicated to application architectures and patterns.

Let's start by analyzing the code proposed by the Visual Studio 2012 template. You have already examined the meaning and functionality of the application manifest and the image folder. Listing 3-1 shows source XAML code of the main page, which has been modified in order to show a *ListView* standard user control that will display the *FullName* property of a list of bound elements.

LISTING 3-1 Modified MainPage.xaml page

```xml
<Page
    x:Class="MyFirstApp.MainPage"
    xmlns="http://schemas.microsoft.com/winfx/2006/xaml/presentation"
    xmlns:x="http://schemas.microsoft.com/winfx/2006/xaml"
    xmlns:local="using:MyFirstApp"
    xmlns:d="http://schemas.microsoft.com/expression/blend/2008"
    xmlns:mc="http://schemas.openxmlformats.org/markup-compatibility/2006"
    mc:Ignorable="d">

    <Grid Background="{StaticResource ApplicationPageBackgroundThemeBrush}">
        <ListView x:Name="list" DisplayMemberPath="FullName" />
    </Grid>
</Page>
```

The page includes the classic XAML definition for a page control that is represented by the MyFirstApp.MainPage class. The user control references four XML namespaces much like in a Silverlight project, as well as a WPF app, or a Windows Phone 7.*x* application.

The default template proposes a *Grid* for the layout, which will be changed in a following procedure where you will do some styling to transform the look and feel of this simple application.

The code-behind for the MainPage.xaml page can be modified as shown in Listing 3-2 to call a fake business layer that returns a list of people represented by the *Person* class you will implement shortly.

LISTING 3-2 Modified MainPage.xaml.cpp code

```cpp
//
// MainPage.xaml.cpp
// Implementation of the MainPage class.
//

#include "pch.h"
#include "MainPage.xaml.h"

using namespace MyFirstApp;

using namespace Platform;
using namespace Windows::Foundation;
using namespace Windows::Foundation::Collections;
using namespace Windows::UI::Xaml;
using namespace Windows::UI::Xaml::Controls;
using namespace Windows::UI::Xaml::Controls::Primitives;
using namespace Windows::UI::Xaml::Data;
using namespace Windows::UI::Xaml::Input;
using namespace Windows::UI::Xaml::Media;
using namespace Windows::UI::Xaml::Navigation;

// The Blank Page item template is documented at
// http://go.microsoft.com/fwlink/?LinkId=234238
```

```
MainPage::MainPage()
{
        InitializeComponent();
        // Fill the ListView
        auto biz = ref new Biz();
        list->ItemsSource = biz->GetPeople();
}


/// <summary>
/// Invoked when this page is about to be displayed in a Frame.
/// </summary>
/// <param name="e">Event data that describes how this page was reached.  The Parameter
/// property is typically used to configure the page.</param>
void MainPage::OnNavigatedTo(NavigationEventArgs^ e)
{
        (void) e;           // Unused parameter
}
```

Modify and test the application

1. Modify the MainPage.xaml file so that its contents are identical to Listing 3-1.

2. Open the code-behind file (MainPage.xaml.cpp) and insert the boldface lines in Listing 3-2.

3. In Solution Explorer, on the shortcut menu for the MyFirstApp project node, choose Add | New Item.

4. Select Header File (.h) from the list of options and name it **Biz.h**. You won't use a separate .cpp file in this example.

5. Replace the code of the Biz.h file with the following code:

```
#pragma once
#include "pch.h"
#include <collection.h>
using namespace Windows::Foundation::Collections;
using namespace Platform::Collections;

namespace MyFirstApp
{
        [Windows::UI::Xaml::Data::Bindable]
        ref class Person sealed
        {
        public:
                Person() {}
                Person( Platform::String^ name ) { FullName = name; }
                property Platform::String^ FullName;
        };
```

```
[Windows::UI::Xaml::Data::Bindable]
ref class Biz sealed
{
public:
        Biz() {}
        ~Biz() {}
        IVector<Person^>^ GetPeople()
        {
                Vector<Person^>^ vec = ref new Vector<Person^>();
                vec->Append( ref new Person("Roberto Brunetti") );
                vec->Append( ref new Person("Paolo Pialorsi") );
                vec->Append( ref new Person("Marco Russo") );
                vec->Append( ref new Person("Luca Regnicoli") );
                vec->Append( ref new Person("Vanni Boncinelli") );
                vec->Append( ref new Person("Guido Zambarda") );
                vec->Append( ref new Person("Jessica Faustinelli") );
                vec->Append( ref new Person("Katia Egiziano") );
                return vec;
        };
    };
}
```

6. Add an *include* directive in the pch.h file, so that it resembles the following code (new lines are in bold):

```
//
// pch.h
// Header for standard system include files.
//

#pragma once

#include <collection.h>
#include "App.xaml.h"
#include "Biz.h"
```

7. Run the application.

The code in the *Biz* class simply returns a list of people represented by the *Person* class. For the sake of simplicity, this class has just one property, *FullName*.

The result will be something similar to Figure 3-4. You can obviously select a person from the list.

Roberto Brunetti

Paolo Pialorsi

Marco Russo

Luca Regnicoli ✓

Vanni Boncinelli

Guido Zambarda

Jessica Faustinelli

Katia Egiziano

FIGURE 3-4 The main page of the application presenting the list of names.

It is time to take off your developer hat and become a designer, to transform the list you just created into something more visually appealing. Stop the debugging session and return to Visual Studio 2012.

Before refining the appearance of the list, you will add some further user interface elements to the page, such as the application's title, in order to make your first app look more integrated with the Windows 8 environment.

To add a title, you need to modify the XAML source in the MainPage.xaml file, as shown in Listing 3-3.

LISTING 3-3 Modified MainPage.xaml code

```
<Page
    x:Class="MyFirstApp.MainPage"
    xmlns="http://schemas.microsoft.com/winfx/2006/xaml/presentation"
    xmlns:x="http://schemas.microsoft.com/winfx/2006/xaml"
    xmlns:local="using:MyFirstApp"
    xmlns:d="http://schemas.microsoft.com/expression/blend/2008"
    xmlns:mc="http://schemas.openxmlformats.org/markup-compatibility/2006"
    mc:Ignorable="d">
```

```xml
<Grid Background="{StaticResource ApplicationPageBackgroundThemeBrush}">
    <Grid.RowDefinitions>
        <RowDefinition Height="140"/>
        <RowDefinition Height="*"/>
    </Grid.RowDefinitions>

    <!-- page title -->
    <Grid Grid.Row="0" Grid.Column="0">
        <Grid.ColumnDefinitions>
            <ColumnDefinition Width="120"/>
            <ColumnDefinition Width="*"/>
        </Grid.ColumnDefinitions>
        <TextBlock x:Name="pageTitle" Grid.Column="1" Text="My First Windows 8 App"
                   Style="{StaticResource PageHeaderTextStyle}"/>
    </Grid>

    <ListView x:Name="list" DisplayMemberPath="FullName"
              Grid.Row="1" Grid.Column="0" Margin="116,0,0,46"/>
</Grid>
</Page>
```

If you press F5 in Visual Studio, your page should look similar to the one shown in Figure 3-5.

FIGURE 3-5 The main page with the title.

The previous listing used a *Grid* as the root element of the page. In XAML, the *Grid* panel allows you to place the child elements in rows and columns, as well as define in advance the number and the properties of each row and column by leveraging the *RowDefinitions* and *ColumnDefinitions* properties. In the example, the main grid has been split into two rows.

Now it is time to go back to the code for a deeper explanation. The first five lines of the *Grid* control definition are as follows:

```
<Grid Background="{StaticResource ApplicationPageBackgroundThemeBrush}">
    <Grid.RowDefinitions>
        <RowDefinition Height="140"/>
        <RowDefinition Height="*"/>
    </Grid.RowDefinitions>
```

To define the rows and columns of the main *Grid*, you used the *Grid.RowDefinitions* property. This syntax (in the form *classtype.propertyname*), also known as *extended property syntax*, represents a standard way to set complex properties using the markup language. Within the *RowDefinitions* property are two instances of *RowDefinition*: the first has height equal to 140 pixels, while the second uses the "*" (star) character to define a dimension that can fill the remaining space on the screen. Keep in mind that it is very important to design a user interface that can adapt itself to the end user's screen resolution, since nowadays tablets and devices are available with various screen resolutions and orientations. The use of relative rather than absolute sizing can go a long way toward helping you achieve this goal.

To assign each graphic element to a cell of the grid is sufficient to set the *Grid.Row* and *Grid. Column* properties of the element itself. These properties are also called *attached properties*, since they do not belong to the object model of the target element, but rather are "attached" to the control itself. In this scenario, two child elements are included in the main grid. First is a secondary *Grid* control that will contain the title page, with the attached property *Grid.Row* with a value of "*0*" and the attached property *Grid.Column* with a value of "*0*", too. That will place it in the first row and first column of the grid. Then there is a *ListView* control, with the properties *Grid.Row = "1"* and *Grid.Column = "0"*, which will place it in the second row of the first column.

Here is further useful information about the use of the *Grid* control:

- It is possible to omit the *Grid.Row* and/or *Grid.Column* property if its value is 0.

- If a *Grid* control does not explicitly set the *RowDefinitions* property, it is regarded as having a single *RowDefinition* definition with the *Height* property set to "*".

- If a *Grid* control does not explicitly set the *ColumnDefinitions* property, it is regarded as having a single *ColumnDefinition* definition with the *Width* property set to "*".

- The *RowDefinition*'s *Height* property can be set to *"Auto"*, in which case its size is defined at run time by the height of the contained controls.

- The *ColumnDefinition*'s *Width* property can be set to *"Auto"*, in which case its size is defined at run time by the width of the contained controls.

Continuing the analysis of the XAML code, you'll find a secondary *Grid* control, further divided into two columns, whose only child is a *TextBlock* control:

```
<TextBlock x:Name="pageTitle" Grid.Column="1"
        Text="My First Windows 8 App"
        Style="{StaticResource PageHeaderTextStyle}"/>
```

The property setting *Grid.Column = "1"* means that the *TextBlock* control will be positioned in the second column of the parent *Grid* control, while the *Style* property references a style called *PageHeaderTextStyle* using the special syntax *{StaticResource}*. You will come back to the basic concepts concerning the styles in the next chapters, but for now it will suffice to understand that a style is simply a container of property settings—a shared object that can be reused in different scenarios.

The property *Grid.Row = "1"* has been added to the *ListView* control so that it will occupy the entire second row of the main grid, and the property *Margin = "116,0,0,46"* places the *ListView* control a few pixels away from the edges of the cell. The *Margin* property is set with four numbers separated by commas, with the first number identifying the distance from the left edge and then continuing clockwise; in our example, the *ListView* control is placed 116 pixels away from the left edge, 0 pixels from the top and right edges, and 46 pixels from the bottom edge.

Now try to add some photos to the project by following these steps:

1. Open Windows Explorer and copy the Photos folder included in the Demo Files of this chapter in the MyFirstApp folder that contains the project files (there are also Assets and Common folders at the same level).

2. In Solution Explorer, on the shortcut menu for the project MyFirstApp node, choose Add | New Filter and rename the new filter to **Photos**.

3. In Solution Explorer, on the shortcut menu for the Photos filter node, choose Add | Existing Item and select all the .jpg files contained in the Photos folder you copied in the MyFirstApp folder in step 1.

As a result of this operation, you will have included in the project a reference to the Photos directory in the project's root containing some .jpg files.

The next step is to modify the *Person* class to add a custom property called *Photo* and refine the business component to set that property. Listing 3-4 shows the modified Biz.h code. Copy this code over the Biz.h file.

LISTING 3-4 Modified Biz.h code

```cpp
#pragma once
#include "pch.h"
#include <collection.h>
using namespace Windows::Foundation::Collections;
using namespace Platform::Collections;

namespace MyFirstApp
{
    [Windows::UI::Xaml::Data::Bindable]
    public ref class Person sealed
        {
        public:
                Person() {}
                Person( Platform::String^ name ) { FullName = name; }
                Person( Platform::String^ name, Platform::String^ photo )
                {
                        FullName = name;
                        Photo = photo;
                }
                property Platform::String^ FullName;
                property Platform::String^ Photo;
        };


        [Windows::UI::Xaml::Data::Bindable]
        public ref class Biz sealed
        {
        public:
                Biz() {}
                IVector<Person^>^ GetPeople()
                {
                        Vector<Person^>^ vec = ref new Vector<Person^>();
                        vec->Append( ref new Person("Roberto Brunetti", "Photos/01.jpg") );
                        vec->Append( ref new Person("Paolo Pialorsi", "Photos/02.jpg") );
                        vec->Append( ref new Person("Marco Russo", "Photos/03.jpg") );
                        vec->Append( ref new Person("Luca Regnicoli", "Photos/04.jpg") );
                        vec->Append( ref new Person("Vanni Boncinelli", "Photos/05.jpg") );
                        vec->Append( ref new Person("Guido Zambarda", "Photos/06.jpg") );
                        vec->Append( ref new Person("Jessica Faustinelli", "Photos/07.jpg") );
                        vec->Append( ref new Person("Katia Egiziano", "Photos/08.jpg") );
                        return vec;
                };
        };
}
```

To make the view of the people contained in the *ListView* control more appealing, you act on the *ItemTemplate* property of the control. It is important to understand that in XAML, a template object is equivalent to the concept of "structure," so the *ItemTemplate* property represents the structure of the individual items in the *ListView* control.

You will start by editing the XAML source code of the MainPage.xaml page with some tweaks to the *ListView* control. Replace the *ListView* definition in MainPage.xaml:

```xml
<ListView x:Name="list" DisplayMemberPath="FullName"
          Grid.Row="1" Grid.Column="0" Margin="116,0,0,46"/>
```

with this markup code:

```xml
<ListView Grid.Row="1" Grid.Column="0" x:Name="list" Margin="116,0,0,46">
    <ListView.ItemTemplate>
        <DataTemplate>
            <TextBlock Text="{Binding FullName}" FontSize="10" />
        </DataTemplate>
    </ListView.ItemTemplate>
</ListView>
```

The difference from the previous example is the removal of the *DisplayMemberPath* property, which displayed only simple strings connected to the *FullName* property of the bound objects, to give space to the *ItemTemplate* property that accepts objects of the *DataTemplate* type. In this scenario, the *DataTemplate* consists of a simple label (*TextBlock*) with its *Text* property connected to the *FullName* property of the bound object. If you run the application, you will see the list of people displayed in a smaller font. It is not a big graphical improvement over the previous version, but these steps serve as the basis for subsequent activities.

In the next step, you will try to change the *DataTemplate* of each item to display both the name and the photo. Replace the *DataTemplate* definition of the *ListView*:

```xml
<DataTemplate>
        <TextBlock Text="{Binding FullName}" FontSize="10" />
</DataTemplate>
```

with this code:

```xml
<DataTemplate>
    <StackPanel Width="200" Height="200">
        <TextBlock Text="{Binding FullName}" />
        <Image Source="{Binding Photo}" />
    </StackPanel>
</DataTemplate>
```

Compared to the previous step, you use a new panel called *StackPanel*, which places the child items under each other or, if the *Orientation* property is set to "*Horizontal*", side by side. In this scenario, each item in the *ListView* will be displayed with a *StackPanel* that will render the person's name and photo by binding the *FullName* property with the *Text* property of a *TextBlock* and the *Photo* property with the *Source* property of an *Image* control.

Until now, you have used the *ListView* control, which can display a series of vertical elements. Now replace the previous *ListView* definition, which was this code:

```
<ListView Grid.Row="1" Grid.Column="0" x:Name="list" Margin="116,0,0,46">
    <ListView.ItemTemplate>
        <DataTemplate>
            <StackPanel Width="200" Height="200">
                <TextBlock Text="{Binding FullName}" />
                <Image Source="{Binding Photo}" />
            </StackPanel>
        </DataTemplate>
    </ListView.ItemTemplate>
</ListView>
```

with this new markup code that uses a *GridView* control:

```
<GridView Grid.Row="1" Grid.Column="0" x:Name="list" Margin="116,0,0,46">
    <GridView.ItemTemplate>
        <DataTemplate>
            <StackPanel Width="200" Height="200">
                <TextBlock Text="{Binding FullName}" />
                <Image Source="{Binding Photo}" />
            </StackPanel>
        </DataTemplate>
    </GridView.ItemTemplate>
</GridView>
```

The *GridView* control, as the name suggests, is able to display its items in a tabular form, or grid.

If you press F5 in Visual Studio, you will see the result shown in Figure 3-6.

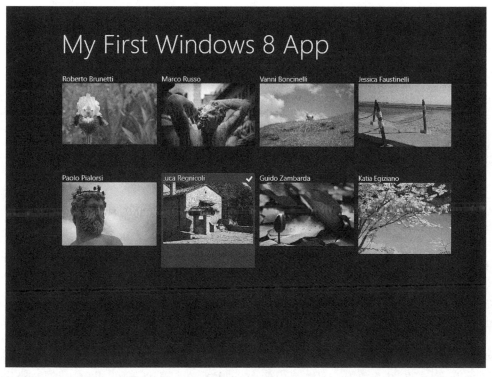

FIGURE 3-6 Element selected in the customized *GridView* control.

The outcome is acceptable, but you can do even better with just a bit of creativity and a few lines of XAML code within the *DataTemplate*. The next listing shows the entire MainPage.xaml page with the code changed from the previous step highlighted in bold. Replace the entire code of MainPage. xaml with the following code:

```
<Page
    x:Class="MyFirstApp.MainPage"
    xmlns="http://schemas.microsoft.com/winfx/2006/xaml/presentation"
    xmlns:x="http://schemas.microsoft.com/winfx/2006/xaml"
    xmlns:local="using:MyFirstApp"
    xmlns:d="http://schemas.microsoft.com/expression/blend/2008"
    xmlns:mc="http://schemas.openxmlformats.org/markup-compatibility/2006"
    mc:Ignorable="d">

    <Grid Background="{StaticResource ApplicationPageBackgroundThemeBrush}">
        <Grid.RowDefinitions>
            <RowDefinition Height="140"/>
            <RowDefinition Height="*"/>
        </Grid.RowDefinitions>

        <!-- Back button and page title -->
        <Grid Grid.Row="0" Grid.Column="0">
            <Grid.ColumnDefinitions>
                <ColumnDefinition Width="120"/>
                <ColumnDefinition Width="*"/>
            </Grid.ColumnDefinitions>
            <TextBlock x:Name="pageTitle"  Grid.Column="1" Text="My First Windows 8 App"
                    Style="{StaticResource PageHeaderTextStyle}"/>
        </Grid>

        <GridView Grid.Row="1" Grid.Column="0" x:Name="list" Margin="116,0,0,46">
            <GridView.ItemTemplate>
                <DataTemplate>
                    <Grid>
                        <Image Source="{Binding Photo}" Width="200" Height="130"
                            Stretch="UniformToFill" />
                        <Border Background="#A5000000" Height="45" VerticalAlignment="Bottom">
                            <StackPanel Margin="10,-2,-2,-2">
                                <TextBlock Text="{Binding FullName}" Margin="0,20,0,0"
                                        Foreground="#7CFFFFFF" HorizontalAlignment="Left"  />
                            </StackPanel>
                        </Border>
                    </Grid>
                </DataTemplate>
            </GridView.ItemTemplate>
        </GridView>
    </Grid>
</Page>
```

The new *DataTemplate* uses a *Grid* as a root element, and there are two elements nested within it: *Image* and *Border*. Given that the *Grid* has neither *RowDefinitions* nor *ColumnDefinitions*, the result is that the grid has a single cell, and the two child elements will be rendered in that cell, following the order defined in the markup—that is, the first element rendered by the runtime will be the image (*Image* control), and the *Border* control (with all its children) will be rendered in overlay. In addition, the XAML markup does not add anything new, except for the *Background* property of the *Border* control that contains the string "*#A5000000*". It is worth noting the first two characters after the number sign (#): they represent the alpha channel, or transparency, of the color defined by the subsequent six characters (black, in this case). In the sample, in fact, the *Border* control does not have a full and "opaque" color as a background; instead, it uses a semitransparent black for graphic purposes.

The result shown in Figure 3-7 is quite in line with the Windows 8 ecosystem and is visually pleasant.

FIGURE 3-7 A different customization of the *GridView* control.

It is worth nothing that the controls provided by the framework support all types of input out of the box, including mouse, keyboard, touch screen, and pen.

Search functionality

In this section, you will add the code that enables the search capability inside the application.

Earlier, you added the Search declaration to the application, causing the operating system to list the application in the Search pane. The declaration in the manifest essentially tells Windows 8, "I'm a searchable application." In other words, the system will present the application as a possible target for a search inside the application itself. A search target is the scope for the user's search, and it can be a file in the file system, an installed application, a setting in Control Panel, or some text inside a searchable application.

When a user selects an application as the target for a search, Windows 8 activates the application for the search and passes the search string typed by the user to the application. The idea is simple: the application is the only component that can display the search result correctly; no other component—or the operating system itself—knows about the application data other than the application. The way the application presents the data is specific to that application's data. In Chapter 6, "Windows Runtime APIs," you will learn more about search integration as well as other WinRT APIs such as Share, Webcam, FilePicker, and so on.

The search feature is implemented by a contract, called the Search contract, that regulates the interaction between the application and the operating system. The Search contract states the following:

- The application needs to be registered (the registration is based on the manifest declaration).

- The manifest declaration must include the name of the executable—that is, the *<application>*.exe file name—the entry point for the application that the system will call when the user chooses that application as the search target.

- The application will present the data in the appropriate format using a page.

- The application will receive the search text entered by the user at the entry point. The application is responsible for presenting a page with appropriate feedback to the user. That feedback can be the list of items found or a message if the search fails. The failure message can be as simple as "Not Found," or it can include graphics or a more specific message, such as "Data not available now, try again later." It's best to be as specific as you can.

- Windows manages the user's search history.

- The application can provide suggestions for amending text entered by the user.

Add a search contract

Visual Studio has a template that provides a simple contract implementation that covers all the points just listed except the last one. In the following procedure, you will first remove the Search declaration you added in the earlier procedure where you were simply exploring the default implementation. Follow these steps to add the search functionality.

1. Remove the Search declaration from the manifest by opening the Package.appxmanifest file, selecting the Declarations tab, selecting Search in the Supported Declaration list, and clicking the Remove button. Save your changes to the manifest.

2. Add a new Search contract item by right-clicking the project in Solution Explorer and choosing Add New Item.

3. In the Add New Item dialog box, select the Search Contract template in the Windows Store folder, and type **SearchPeople.xaml** as the name of the item, as shown in the following image.

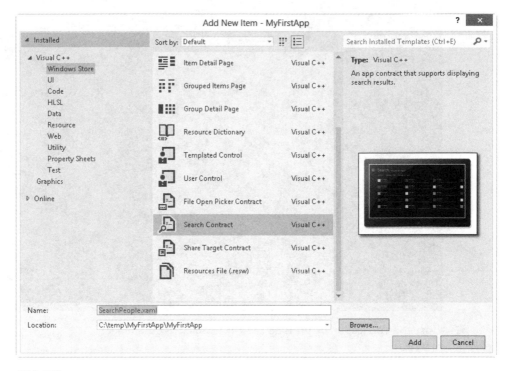

4. Click OK.

5. Click the Yes button in the dialog box that asks if you want to add all the files you need to implement the contract.

Test the default search component

You can test the application now. Doing so should help you fully understand the complete flow of the application. You will implement the people search in the next procedure.

1. Deploy the application from Visual Studio by right-clicking the project element in Solution Explorer and choosing the Deploy menu item.

2. Press Windows+Q to activate the Search pane.

3. Type some text in the Search box, and choose MyFirstApp from the list of applications. The operating system will launch the application—which was not already running because you just deployed it—and then activate the search inside the application using a call to the Search contract entry point. The application shows the SearchPeople.xaml page, which presents no results yet, as shown in the following image.

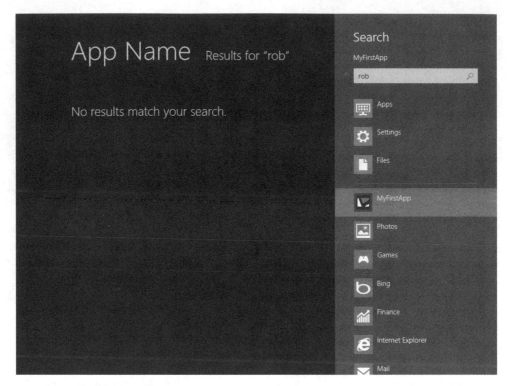

4. Close the application by pressing Alt+F4 or using Task Manager.

5. Launch the application from the Start screen.

6. Press Windows+Q to start a new search.

7. Type some text in the Search box and choose MyFirstApp from the application list. The results page is identical to the one presented earlier, but the back button is now enabled, because the search target (your application) was already running when you activated the search.

8. Click the back button and note that the application will be in the same state.

9. Go to the Start screen, open another application (Mail is fine), and repeat steps 6 through 8. The result will be always a blank page, but if you press the back button, you will see the page that shows the previous search. This demonstrates that the application was put into the suspended state and resumed when activated as the search target.

10. Press Alt+Tab (yes, that key combination still works in Windows 8) to select another application for the foreground.

11. Go to the Start screen and launch your application. The application presents the search results because Windows 8 suspends the application and restores it when the user returns to the application.

Now that you have explored the search flow, you need to understand the Search Contract template. The template adds the Search declaration to Package.appxmanifest, as you can verify by double-clicking the file and selecting the Declarations tab.

This template also modifies the project, adding, among other things, a new page to display the search results (SearchPeople.xaml or whatever name you used in the Add New Item dialog box)—you already saw this in the preceding procedure when you chose MyFirstApp as the target for the search. This page is displayed when a search is activated: the contract defines the entry point for the "search call," which by default is the *App* class.

The Search Contract Visual Studio template also modified the App.xaml.h and App.xaml.cpp files, overriding the *OnSearchActivated* method of the base class to show the search results page. Listings 3-5 and 3-6 show the complete code for App.xaml.h and App.xaml.cpp, respectively.

LISTING 3-5 Code-behind file for the *App* class: App.xaml.h

```
//
// App.xaml.h
// Declaration of the App class.
//

#pragma once

#include "App.g.h"

namespace MyFirstApp
{
        /// <summary>
        /// Provides application-specific behavior to supplement
        /// the default Application class.
        /// </summary>
        ref class App sealed
        {
        public:
                App();
                virtual void
                    OnLaunched(
                        Windows::ApplicationModel::Activation::LaunchActivatedEventArgs^
                        args) override;

        private:
                void OnSuspending(Platform::Object^ sender,
                    Windows::ApplicationModel::SuspendingEventArgs^ e);
        protected:

                virtual void OnSearchActivated(
                    Windows::ApplicationModel::Activation::SearchActivatedEventArgs^
                    pArgs) override;
        };
}
```

LISTING 3-6 Code-behind file for the *App* class: App.xaml.cpp

```cpp
//
// App.xaml.cpp
// Implementation of the App class.
//

#include "pch.h"
#include "MainPage.xaml.h"
#include "SearchPeople.xaml.h"

using namespace MyFirstApp;

using namespace Platform;
using namespace Windows::ApplicationModel;
using namespace Windows::ApplicationModel::Activation;
using namespace Windows::Foundation;
using namespace Windows::Foundation::Collections;
using namespace Windows::UI::Xaml;
using namespace Windows::UI::Xaml::Controls;
using namespace Windows::UI::Xaml::Controls::Primitives;
using namespace Windows::UI::Xaml::Data;
using namespace Windows::UI::Xaml::Input;
using namespace Windows::UI::Xaml::Interop;
using namespace Windows::UI::Xaml::Media;
using namespace Windows::UI::Xaml::Navigation;

// The Blank Application template is documented at http://go.microsoft.com/fwlink/?LinkId=234227

/// <summary>
/// Initializes the singleton application object.  This is the first line of authored code
/// executed, and as such is the logical equivalent of main() or WinMain().
/// </summary>
App::App()
{
        InitializeComponent();
        Suspending += ref new SuspendingEventHandler(this, &App::OnSuspending);
}

/// <summary>
/// Invoked when the application is launched normally by the end user.  Other entry points
/// will be used when the application is launched to open a specific file, to display
/// search results, and so forth.
/// </summary>
/// <param name="args">Details about the launch request and process.</param>
void App::OnLaunched(Windows::ApplicationModel::Activation::LaunchActivatedEventArgs^ args)
{
        auto rootFrame = dynamic_cast<Frame^>(Window::Current->Content);

        // Do not repeat app initialization when the Window already has content,
        // just ensure that the window is active
        if (rootFrame == nullptr)
        {
                // Create a Frame to act as the navigation context and associate it with
                // a SuspensionManager key
                rootFrame = ref new Frame();
```

```cpp
            if (args->PreviousExecutionState == ApplicationExecutionState::Terminated)
            {
                    // TODO: Restore the saved session state only when appropriate,
                    // scheduling the final launch steps after the restore is complete

            }

            if (rootFrame->Content == nullptr)
            {
                    // When the navigation stack isn't restored navigate
                    // to the first page,
                    // configuring the new page by passing required information
                    // as a navigation
                    // parameter
                    if (!rootFrame->Navigate(TypeName(MainPage::typeid),
                        args->Arguments))
                    {
                        throw ref new FailureException(
                            "Failed to create initial page");
                    }
            }
            // Place the frame in the current Window
            Window::Current->Content = rootFrame;
            // Ensure the current window is active
            Window::Current->Activate();
    }
    else
    {
            if (rootFrame->Content == nullptr)
            {
                // When the navigation stack isn't restored navigate to the first page,
                // configuring the new page by passing required information as a navigation
                // parameter
                if (!rootFrame->Navigate(TypeName(MainPage::typeid), args->Arguments))
                {
                    throw ref new FailureException("Failed to create initial page");
                }
            }
            // Ensure the current window is active
            Window::Current->Activate();
    }
}

/// <summary>
/// Invoked when application execution is being suspended.  Application state is saved
/// without knowing whether the application will be terminated or resumed with the contents
/// of memory still intact.
/// </summary>
/// <param name="sender">The source of the suspend request.</param>
/// <param name="e">Details about the suspend request.</param>
void App::OnSuspending(Object^ sender, SuspendingEventArgs^ e)
{
        (void) sender;          // Unused parameter
        (void) e;          // Unused parameter

        //TODO: Save application state and stop any background activity
}
```

```cpp
/// <summary>
/// Invoked when the application is activated to display search results.
/// </summary>
/// <param name="args">Details about the activation request.</param>
void MyFirstApp::App::OnSearchActivated(
    Windows::ApplicationModel::Activation::SearchActivatedEventArgs^ args)
{

        // TODO: Register the Windows::ApplicationModel::Search::SearchPane::
        // GetForCurrentView()->QuerySubmitted
        // event in OnWindowCreated to speed up searches once the application is already running

        // If the app does not contain a top-level frame, it is possible that this
        // is the initial launch of the app. Typically this method and OnLaunched
        // in App.xaml.cpp can call a common method.
    auto previousContent = Window::Current->Content;
    auto rootFrame =
        dynamic_cast<Windows::UI::Xaml::Controls::Frame^>(previousContent);
    if (rootFrame == nullptr)
    {
            // Create a Frame to act as the navigation context and associate it with
            // a SuspensionManager key
            rootFrame = ref new Frame();
            Common::SuspensionManager::RegisterFrame(rootFrame, "AppFrame");

            auto prerequisite = Concurrency::task<void>([](){});
            if (args->PreviousExecutionState == ApplicationExecutionState::Terminated)
            {
                    // Restore the saved session state only when appropriate,
                    // scheduling the
                    // final launch steps after the restore is complete
                    prerequisite = Common::SuspensionManager::RestoreAsync();
            }
            prerequisite.then([=](Concurrency::task<void> prerequisite)
            {
                    try
                    {
                            prerequisite.get();
                    }
                    catch (Platform::Exception^)
                    {
                            // If restore fails, the app should proceed as though
                            // there was no restored state.
                    }

                    // TODO: Navigate to the initial landing page of the app as if you
                    // were launched. This
                    // allows the user to return to your app from the search results page
                    // by using the back button.
```

```
                        //Navigate to the search page
                        rootFrame->Navigate(TypeName(SearchPeople::typeid),
                            args->QueryText);
                        // Place the frame in the current Window
                        Window::Current->Content = rootFrame;
                        // Ensure the current window is active
                        Window::Current->Activate();

                }, Concurrency::task_continuation_context::use_current());
        }
        else
        {

                //Navigate to the search page
                rootFrame->Navigate(TypeName(SearchPeople::typeid), args->QueryText);
                // Ensure the current window is active
                Window::Current->Activate();
        }
}
```

The *OnLaunched* method is the standard code suggested by the Windows Store Application template and is needed to activate the main page when the user launches the application. An application is "launched" when its state is not running.

The *OnSearchActivated* method is the code for the Search Contract default implementation. The code instantiates the designated page and calls the *Activate* custom method, passing the received arguments.

The *SearchActivatedEventArgs* class used by the *OnSearchActivated* method and the *LaunchActivatedEventArgs* class used by the *OnLaunched* method both implement the *IActivatedEventArgs* interface.

The first property of the interface is *Kind* and can be one of the values defined in the *ActivationKind* enumeration. This property lets the developer ask for the kind of activation during launch—for instance, if the application is launched by the user, this property will be *ActivationKind. Launch*; if the application is launched by the system when the user designates it as search target, the property will be *ActivationKind.Search*. If the application is activated to receive something from other applications using a Share contract, the property will be *ActivationKind.ShareTarget*.

The *QueryText* property of the *SearchActivatedEventArgs* class contains the text entered by the user in the Search pane. This property is used in the default *OnSearchActivated* method during the navigation to the search page, as shown in the following excerpt:

```
//Navigate to the search page
rootFrame->Navigate(TypeName(SearchPeople::typeid), args->QueryText);
// Place the frame in the current Window
Window::Current->Content = rootFrame;
// Ensure the current window is active
Window::Current->Activate();
```

As you can see, the search terms are received in the *navigationParameter* parameter of the *LoadState* method of the SearchPeople.xaml.cs page and used to build the *QueryText* property of the user interface in the *DefaultViewModel* property of the page. Listing 3-7 shows the code for this method.

LISTING 3-7 Excerpt of SearchPeople.xaml.cpp code-behind

```
void SearchPeople::LoadState(Object^ navigationParameter, IMap<String^, Object^>^ pageState)
{
        (void) pageState;           // Unused parameter

        // Unpack the two values passed in the parameter object: query text and previous
        // Window content
        auto queryText = safe_cast<String^>(navigationParameter);

        // TODO: Application-specific searching logic.  The search process is responsible for
        //       creating a list of user-selectable result categories:
        //
        //       filterList->Append(ref new SearchPeopleFilter("<filter name>",
        //          <result count>), false);
        //
        //       Only the first filter, typically "All", should pass true as a
        //       third argument in
        //       order to start in an active state.  Results for the active filter are
        //       provided in Filter_SelectionChanged below.

        auto filterList = ref new Vector<Object^>();
        filterList->Append(ref new SearchPeopleFilter("All", 0, true));

        // Communicate results through the view model
        DefaultViewModel->Insert("QueryText", "\u201c" + queryText + "\u201d");
        DefaultViewModel->Insert("Filters", filterList);
        DefaultViewModel->Insert("ShowFilters", filterList->Size >= 1);
}
```

The code is relatively simple: it defines a local variable called *queryText* to host the text entered by the user in the Search box. This text is passed in the Search contract as the *QueryText* property of the *SearchActivatedEventArgs* class.

The placeholder lets you choose the business logic to look for the text in your data, and it represents the most important part of this code.

The last three lines of code are useful if you decide to use the default layout to display the search results. The code assigns the text for the query, the filters list, and a Boolean value to indicate whether to show the filters list in the bindable dictionary (*IObservableMap* derives, in fact, from *IDictionary*). Next, you'll try to implement the search reusing the business layer you saw at the beginning of this chapter.

Implement the search logic

In the following procedure, you will implement the logic for retrieving results in a people search. Although you can implement the logic using a Language-Integrated Query (LINQ) query on the results from the business logic component *List* method, consider passing the search parameter to the business logic component to perform the search in lower layers. Generally speaking, it is a bad idea to filter the entire set of data in memory, in the user interface layer. For the sake of simplicity, this sample application has no persistence layer. Thus, you will implement the search in memory, inside the business layer.

1. Add a method to the business logic component (the *Biz* class in Biz.h) to filter the data source using the following code (please note that the comparison is case-sensitive):

```
IVector<Person ^>^ GetPeople(Platform::String^ search)
{
        Vector<Person^>^ vec = ref new Vector<Person^>();
        std::wstring _search = std::wstring( search->Data() );
        for each( Person^ p in GetPeople() ) {
                std::wstring name = std::wstring( p->FullName->Data() );
            int pos = name.find(_search);
                if (pos> 0) {
                        vec->Append( p );
                }
        }
        return vec;
}
```

2. Add a call to the new *GetPeople* method from the SearchPeople.xaml.cpp *LoadState* method, and assign the result to the *DefaultViewModel* property. Use the following code as a reference (the lines to add are in bold):

```
void SearchPeople::LoadState(Object^ navigationParameter, IMap<String^, Object^>^
    pageState)
{
    (void) pageState;          // Unused parameter

    // Unpack the two values passed in the parameter object: query text and
    // previous Window content
    auto queryText = safe_cast<String^>(navigationParameter);

    // TODO: Application specific searching logic.  The search process is responsible
    //       for
    //       creating a list of user-selectable result categories:
    //
    //       filterList->Append(ref new SearchPeopleFilter("<filter name>",
    //           <result count>), false);
    //
    //       Only the first filter, typically "All", should pass true as a third
    //       argument in
    //       order to start in an active state.  Results for the active filter are
    //       provided
    //       in Filter_SelectionChanged below.
```

```
auto biz = ref new Biz();
auto people = biz->GetPeople(queryText);
DefaultViewModel->Insert("Results", people );

auto filterList = ref new Vector<Object^>();
filterList->Append(ref new SearchPeopleFilter("All", 0, true));

// Communicate results through the view model
DefaultViewModel->Insert("QueryText", "\u201c" + queryText + "\u201d");
DefaultViewModel->Insert("Filters", filterList);
DefaultViewModel->Insert("ShowFilters", filterList->Size >= 1);
}
```

3. Open SearchPeople.xaml and find the *GridView* control named *resultGridView*. Remove the *ItemTemplate* default definition and define a new one to show the person's name for each result. The following code shows the control's complete definition:

```
<GridView
  x:Name="resultsGridView"
  AutomationProperties.AutomationId="ResultsGridView"
  AutomationProperties.Name="Search Results"
  TabIndex="1"
  Grid.Row="1"
  Margin="0,-238,0,0"
  Padding="110,240,110,46"
  SelectionMode="None"
  IsSwipeEnabled="false"
  IsItemClickEnabled="True"
  ItemsSource="{Binding Source={StaticResource resultsViewSource}}">
    <GridView.ItemTemplate>
        <DataTemplate>
          <TextBlock Text="{Binding FullName}" Margin="0,20,0,0"
             Foreground="#7CFFFFFF" HorizontalAlignment="Left"  />
        </DataTemplate>
    </GridView.ItemTemplate>
    <GridView.ItemContainerStyle>
        <Style TargetType="Control">
            <Setter Property="Height" Value="70"/>
            <Setter Property="Margin" Value="0,0,38,8"/>
        </Style>
    </GridView.ItemContainerStyle>
</GridView>
```

4. Deploy the application and test a search from the Search pane as you learned in the "Test the default search component" procedure earlier in this chapter.

The result is shown in Figure 3-8.

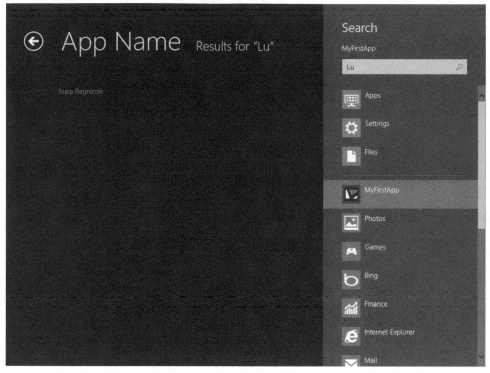

FIGURE 3-8 The result of a new search.

The last thing to do to complete this sample is change the *DefaultViewModel* property value to display the actual number of people retrieved by the search.

Modify the ViewModel properties

In this procedure, you will modify the code to show the actual number of people retrieved by the search. The procedure is very straightforward.

1. Modify the *LoadState* method in SearchPeople.xaml.cpp as follows. The bold code shows the changes.

```
void SearchPeople::LoadState(Object^ navigationParameter, IMap<String^, Object^>^
    pageState)
{
        (void) pageState;        // Unused parameter

        // Unpack the two values passed in the parameter object: query text
        // and previous Window content
        auto queryText = safe_cast<String^>(navigationParameter);
```

```
// TODO: Application-specific searching logic.  The search process is responsible
//         for
//         creating a list of user-selectable result categories:
//
//         filterList->Append(ref new SearchPeopleFilter("<filter name>",
//             <result count>), false);
//
//         Only the first filter, typically "All", should pass true as a third
//         argument in
//         order to start in an active state.  Results for the active filter are
//         provided
//         in Filter_SelectionChanged below.

auto biz = ref new Biz();
auto people = biz->GetPeople(queryText);
DefaultViewModel->Insert("Results", people );

auto filterList = ref new Vector<Object^>();
filterList->Append(ref new SearchPeopleFilter("All", people->Size, true));

// Communicate results through the view model
DefaultViewModel->Insert("QueryText", "\u201c" + queryText + "\u201d");
DefaultViewModel->Insert("Filters", filterList);
DefaultViewModel->Insert("ShowFilters", filterList->Size >= 1);
}
```

In practice, the first filter that shows the *All* keyword will contain the actual number of retrieved results, and the *ShowFilters* Boolean property indicates whether to show the various filters to the user. Obviously, you have to implement the various filters and the corresponding code.

2. Kill the application using Task Manager because the process is probably already running from the previous procedure.

3. Deploy the application and test it again using the Search pane.

The result of a search for "Rob" should be identical to that shown in Figure 3-9.

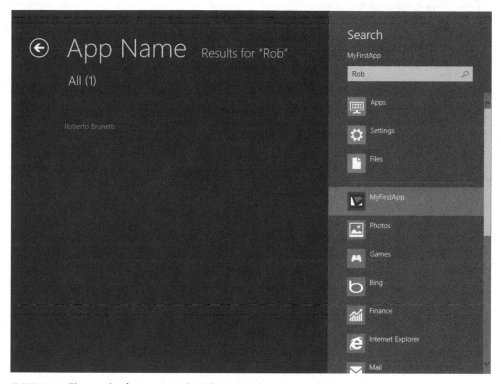

FIGURE 3-9 The result of a new search with the number of items found.

Summary

In this chapter, you reviewed the complete cycle of creating, testing, and deploying a simple Windows 8 application. You learned about the available templates and how to describe the application using the manifest. You also added code to implement the Search contract using a provided template.

Quick reference

To	Do this
Arrange controls inside a flexible grid area	Use the *Grid* control.
Arrange child elements into a single line that can be oriented horizontally or vertically	Use the *StackPanel* control.
Deploy a Windows Store application	Use the deployment feature of Visual Studio 2012.
Deploy and test the application	In Visual Studio, press F5.
Implement the Search contract	Use the SDK template called Search Contract, which adds the search results page, the manifest declaration, and some sample code to the solution.
Define an application feature	Use the Visual Studio IDE Designer and open the Package.appxmanifest file.
Close an application	Stop the debugger (in case you are debugging), press Alt+F4, use the closing gesture, or use the new Task Manager to terminate the process.

CHAPTER 4

Application life-cycle management

After completing this chapter, you will be able to

- Understand the application manifest settings.

- Use the application manifest to modify application capability and appearance.

- Deploy and test an application.

- Understand the way Windows 8 manages the different running states of an application.

- Respond to launching, activating, suspending, and resuming events.

- Use the application data store to save data locally.

In preceding chapters, you saw how Windows 8 provides a new user interface, offers a completely new user experience, and exposes a new set of APIs called Windows Runtime (WinRT) APIs through which you can interact with the operating system. You also developed a simple application in Chapter 3, "My first Windows 8 app."

This chapter introduces the complete application life cycle in Microsoft Windows 8, from deployment, to launch, to uninstallation. You will start by analyzing the various settings in the application manifest. The *application manifest* is a file that defines an application's appearance on the Start screen and informs Windows 8 about which WinRT features the application will use. You will also explore how WinRT manages an application's life cycle at run time, by launching, suspending, resuming, and terminating the application as needed.

First, a Windows 8 application cannot include an app.config file. This means that—just as in a Microsoft Windows Phone or Windows Presentation Foundation (WPF) Web Browser Application (WBA)—you cannot use the classic .NET configuration mechanism to provide application and system settings. There is no *System.Configuration* namespace or any equivalent classes in the WinRT APIs. The Windows 8 runtime system executes Windows Store applications in a sandboxed process, similar to a Silverlight or WPF WBA. Users cannot navigate to the file system where the application is installed and change files, because Windows 8 apps are mainly downloaded and installed from the Windows Store.

Application manifest

As in a Windows Phone 7.*x* project, deployment information and many configuration settings are stored in a manifest file that WinRT calls Package.appxmanifest, which is an XML-formatted file that describes various aspects of the project, as you can see in the following listing, taken from a real Windows Store application.

```xml
<?xml version="1.0" encoding="utf-8"?>

<Package xmlns="http://schemas.microsoft.com/appx/2010/manifest">

 <Identity Name="ea15f786-9bb0-4d64-98b0-d251fa375633" Publisher="CN=Devleap"
    Version="1.0.0.1" />

 <Properties>
    <DisplayName>Learn with the Animals</DisplayName>
    <PublisherDisplayName>ThinkAhead</PublisherDisplayName>
    <Logo>Assets\Store_Logo.png</Logo>
 </Properties>
 <Prerequisites>
    <OSMinVersion>6.2.1</OSMinVersion>
    <OSMaxVersionTested>6.2.1</OSMaxVersionTested>
 </Prerequisites>
 <Resources>
    <Resource Language="x-generate" />
 </Resources>
 <Applications>
    <Application Id="App" Executable="$targetnametoken$.exe"
      EntryPoint="ThinkAhead.Windows8KidsGames.App">
     <VisualElements DisplayName="Learn with the Animals" Logo="Assets\logo.png"
       SmallLogo="Assets\small_logo.png" Description="Learn animal noises, names,
       guess their noises and names, try to read and try to write their names"
       ForegroundText="dark"
       BackgroundColor="#464646">
       <DefaultTile ShowName="noLogos" WideLogo="Assets\wide_logo.png"
          ShortName="Learn with the Animals" />
       <SplashScreen Image="Assets\splash_screen.png" BackgroundColor="#b4dfba" />
       <InitialRotationPreference>
         <Rotation Preference="landscape" />
         <Rotation Preference="landscapeFlipped" />
       </InitialRotationPreference>
     </VisualElements>
    </Application>
 </Applications>
</Package>
```

The first section, called *Properties*, contains information for the Windows Store, such as the title for the application, the name of the publisher, the official logo, and a brief description.

The last section, called *Capabilities*, contains a list of all the operating system features the application needs to access on the user's PC or tablet. When application code requests one of these features, the user receives a direct request to give the application specific permission to use the feature. The user can revoke this permission at any time; your code has to fail gracefully if the user denies the permission to use a capability.

This way of working is similar to a Windows Phone 7.x project, where WMAppManifest.xml tells the operating system the capabilities the application requires to run. You can find more information on application capabilities in Chapter 6, "Windows Runtime APIs."

Figure 4-1 shows the Manifest Designer that Microsoft Visual Studio 2012 provides to simplify the application definition. To open the designer, simply double-click the Package.appxmanifest file in Solution Explorer. The figure shows the real manifest for one of the authors' applications, called Learn with the Animals. The Application UI tab lets you choose the display name of the application (the name used for the Start screen), a description of the application, three logos for the application, and so on.

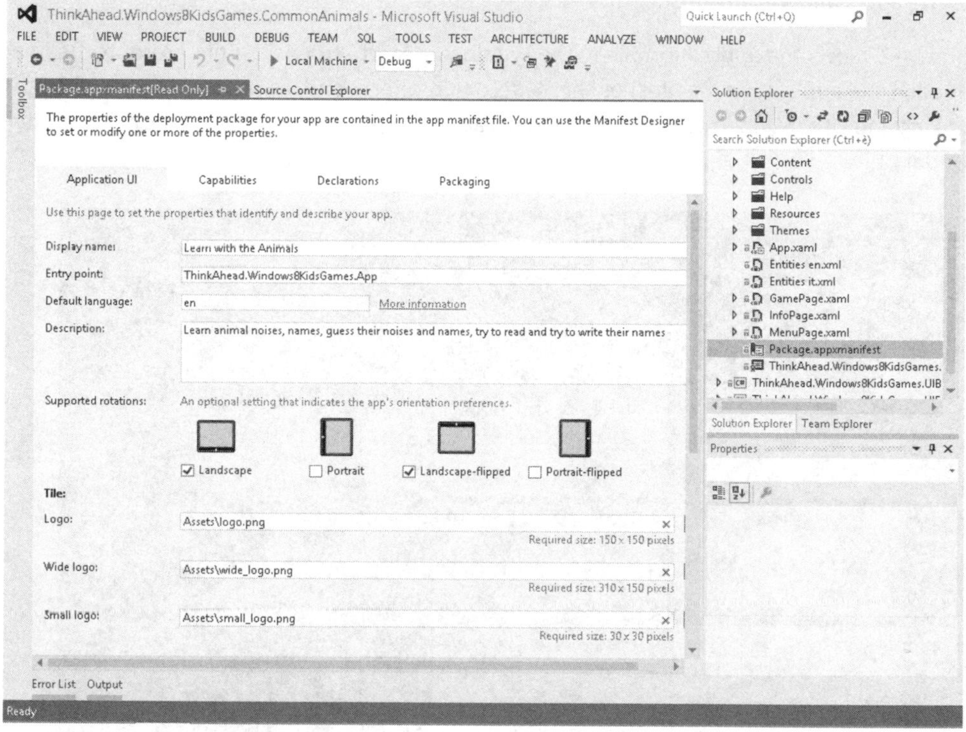

FIGURE 4-1 The Application UI tab.

The first tab of the Visual Studio Manifest Designer produces the following section in the application manifest:

```
<VisualElements DisplayName="Save The Planet" Logo="Assets\Logo.png"
    SmallLogo="Assets\SmallLogo.png" Description="ThinkAhead.SaveThePlanet.Win8.UI"
    ForegroundText="light" BackgroundColor="#222222" ToastCapable="true">
        <LockScreen Notification="badgeAndTileText" BadgeLogo="Assets\BadgeLogo.png" />
        <DefaultTile ShowName="allLogos"  />
        <SplashScreen Image="Assets\SplashScreen.png" BackgroundColor="#000000" />
</VisualElements>
```

VisualElements, as the name implies, defines the display name for the Windows 8 Start screen, the various logos for the tile (*Logo*), the small tile (*SmallLogo*), and the wide tile (*WideLogo*), as well as the supported rotation and the default one, the badge default logo, and the image for the splash screen.

All the required images referenced by the application package manifest are provided as placeholders by the Visual Studio templates for Windows Store applications and are placed in the Assets folder of the project. The default template uses an image for the application logo that displays on the default application tile (Logo.png), an image for the initial splash screen (SplashScreen.png), a small logo image that is shown in the tile if the application switches its tile from code (SmallLogo.png) and, last but not least, an image used by the Windows Store to represent the application (StoreLogo.png). As you can see in Figure 4-1, you can also provide a wide logo that displays if the user chooses a wide tile for the application from the Start screen.

Figure 4-2 shows the application tile in the Windows 8 Start screen. The tile presents the image described in the application manifest as the *WideLogo* property and, as you will learn in Chapter 9, "Rethinking the UI for Windows 8 apps," the application can also modify the tile from code or create a secondary tile.

FIGURE 4-2 The Learn with the Animals wide tile on the Start screen.

Application package

The application manifest contains all the application information the system needs to deploy it on a target machine. That could be the local machine or the Windows 8 Simulator, which you can use for testing and debugging purposes. The manifest also contains all the information needed to package the application for the Windows Store.

When you run an application using the F5 button, Visual Studio 2012 compiles the application, builds the application package, and asks the operating system to install the package on the developer machine or the Windows 8 Simulator.

Visual Studio lets you package and deploy the application on the Windows Store by using the Store | Create App Package feature. This menu item launches a Create App Packages wizard that guides you through the process to package the application and upload it to the store, or to simply build the package to use it on a developer machine, as you can see from the two options and associated descriptions in Figure 4-3.

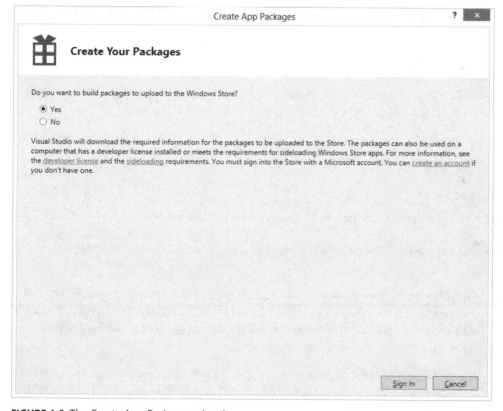

FIGURE 4-3 The Create App Packages wizard.

If you choose the first option, you will be asked for the Windows Live ID associated with your Windows Store account to publish the application. In both cases, the last step of the wizard lets you choose the processor architecture for which to build the application, and then it creates the package (see Figure 4-4).

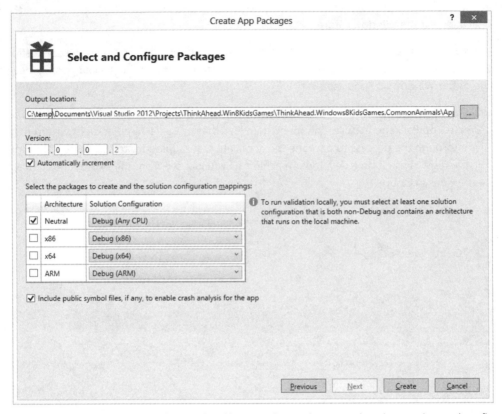

FIGURE 4-4 The Create App Packages wizard lets you choose the output location, version, and configuration.

The package contains one binary file that represents the application and a folder with four different files:

- **<App Name_Version_Compilation>.appxupload** This is the real "package," and it contains the compiled application to be installed. For example, the application Learn with the Animals, version 1.0.0.6 for Any CPU is packaged in a file called LearnwiththeAnimals_1.0.0.6_AnyCPU. appxupload. This is the file for the Windows Store.

- **<App Name_Version_Compilation>.cer** This is a certificate used to sign the application in the local development environment. The private key is contained in the .pfx file of the Visual Studio 2012 project. During the installation process, this certificate is added to the Trusted Root Certification Authorities of the local machine.

- ***<App Name_Version_Compilation>*.appxsym** This file contains the debugging symbols.

- **Add-AppxDevPakage.bat** This file contains the script to install the application, the signing certificate in the Trusted Root Certification Authorities, and all the dependencies the application needs to run.

Note The directory name is also dependent on and formed by the compilation type (Debug, Release, Platform) and the current user name, and it contains all the deployed application files.

When the application is installed on the system, Windows 8 creates a directory in X:\Users\<*username*>\AppData\Local\Packages\ using the globally unique identifier (GUID) associated with the application. This GUID is automatically generated when the Create App Packages wizard creates a new Windows Store application and is stored in the application manifest in the *Identity* tag, as shown in the following excerpt:

```
<Identity Name="380ac04e-991e-4e5f-8758-5f56e68b0e94" Publisher="CN=DevLeap"
    Version="1.0.0.2" />
```

You can uninstall an application at any time by selecting its tile and choosing Uninstall from the Windows 8 Start screen. As shown in Figure 4-5, you can also unpin the application by choosing the Unpin from Start item in the app bar. Doing so simply removes the tile from the Start screen and does *not* uninstall the application from the system. You can always reach the application again by pressing Windows+Q and searching within the installed apps.

Note You can use the batch file to install the application on a developer machine manually.

FIGURE 4-5 The Windows 8 Start screen app bar.

Windows Store

The Windows Store enables users to search for, download, install, and review applications. As a developer, you can upload your applications to the Windows Store, making them available for download or purchase on every tablet and PC running Windows 8 around the globe.

To upload an application, you first need to create a Windows Store account and bind it to a Windows Live ID. This procedure is quite straightforward. It also lets you define the application's publisher name, the name that appears in many Windows Store screens near the application name. Users can search for apps in the Windows Store by name, by keyword, and by publisher.

After you have created an account, you can upload an application immediately. Alternatively, you can reserve a name for an application you plan to develop within a year. If you plan to sell the application, you must also fill out the fiscal profile for the person or company specified as the publisher. You will also need to complete the IRS module related to your fiscal position. For example, if you are the publisher and you live outside the United States, you will need to fill out the W-8BEN form. Fortunately, a wizard will guide you during the process of choosing the right module and filling it out online.

You can upload and sell an application before you have filled in all the fiscal data, but you will receive no money until you have completed the financial profile.

Aside from these administrative tasks, the process of publishing an application is straightforward. First, you should verify that the application conforms to Windows Store requirements locally. This step is not required, but it's very useful to validate your application quickly before performing any upload. You can validate your app with the application verifier (Windows App Certification Kit, or ACK) which, as shown in Figure 4-6, validates an application for technical compliance with Windows Store rules.

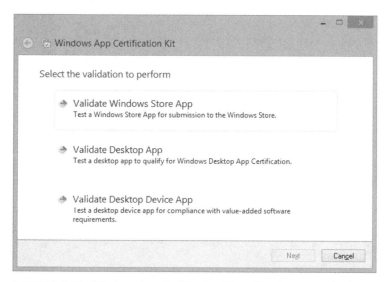

FIGURE 4-6 The Windows App Certification Kit verifies that an application conforms to Windows Store rules.

The tool can also validate a desktop application and a desktop device application for Windows 8 Desktop App Certification. The Windows App Certification Kit is installed on your system together with Visual Studio Express for Windows 8; you can launch it from the Start screen.

The next step lets you choose the application to validate (remember to deploy it to the local system compiling the project in release mode). The validation begins by launching the application. It is very important that you *do not interact* with the application (and the system) during the test, because the test also verifies how the application is suspended and how it resumes, as well as whether it closes and terminates correctly.

If your application does not pass all the tests performed by the Windows App Certification Kit, there's no point in trying to upload the application package to the Windows Store. The Windows Store service performs exactly the same verification process, so there is no way an app that fails local certification can pass the store certification. At the end of the process, you will receive detailed information on any application problems, presented as errors or warnings. As stated earlier, the local verification step is not required, but it is very useful and recommended.

When you have completed local certification, if you haven't reserved a name for your app, you must choose an application name before uploading the package.

For each application you upload to the Windows Store, you need to provide required information, including the application name and sales details (price, country availability, trial version availability, and so on). You can enrich this information by providing details such as an age rating (especially if your app is a game), the cryptography mechanism your app uses (if any), and notes to testers, as shown in Figure 4-7.

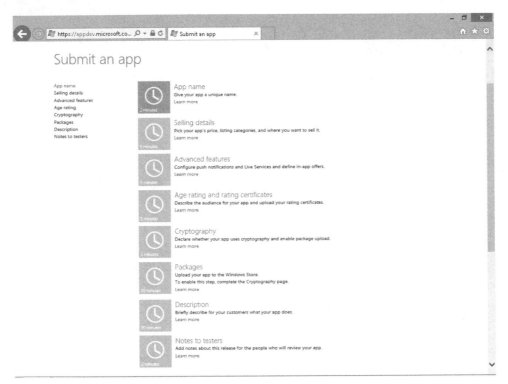

FIGURE 4-7 The Submit an App page allows you to fill in information about your application when submitting it to the Windows Store.

After completing the information on the Submit an App page, you need to upload the package. You can build the package directly from Visual Studio 2012 as you saw in the previous section of this chapter, choosing the option to associate the package with the application in the store. From a practical viewpoint, after you create an application using the Windows Store dashboard, you can associate it with the Visual Studio project using the Store menu. This association modifies the application manifest using the publisher name and publisher ID taken from the store services.

To do that, from the Store menu, select the Associate App with the Store menu item to bind the project to an application and import the publisher name and certificate to the project. Alternatively, you can perform the binding operation when you build the application package, as shown in Figure 4-8.

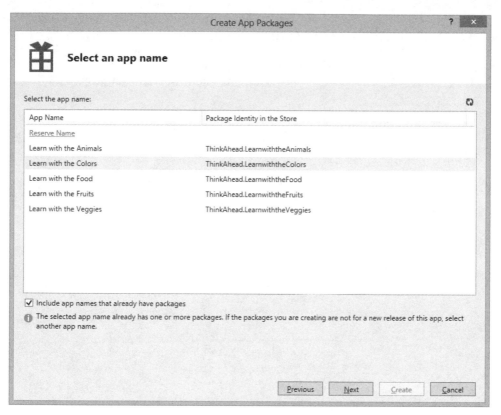

FIGURE 4-8 Associate an application Visual Studio project with the real Windows Store application.

After the upload operation completes, you need to fill in an important form linked to the Description button that allows you to define all of the marketing information for your app:

- Description of the application (free text)

- Two lines describing major application features

- Seven keywords (may be more in future releases)

- Optional copyright information and license terms

- Eight optional screen shots, each one with a required description

- Promotional images that will be used by the system if your app is selected to appear on the New Apps or Top Apps page of the store

- Application minimum hardware requirements

- An email address that users can write to if they have support requests

- A privacy policy

For example, Figure 4-9 shows the attributes used for the Learn with the Colors application, which is a Windows 8 app the authors published to the Windows Store.

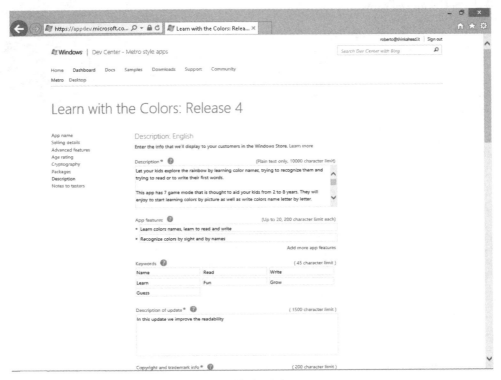

FIGURE 4-9 Attributes for the authors' Learn with the Colors app.

For each application you distribute through the Windows Store, the store service provides statistics such as store trends, a financial summary, the number of downloads, and reviews and rating information.

Launching

When you create a new Windows Store application using the Visual Studio template, you will end up with a solution containing one project with a default page called MainPage.xaml and a class that represents the application defined in the App.xaml.cpp and App.xaml.h files. WinRT invokes the method called *OnLaunched* immediately after creating the application instance. You can override this method in your application to perform some activities.

Understand the *OnLaunched* event

In this procedure, you will start coding the event handlers for application events.

1. Create a new application project. To do so, open Visual Studio 2012 and select New Project from the File menu (the sequence can be File | New | Project for full-featured versions of Visual Studio). Choose Visual C++ in the Templates tree and then Windows Store from the list of installed templates. Then choose Blank App (XAML) from the list of available projects.

2. Name the new project **ALMEvents**, and then choose a location on your file system and accept the default solution name. When you've finished, click OK.

   As you learned in Chapter 3, the Windows Store Application template provides a default page (MainPage.xaml), an application entry point in the *App* class (App.xaml.cpp and App.xaml.h files), and a default application description in Package.appxmanifest.

3. Open the App.xaml.cpp file and scroll down until you can see the *OnLaunched* method.

   This method is called by WinRT when the user launches the application. An application is launched when the user clicks the application tile. The default code inside the method simply instantiates a new *Frame* class, sets it as the current content, and then navigates to the main page, calling the *Navigate* method on the frame and passing the *MainPage* class. The last line activates the current content that is the Main Page. The code also contains a test to check for the presence of an existing frame (meaning the application is already running), which will be explained later in this chapter.

   The following snippet shows the *OnLaunched* method:

```
void App::OnLaunched(Windows::ApplicationModel::Activation::LaunchActivatedEventArgs^
    args)
{
        auto rootFrame = dynamic_cast<Frame^>(Window::Current->Content);

        // Do not repeat app initialization when the Window already has content,
        // just ensure that the window is active
        if (rootFrame == nullptr)
        {
                // Create a Frame to act as the navigation context and associate it with
                // a SuspensionManager key
                rootFrame = ref new Frame();

                if (args->PreviousExecutionState ==
                    ApplicationExecutionState::Terminated)
                {
                        // TODO: Restore the saved session state only when appropriate,
                        // scheduling the final launch steps after the restore is
                        // complete
                }
        }
```

```
                            if (rootFrame->Content == nullptr)
                            {
                                    // When the navigation stack isn't restored, navigate to the
                                    // first
                                    // page, configuring the new page by passing required
                                    // information as a navigation parameter
                                    if (!rootFrame->Navigate(TypeName(MainPage::typeid),
                                            args->Arguments))
                                    {
                                            throw ref new FailureException(
                                                "Failed to create initial page");
                                    }
                            }
                            // Place the frame in the current Window
                            Window::Current->Content = rootFrame;
                            // Ensure the current window is active
                            Window::Current->Activate();
                }
                else
                {
                            if (rootFrame->Content == nullptr)
                            {
                                    // When the navigation stack isn't restored, navigate to the
                                    // first
                                    // page, configuring the new page by passing required information
                                    // as a navigation parameter
                                    if (!rootFrame->Navigate(TypeName(MainPage::typeid),
                                            args->Arguments))
                                    {
                                            throw ref new FailureException(
                                                "Failed to create initial page");
                                    }
                            }
                            // Ensure the current window is active
                            Window::Current->Activate();
                }
        }
}
```

4. Add the following two lines just at the beginning of the method, before the rest of the code, as presented in the previous step:

```
auto dia = ref new Windows::UI::Popups::MessageDialog(
            "App OnLaunched",
            "ALM Events");
dia->ShowAsync();
.....
```

The first line instantiates the *MessageDialog* class, passing to it the content and the title as string parameters. This class represents what in the past was called a *message box*. The second line of code shows the message dialog box in the default location and begins an asynchronous operation for processing the dialog box, and then calls the *Start* method to start the operation.

5. Press F5 to start the application or deploy the application as you learned in Chapter 3, and tap or click the application tile. The following image shows the message dialog box.

ALM Events

App OnLaunched

Close

As you can see, the dialog box is shown full screen, and it displays the title and the content passed as parameters in the class constructor.

6. Click or tap the Close button to close the dialog box. You will see a completely black page—this is because the default page presents nothing.

7. Press the Windows button to open the Start screen (you can also move the mouse in the lower-left corner of the screen and choose Start from the Start menu).

8. Scroll right until you find the ALMEvents application, and tap or click the application tile to launch it again. The application is already running, and you will not see the dialog box; in fact, WinRT does not call the *OnLaunched* method on the application when the application instance is already loaded.

This behavior is significantly different than in previous versions of Windows, where the system started a new instance of the application each time the user launched it. In Windows 8, there can be only one instance running at the same time. When the user launches an already running application, WinRT just brings the application to the foreground.

9. Close the application by pressing Alt+F4 and repeat steps 5–7 to verify the application flow again.

The parameter received by the *OnLaunched* method is of type *LaunchActivatedEventArgs*, a class that implements the *IActivatedEventArgs* interface you saw in Chapter 3. This interface is implemented by different classes that serve as event arguments for different activation events. The first property of the interface is *Kind*, and it can assume one of the values defined in the *ActivationKind* enumeration. This property lets the developer ask for the kind of launch. For instance, if the application is launched by the user, this property will be *ActivationKind.Launch*; if the application is launched by the system when the user selects it as search target, the property will be *ActivationKind.Search*; if the application is activated to receive something from other applications using a Share contract, the property will be *ActivationKind.ShareTarget*. There are two different methods in the base class to react to this activation. You will see these differences in this chapter.

Show the launch kind

In this procedure, you will change the code of the previous procedure to show the activation kind.

1. Replace the code you inserted in the previous procedure for the *OnLaunched* method to create a message that contains the activation kind as follows. You will need to insert the lines in bold:

```
Platform::String^ message = "App Launched: " + args->Kind.ToString();
auto dia = ref new Windows::UI::Popups::MessageDialog(message, "ALM Events");
dia->ShowAsync

. . .
```

   The first line uses the *Kind* property of the event args to build the message text, and the second line presents it in a message dialog box.

2. Run the application, deploying it from the Build menu, and start the application by clicking the application tile on the Start screen. You will see the dialog box presenting the message "App Launched: Launch."

3. Click the Close button and do not close the application.

4. Go to the Start screen and click the application tile. You won't see any messages because the application is already running.

5. Close the application using Alt+F4.

Understand the previous state

In this procedure, you will modify the code for the *OnLaunched* method to test the execution state for the previous launch of the application. If the user closes the application normally, the previous execution state will be *ClosedByUser*, telling you that everything went well for the user. If the user has never launched the application, the previous execution state will be *NotRunning*.

1. Change again the first line of the *OnLaunched* event to build a more detailed message that shows the activation kind and the previous execution state by replacing the first line of the method with the one shown in the following code excerpt (bold line):

```
Platform::String^ message = "App Launched: " + args->Kind.ToString()
            + " - Previous State: " + args->PreviousExecutionState.ToString();
auto dia = ref new Windows::UI::Popups::MessageDialog(message, "ALM Events");
dia->ShowAsync();
...
```

2. Deploy the application using the Deploy menu item on the Build menu.

3. Start the application by launching it from the Start screen.

4. Verify that the message "App Launched: Launch – Previous State: ClosedByUser" displays, meaning the application was closed by you previously (if, in fact, you closed it in the previous procedure). The message can be "App Launched: Launch – Previous State: NotRunning" if the application was closed immediately before. Try it closing and launching it from the Start screen quickly.

5. Close the application using Alt+F4.

6. Modify MainPage.xaml by adding two buttons and their corresponding click events in the *Grid* control as follows:

```
<Grid Background="{StaticResource ApplicationPageBackgroundThemeBrush}">
    <StackPanel Orientation="Horizontal" VerticalAlignment="Top">
        <Button Click="Crash_Click" Content="Crash" />
        <Button Click="Close_Click" Content="Close" />
    </StackPanel>
</Grid>
```

The first one will be used to perform an invalid operation that causes a crash of the application. The second will be used to gracefully close the application from code.

7. Implement the event handlers for the *Crash* and the *Close* click events (highlighted in bold) using the following code in the MainPage.xaml.h (Listing 4-1) and MainPage.xaml.cpp (Listing 4-2) files, respectively.

LISTING 4-1 Code-behind file for the *App* class: MainPage.xaml.h

```cpp
#pragma once

#include "MainPage.g.h"

namespace ALMEvents
{
    /// <summary>
    /// An empty page that can be used on its own or navigated to within a Frame.
    /// </summary>
    public ref class MainPage sealed
    {
    public:
        MainPage();

    protected:
        virtual void OnNavigatedTo(Windows::UI::Xaml::Navigation::NavigationEventArgs^ e)
            override;
    private:
        void Crash_Click(Platform::Object^ sender,
            Windows::UI::Xaml::RoutedEventArgs^ e);
        void Close_Click(Platform::Object^ sender,
            Windows::UI::Xaml::RoutedEventArgs^ e);
        };
}
```

LISTING 4-2 Code-behind file for the *App* class: MainPage.xaml.cpp

```cpp
#include "pch.h"
#include "MainPage.xaml.h"

using namespace ALMEvents;

using namespace Platform;
using namespace Windows::Foundation;
using namespace Windows::Foundation::Collections;
using namespace Windows::UI::Xaml;
using namespace Windows::UI::Xaml::Controls;
using namespace Windows::UI::Xaml::Controls::Primitives;
using namespace Windows::UI::Xaml::Data;
using namespace Windows::UI::Xaml::Input;
using namespace Windows::UI::Xaml::Media;
using namespace Windows::UI::Xaml::Navigation;

// The Blank Page item template is documented at
// http://go.microsoft.com/fwlink/?LinkId=234238

MainPage::MainPage()
{
        InitializeComponent();
}
```

```
/// <summary>
/// Invoked when this page is about to be displayed in a Frame.
/// </summary>
/// <param name="e">Event data that describes how this page was reached. The Parameter
/// property is typically used to configure the page.</param>
void MainPage::OnNavigatedTo(NavigationEventArgs^ e)
{
        (void) e;          // Unused parameter
}


void ALMEvents::MainPage::Crash_Click(Platform::Object^ sender,
    Windows::UI::Xaml::RoutedEventArgs^ e)
{
        int a = 10;
        int b = 0;
        int c = a / b;
}


void ALMEvents::MainPage::Close_Click(Platform::Object^ sender,
    Windows::UI::Xaml::RoutedEventArgs^ e)
{
        Application::Current->Exit();
}
```

8. Deploy the application by right-clicking the project in the solution and choosing Deploy from the context menu.

9. Launch the application from the Start screen, click Close on the dialog box, and click the Crash button on the main page. The application should crash, returning to the Start screen in a few seconds. Be patient.

10. Launch the application again from the Start screen. The dialog box will show NotRunning as the previous state.

11. Close the dialog box and then click the Close button to gracefully close the application.

12. Launch the application again from the Start screen to verify that the dialog box shows NotRunning as the previous state.

13. Close the dialog box and then close the application by using Alt+F4 or swiping your mouse or finger from the upper-center of the screen to the lower-center to close the application in the canonical way.

14. Wait for at least 20 seconds and then launch the application again from the Start screen to verify that the dialog box shows ClosedByUser as the previous state.

To summarize, an application receives a call to the *OnLaunched* method from WinRT when the user launches the application and the application is not already running. This method receives the launch kind and the previous state. Also note that there can be only one instance of a Windows Store application in Windows 8.

Activating

If the user "launches" the application using the Search contract, the application receives a call to the *OnSearchActivated* method, as you learned in Chapter 3. In this case, WinRT calls this procedure *activation*, as the name of the method implies. Activation is a more correct term, since the application is not launched by the user. The parameter args received by the *OnLaunched* method, as you learned in the preceding procedure, has a property called *Kind* that can assume the value of *Search*, but don't be confused by this. When the user selects the target of a search, WinRT invokes the *OnSearchActivated* method on the *App* class and never invokes the *OnLaunched* events. Both event arguments, as well as other event args for other activation methods, implement a common interface; this explains why both of them have the same property. The following procedure clarifies these concepts.

Understand the *OnSearchActivated* method

In this procedure, you will modify the code for the App.xaml.cpp file to test the activation for search. You will use the Search Contract template from Visual Studio, which you learned about in Chapter 3.

1. Implement the Search contract by right-clicking the project in Solution Explorer and choosing Add New Item.

2. Scroll down in the Windows Store folder until you find the Search Contract item.

3. Click the Add button without changing the default name, and click Yes when the dialog box asks you to add the requested files.

   You will not implement a real search page in this procedure; you will just test the activation for searching.

   Adding the Search Contract item modifies the Package.appxmanifest file to declare the Search contract and adds the following line in the App.xaml.cpp file:

```
void ALMEvents::App::OnSearchActivated(
    Windows::ApplicationModel::Activation::SearchActivatedEventArgs^ args)
{

        // TODO: Register the Windows::ApplicationModel::Search::
        //    SearchPane::GetForCurrentView()->QuerySubmitted
        // event in OnWindowCreated to speed up searches once the
        // application is already running

        // If the app does not contain a top-level frame, it is possible that this
        // is the initial launch of the app. Typically this method and OnLaunched
        // in App.xaml.cpp can call a common method.
        auto previousContent = Window::Current->Content;
        auto rootFrame = dynamic_cast<Windows::UI::Xaml::Controls::Frame^>
            (previousContent);
        if (rootFrame == nullptr)
        {
```

```cpp
// Create a Frame to act as the navigation context and associate it with
// a SuspensionManager key
rootFrame = ref new Frame();
Common::SuspensionManager::RegisterFrame(rootFrame, "AppFrame");

auto prerequisite = Concurrency::task<void>([](){});
if (args->PreviousExecutionState ==
    ApplicationExecutionState::Terminated)
{
        // Restore the saved session state only when appropriate,
        // scheduling the final launch steps after the restore is
        // complete
        prerequisite = Common::SuspensionManager::RestoreAsync();
}
prerequisite.then([=](Concurrency::task<void> prerequisite)
{
        try
        {
                prerequisite.get();
        }
        catch (Platform::Exception^)
        {
                // If restore fails, the app should proceed as though
                // there
                // was no restored state.
        }

        // TODO: Navigate to the initial landing page of the app as if
        // it were launched. This allows the user to return to your app
        // from the search results page by using the back button.

        //Navigate to the search page
        rootFrame->Navigate(TypeName(
            SearchResultsPage::typeid), args->QueryText);
        // Place the frame in the current Window
        Window::Current->Content = rootFrame;
        // Ensure the current window is active
        Window::Current->Activate();

}, Concurrency::task_continuation_context::use_current());
}
else
{
        //Navigate to the search page
        rootFrame->Navigate(TypeName(SearchResultsPage::typeid),
            args->QueryText);
        // Ensure the current window is active
        Window::Current->Activate();
}
}
```

4. Add the following three bold lines just at the beginning of the *OnSearchActivated* method:

```
void ALMEvents::App::OnSearchActivated(
    Windows::ApplicationModel::Activation::SearchActivatedEventArgs^ args)
{
    Platform::String^ message = "App Activated by the Search Contract";
    auto dia = ref new Windows::UI::Popups::MessageDialog(message, "ALM Events");
    dia->ShowAsync();

    ...
```

5. Deploy the application. If you haven't closed the application in the previous procedure yet, activate it and press the Close button or use Task Manager to kill the application.

6. Press Windows+Q, type something in the Search box, and select the ALMEvents application.

7. Verify that the dialog box displays the message "App Activated by the Search Contract."

You will not receive the dialog box for the application launching because the application was not launched by the user but activated for a search. Visual Basic, C#, and C++ application base classes expose different methods to respond to launch and search activations, while WinJS exposes just a generic activation function where you can test the activation kind property of the event args.

8. Close the application using Alt+F4.

If the user shares some content from another application, the target application receives a different activation called *sharing target activation* (*OnSharingTargetActivated* is the name of the corresponding method). You will learn about this kind of activation and the Sharing contract in Chapter 6.

There are other types of activation, each one corresponding to an operation done by the user. Table 4-1 summarizes the principal activation types.

TABLE 4-1 List of Windows Runtime activations

Method name	Description
Activated	Invoked when the application is activated by tile activation
File Activated	Invoked when the application is activated through file open
File Picker Activated	Invoked when the application is activated through file-dialog association
Search Activated	Invoked when the application is activated through search association
Sharing Target Activated	Invoked when the application is activated through sharing association

Since there are many types of activations, if you want to perform some action not related to a specific type of activation, you can override the *OnInitialize* method on the application class. This method is called from the runtime immediately after the creation of the application instance and before the specific method for a particular activation.

Suspending

WinRT introduces a new concept in the application life cycle that consists of a two-phase process in which the application is suspended when the user leaves it to launch or activate a different one and resumed when the user switches back to it.

The idea behind this mechanism is to maintain the system responsiveness even if the user launches many applications. Only the foreground application uses processor time, while other applications are suspended by the system. There can be a maximum of two running apps when they are in snapped mode. Usually, when not in snapped mode, there will be only one foreground app. To avoid latency when the user comes back to a previously launched application, WinRT freezes the application memory when suspending an application and places it in a special idle state. No CPU cycle, disk, or network access is given to a suspended application. The result of this mechanism is that the system remains responsive while the resuming phase is practically instantaneous.

Verify the suspension of the application

In this procedure, you will test the suspension mechanism using the application you are building in this chapter.

1. Launch the application from the Start screen. Avoid using the Visual Studio 2012 debugger to test the standard suspension behavior, because while debugging this behavior changes slightly.

2. Close the dialog box that displays the launch message.

3. Press Alt+Tab or the Windows key to put the current application in the background.

4. Open Task Manager and wait until the application goes into the suspended status. To open Task Manager, you can press Windows+Q and search the term "Task Manager" in the Apps list, or you can activate the desktop from the Start screen and right-click the taskbar.

The result of this procedure is shown in Figure 4-10.

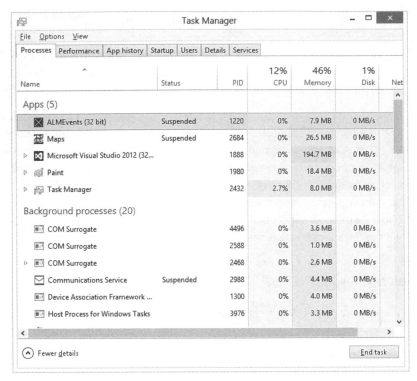

FIGURE 4-10 Using Task Manager to determine application state and resources.

> **Note** Your screen may be slightly different from Figure 4-10 depending on the columns shown by Task Manager. For instance, the suspension status column has to be manually enabled in order to be shown.

As you can see, the ALMEvents application (PID 1220) is placed in the suspended state. It uses no processor time or disk access at all but, as stated earlier, it uses 7.9 MB of frozen memory. This value may be different on your system.

Switch back to the application by pressing Alt+Tab again and note that the application resumes instantly without showing a launch message dialog box because the application was just resumed from the suspended state.

WinRT will suspend the app as soon as it is in the background at least for 10 seconds. In case you put the app in the background for a time shorter than 10 seconds and you come back, the app probably will not be suspended.

In case of suspension, the system informs the application immediately before the suspension manager starts its work, and the application will have only five seconds to perform any suspension operations. If the app takes longer than five seconds to perform suspension operations, WinRT will terminate it forcibly.

It is very important to understand the complete flow of suspension/resuming before coding against it. The system suspends your app whenever the user switches to another app or to the desktop. The system resumes your app whenever the user switches back to it. When the system resumes your app, the content of your variables and data structures is the same as it was before the system suspended the app. The system restores the app exactly where it left off, so that it appears to the user as if it's been running in the background. In practice, there is no need to save the data the user is working on during the suspension phase if the user comes back to the application. However, if the system does not have the resources to keep your app in memory, or it needs more resources for other applications launched by the user, the system will terminate your app. Your app will not be notified of the termination because WinRT assumes you have already saved any data or state information in the suspension phase. When the user switches back to a suspended app that has been terminated, the app receives a different launch, where you have to write the code that restores the application data.

Now that you understand the complete flow, you will add some code to the application you are developing in this chapter.

Use the *Suspending* event

In this procedure, you will modify the code for the App.xaml.cpp file to intercept the suspension and display a message dialog box. This is not what you would do in a real application, but it is important to understand the complete process.

1. Open the App.xaml.cpp file.

2. In the constructor, the Visual Studio Blank App template prepares the code to hook up the *Suspending* event as follows:

```
App::App()
{
        InitializeComponent();
        Suspending += ref new SuspendingEventHandler(this, &App::OnSuspending);
}
```

3. Use the following code for the event handler for the *Suspending* event, replacing the existing code:

```
void App::OnSuspending(Object^ sender, SuspendingEventArgs^ e)
{
        (void) sender;        // Unused parameter
        (void) e;        // Unused parameter

        Platform::String^ message = "App Suspending";
        auto dia = ref new Windows::UI::Popups::MessageDialog(message, "ALM Events");
        dia->ShowAsync();
}
```

4. Deploy the application and launch it from the Start screen.

5. Close the dialog box that displays the launch.

6. Press the Windows key to put the current application in the background.

7. Open Task Manager and wait until the application is suspended.

8. When the application is suspended, press Alt+Tab again to return to the application and verify that the message "App Suspending" appears.

This dialog box was shown during application suspension but, since the application was not in the foreground anymore, you saw nothing during the system operation. When you reactivate the application, WinRT resumes the application as it was prior to the suspension; this is why you can see the dialog box on the screen only during the resuming operation.

In practice, the dialog box is shown because the application has been resumed exactly where it was left off. The last thing the application did before the suspension was execute the call to display this message. You did not see this message during the suspension because the application was sent to the background.

Simulate an incorrect suspension

The application has only five seconds to respond to the suspension event. If the application needs more time, WinRT kills the application. In this procedure, you will try this behavior.

1. Close the application if you left it open in the previous procedure.

2. Open the App.xaml.cpp file, comment out the existing code of the *OnSuspending* method, and insert the bold line of code in the following excerpt:

```
void App::OnSuspending(Object^ sender, SuspendingEventArgs^ e)
{
        (void) sender;          // Unused parameter
        (void) e;          // Unused parameter

        //Platform::String^ message = "App Suspending";
        //auto dia = ref new Windows::UI::Popups::MessageDialog(message, "ALM Events");
        //dia->ShowAsync();
        Concurrency::wait( 10000 );
}
```

This code simply waits 10 seconds—too much time for the system, which will kill the application after 5 seconds.

3. Deploy the application.

4. Open an instance of Task Manager and minimize it.

5. Go to the Start screen by pressing the Windows key and launch the application.

6. Maximize Task Manager.

You can verify that after some time (maybe 20 seconds or more, depending on the system) the application disappears from the application list. This means that the application was killed by the system because the code for the suspending event exceeded the allowed time.

7. Launch the application again and verify the message in the dialog box, which indicates the previous state as Terminated because the application was terminated (killed) by WinRT. This procedure can be slightly unpredictable since the runtime can decide to terminate the application later. This mechanism makes the debugging of the *OnLaunched* event very difficult and time consuming if you are trying to test for a previous termination, but don't worry—at the end of this chapter, you will learn how you can simulate suspension, resuming, and termination from Visual Studio 2012 during a debugging phase.

Request more suspension time

If you need some more time—for instance, to persist some temporary data via web services or in the cloud—you can inform the system that you are executing an asynchronous operation. Call the *SuspendingOperation.GetDeferral* method to indicate that the app is saving its application data asynchronously. When the operation completes, the handler calls the *SuspendingDeferral.Complete* method to indicate that the app's application data has been saved. If the app does not call the *Complete* method, the system assumes the app is not responding and terminates it. When the user launches the application, you should not rely on the validity of the saved application data.

The *SuspendingOperation* method has a deadline time. Make sure all your operations are completed by that time. You can ask the system for the deadline using the *Deadline* property of the *SuspendingOperation* method.

In this procedure, you will change the code for the event handler to write the suspension time on disk using an asynchronous deferred operation. Theoretically, this operation cannot last longer than five seconds, but this example shows the correct code to implement an asynchronous operation.

1. Comment the line with the wait call.

2. Add the code shown in bold in the following block:

```
void App::OnSuspending(Object^ sender, SuspendingEventArgs^ e)
{
    (void) sender;        // Unused parameter

    //Platform::String^ message = "App Suspending";
    //auto dia = ref new Windows::UI::Popups::MessageDialog(message, "ALM Events");
    //dia->ShowAsync();
    //Concurrency::wait( 10000 );
```

```
auto deferral = e->SuspendingOperation->GetDeferral();

auto settingsValues = Windows::Storage::ApplicationData::Current->
    LocalSettings->Values;
if (settingsValues->HasKey("SuspendedTime"))
{
    settingsValues->Remove("SuspendedTime");
}

Windows::Globalization::Calendar^ now = ref new Windows::Globalization::Calendar();
now->SetToNow();
settingsValues->Insert("SuspendedTime", DateTimeFormatter::LongTime::get()->Format(
    now->GetDateTime()));
// Perform the async operation
deferral->Complete();
```

The first uncommented line gets the deferral from the *SuspendingOperation* property of the *SuspendingEventArgs* class. At the end, the code reports the completion of the deferred operation to the system.

The code gets the *LocalSettings* property of the application data and inserts a key called *SuspendedTime* with the current time in the collection. The *LocalSettings* class lets the developer save simple key/value pairs in the local application data folder. As you will learn in Chapter 10, "Architecting a Windows 8 app," WinRT denies access to the classic file system and provides a local or roaming space, called *application data*, that applications can use to store data. This kind of storage recalls in many aspects the *IsolatedStorage* provided by the Silverlight and the Windows Phone runtime. You can also use a *RoamingSettings* property, instead of the *LocalSettings* one, if you want to share your app data across multiple devices. The *RoamingSettings* property is a cloud-based isolated storage, which relates the data to the current user's Windows Live ID account.

 Warning Remember that the entire method must return within the deadline.

You can also hook the suspending event inside the code of an application page. This is very useful to save the state of the page during the suspension to restore it in case of termination. Be aware that the *Suspending* event is not raised in the UI thread, so if you have to perform some UI operations, you need to use a dispatcher.

You can debug the code for the suspending method as usual, and you can also force a suspension during a debugging session from Visual Studio. You will try this functionality during the next procedure.

Resuming

In the "Suspending" section of this chapter, you implemented a suspension event handler in the application class to calculate and save the current suspension time to the application data storage.

In this procedure, you will read the saved time from the application data storage during the resume operation from the application class, and then you will implement the code to show the same data within a page.

The resume operation is useless if the application was suspended by the system because the memory dedicated to the application is just frozen and not cleared. Instead, if the system needed more memory and decided to terminate the application, the resume operation is the right place to read the data saved in the suspension procedure.

You can intercept the resume operation hooking up the *Resuming* event of the application class if you want to perform some operations on the application. For instance, you can save the page the user had open before the suspension and, in case of application termination, open that page instead of the default one, as you can see in the following code sample:

```
static Platform::String^ currentPage;

App::App()
{
        InitializeComponent();
        Suspending += ref new SuspendingEventHandler(this, &App::OnSuspending);
        Resuming += ref new EventHandler<Platform::Object^>(this, &App::OnResuming);
}

void App::OnSuspending(Object^ sender, SuspendingEventArgs^ e)
{
    (void) sender;          // Unused parameter

    auto def = e->SuspendingOperation->GetDeferral();

    auto settingsValues = Windows::Storage::ApplicationData::Current->LocalSettings->Values;
    if (settingsValues->HasKey("Page"))
    {
            settingsValues->Remove("Page");
    }
    settingsValues->Insert("Page", currentPage);

    def->Complete();

}

void App::OnResuming(Object^ sender, Platform::Object^ e)
{
    (void) sender;          // Unused parameter
    auto settingsValues = Windows::Storage::ApplicationData::Current->LocalSettings->Values;
    if (settingsValues->HasKey("Page"))
    {
        if (dynamic_cast<Platform::String^>(settingsValues->Lookup("Page")) ==
            "CustomerDetails")
        {
            // Activate the Customer Details Page
        }
    }

}
```

The code is straightforward: the *OnSuspending* event handler saves the name of the current page in the local application data store, and the *OnResuming* event handler reads that value when the application is resumed from a terminated state.

An application can leverage the resuming operation, performing some actions even if the application was not terminated. For instance, you can request data taken from a web service or remote source if the suspend operation was done some minutes before the resume, in order to present fresh content to the user.

Refresh data during resume

In this procedure, you will modify the code for the MainPage.xaml.cpp file to display the time the page was launched, suspended, and resumed.

1. Open the MainPage.xaml file and add three *TextBlock*s. The first one will display the time the page was first opened, the second will display the time the page was suspended, and the third will display the time the page was resumed. Use this code as a reference:

```
<Page
    x:Class="ALMEvents.MainPage"
    xmlns="http://schemas.microsoft.com/winfx/2006/xaml/presentation"
    xmlns:x="http://schemas.microsoft.com/winfx/2006/xaml"
    xmlns:local="using:ALMEvents"
    xmlns:d="http://schemas.microsoft.com/expression/blend/2008"
    xmlns:mc="http://schemas.openxmlformats.org/markup-compatibility/2006"
    mc:Ignorable="d">

    <Grid Background="{StaticResource ApplicationPageBackgroundThemeBrush}">
        <StackPanel Orientation="Vertical" VerticalAlignment="Top" Margin="10,01,10,10">
            <Button Click="Close_Click" Content="Close" />
            <TextBlock Name="firstTime" FontSize="24" Margin="10,10,10,10" />
            <TextBlock Name="suspendTime" FontSize="24" Margin="10,10,10,10" />
            <TextBlock Name="resumeTime" FontSize="24" Margin="10,10,10,10" />
        </StackPanel>
    </Grid>
</Page>
```

2. Open the MainPage.xaml.h file and add check that the code corresponds to the following listing:

```
#pragma once
#include "MainPage.g.h"
namespace ALMEvents
{
        /// <summary>
        /// An empty page that can be used on its own or navigated to within a Frame.
        /// </summary>
        public ref class MainPage sealed
        {
        public:
                MainPage();
```

```
        protected:
                virtual void OnNavigatedTo(
                    Windows::UI::Xaml::Navigation::NavigationEventArgs^ e) override;
        private:
                void Close_Click(Platform::Object^ sender,
                    Windows::UI::Xaml::RoutedEventArgs^ e);
                void Current_Resuming(
                    Platform::Object^ sender, Platform::Object^ e);
        };
}
```

3. Open the MainPage.xaml.cpp file and use the following code as a reference to hook up the resuming event to display the suspended time restored from the application state and the resumed time.

```
#include "pch.h"
#include "MainPage.xaml.h"

using namespace ALMEvents;

using namespace Platform;
using namespace Windows::Foundation;
using namespace Windows::Foundation::Collections;
using namespace Windows::UI::Xaml;
using namespace Windows::UI::Xaml::Controls;
using namespace Windows::UI::Xaml::Controls::Primitives;
using namespace Windows::UI::Xaml::Data;
using namespace Windows::UI::Xaml::Input;
using namespace Windows::UI::Xaml::Media;
using namespace Windows::UI::Xaml::Navigation;
using namespace Windows::Globalization::DateTimeFormatting;

// The Blank Page item template is documented at
// http://go.microsoft.com/fwlink/?LinkId=234238

MainPage::MainPage()
{
    InitializeComponent();
    Windows::Globalization::Calendar^ now = ref new Windows::Globalization::Calendar();
    now->SetToNow();
    firstTime->Text = "Ctor : " + DateTimeFormatter::LongTime::get()->
        Format(now->GetDateTime());
    App::Current->Resuming += ref new EventHandler<Platform::Object^>(this,
        &MainPage::Current_Resuming);
}
```

```
void MainPage::Current_Resuming(Platform::Object^ sender, Platform::Object^ e)
{
    this->Dispatcher->RunAsync(
        Windows::UI::Core::CoreDispatcherPriority::Normal,
            ref new Windows::UI::Core::DispatchedHandler(
                [this]() {
                auto settingsValues = Windows::Storage::ApplicationData::Current->
                    LocalSettings->Values;
                if (settingsValues->HasKey("SuspendedTime"))
                {
                    suspendTime->Text = "Suspended : " + settingsValues->
                        Lookup("SuspendedTime")->ToString();
                }
                Windows::Globalization::Calendar^ now =
                    ref new Windows::Globalization::Calendar();
                now->SetToNow();
                resumeTime->Text = "Resumed :" + DateTimeFormatter::LongTime::get()->
                    Format(now->GetDateTime());
            }));
}

void ALMEvents::MainPage::Close_Click(Platform::Object^ sender,
    Windows::UI::Xaml::RoutedEventArgs^ e)
{
        Application::Current->Exit();
}

/// <summary>
/// Invoked when this page is about to be displayed in a Frame.
/// </summary>
/// <param name="e">Event data that describes how this page was reached. The Parameter
/// property is typically used to configure the page.</param>
void MainPage::OnNavigatedTo(NavigationEventArgs^ e)
{
        (void) e;           // Unused parameter
}
```

In the *MainPage* class constructor, the second and subsequent lines of code assign the current time to the first label. This code is executed only when the application instantiates the page, which occurs when the user launches the application or when the application is resumed from a terminated state. This code is not executed when the application is resumed from the suspended state.

The *Current_Resuming* event handler reads the value of the *SuspendedTime* key in the application data store and assigns it to the second label. It then assigns the current time to the last label. This code is not executed in the UI thread, which is why the code is executed by a dispatcher.

4. Deploy the application.

5. Launch the application from the application tile on the Start screen and close the initial dialog box.

6. Press the Windows key and then go to the desktop.

7. Open Task Manager and wait until the application is suspended by the system.

8. Minimize Task Manager.

9. Return to the application by pressing Alt+Tab. The result is shown in the following screen shot.

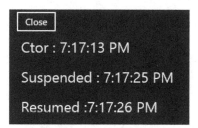

10. Close the application using the Close button.

To facilitate debugging the suspending and resuming events, Visual Studio provides two menu items that enable you to ask WinRT to suspend and resume the application during a debugging session. This feature is useful because it lets you avoid using Task Manager, and you can invoke this event as needed.

Use Visual Studio to debug the suspending and resuming events

In this procedure, you will use Visual Studio to debug the suspending and resuming events.

1. Open the App.xaml.cpp file and place a breakpoint in the first line of the *OnSuspending* method.

2. Open the MainPage.xaml.cpp file and place a breakpoint in the first line of the *Current_Resuming* method.

3. Press F5 to start a debugging session and wait until the application is visible on the screen.

4. Press Alt+F4 to return to Visual Studio, and in the Debug Location toolbar choose Suspend. If this toolbar is not visible, you can enable it by choosing the Toolbars item from the View menu, and then selecting the Debug Location item. The toolbar is visible in the following graphic.

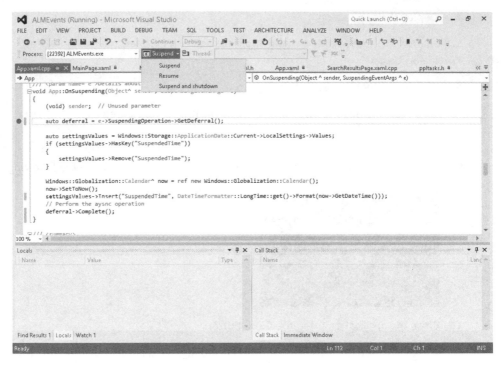

The breakpoint in the suspend event handler will be hit. Press F5 to continue. The breakpoint in the resume event handler will be hit soon because the application was taken to the foreground by Visual Studio when you pressed F5.

5. Press F5 again and verify that the application is visible and presents the three labels with different times.

6. Press Alt+F4 to return to Visual Studio, and use the Debug Location toolbar to select Resume to verify you can debug directly the resume procedure without the need to debug the suspend procedure first. You can also click the Resume button on the Debug Location toolbar.

7. Using the Debug Location toolbar, select Suspend and Shutdown. The application will first go in the suspended state and then will be terminated by the runtime. With this option, you can debug the code for the *OnLaunched* event to test a previous termination.

To summarize, the system suspends your app whenever the user switches to another app or to the desktop, and the system resumes your app whenever the user switches back to it. When the system resumes your app, the content of your variables and data structures is the same as it was before the system suspended the app—in other words, the system restores the app exactly where it left off, so that it appears to the user as if it's been running in the background the whole time. However, the app may have been suspended for a significant amount of time, so it should refresh any displayed content that might have changed while the app was suspended, such as news feeds or the user's location.

Summary

In this chapter, you saw the complete application life cycle at run time. You saw how to package and install an application in the local system, and how to create a package for the Windows Store. Finally, you were treated to an exploration of the various events that the Windows Runtime (WinRT) fires to launch, activate, suspend, resume, and terminate a Windows 8 application.

Quick reference

To	Do this
Create the application package	Access the Store menu from Visual Studio, and choose Create App Package.
Install an application locally for testing	You can use the classic F5 button to deploy and run the app automatically, or you can choose Deploy from the project contextual menu, or you can create the app package and launch the batch file.
Save temporary data	Use the *Suspending* event from the application class.
Test suspend and resume	Debug the application and use the Suspend and Resume buttons on the Visual Studio Debug Location toolbar.
Uninstall an application	Go to the Start screen, right-click the tile, and choose Uninstall. You can also swipe down your finger on the tile to activate the lower toolbar.

CHAPTER 5

Introduction to the Windows Runtime

After completing this chapter, you will be able to

- Understand the architecture of the Windows Runtime (WinRT).

- Leverage the new Windows 8 APIs across multiple languages.

- Create custom Windows Metadata (WinMD) libraries.

This chapter introduces the WinRT APIs, which are the new APIs that are the very foundation of every Windows 8 app.

What is WinRT?

Microsoft Windows, since its early versions, has always provided developers with libraries and APIs to interact with the operating system. However, before the release of Windows 8, those APIs and libraries were sometimes complex and stressful to use. Moreover, many different standards were used to expose libraries' functions, ranging from pure Win32 function calls to Component Object Model (COM) interfaces. The lack of a full set of metadata required an effort to call these APIs from different programming languages, and C++ developers also needed the corresponding version of include files in order to call a library function. As an example, consider the code excerpt in Listing 5-1.

LISTING 5-1 Code excerpt leveraging Win32 in C#

```
HWND hWndC = capCreateCaptureWindow (
    TEXT("My Capture Window"),   // window name if pop-up
    WS_CHILD | WS_VISIBLE,       // window style
    0, 0, 640, 480,              // window position and dimensions
    (HWND) hWndParent,           // parent window
    (int) 1 );                   // window id

capDriverConnect( hWndC, 0 );
capPreviewRate( hWndC, 66 );
capPreview( hWndC, TRUE );
```

This sample C++ code opens a preview video capture window, using a couple of Win32 APIs to leverage the video capture features of a PC.

With Windows 8 and WinRT, Microsoft realized the complexity of the previously existing scenario and made a huge investment to simplify interaction with the native operating system—not just from C++, but from any language. In fact, WinRT is a set of fresh, new APIs that were reimagined from the developer perspective to make previously complex tasks easy, simple, and fast. And WinRT was developed with the idea of developing Windows 8 apps with many of the available programming languages/environments (HTML5/WinJS, CLR, and C++).

In Listing 5-2 you can see how you can write, using WinRT and C++, the code illustrated in Listing 5-1.

LISTING 5-2 A sample code excerpt leveraging WinRT in C++

```
CameraCaptureUI^ dialog = ref new CameraCaptureUI();
dialog->PhotoSettings->CroppedAspectRatio = Size(4,3);
concurrency::task<StorageFile^> (
    dialog->CaptureFileAsync(CameraCaptureUIMode::Video))
    .then([this] (StorageFile^ file)
    {
        if (nullptr != file)
        {
            concurrency::task<Streams::IRandomAccessStream^> (
                file->OpenAsync(FileAccessMode::Read))
                .then([this] (Streams::IRandomAccessStream^ stream)
                {
                    BitmapImage^ bitmapImage = ref new BitmapImage();
                    bitmapImage->SetSource(stream);
                    CaptureArea->Source = bitmapImage;
                });
        }
    });
```

As the code illustrates, the syntax is clearer and easier to write, read, and maintain. In this example, *CaptureArea* is a XAML *Image* control.

As mentioned previously, for people who instead prefer to write code using WinJS and HTML5, the code is similar to the C++ version, as you can see in Listing 5-3.

LISTING 5-3 A sample code excerpt leveraging WinRT in WinJS

```
var camera = new capture.CameraCaptureUI();

camera.captureFileAsync(capture.CameraCaptureUIMode.photo)
    .then(function (file) {
        if (file != null) {
            media.shareFile = file;
        }
    });
```

Basically, WinRT is a rich set of APIs built upon the Windows 8 operating system that provides direct and simplified access to all the main primitives, devices, and capabilities using any language suitable for developing Windows 8 apps. WinRT is available only to Windows 8 apps. Its main goal is to unify the development experience of building a Windows 8 app—regardless of the programming language being used.

Figure 5-1 shows the overall architecture of WinRT.

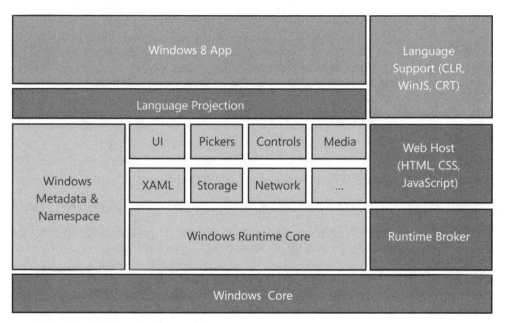

FIGURE 5-1 The Windows Runtime architecture.

As you can see from Figure 5-1, WinRT sits on top of the WinRT core engine, which is a set of C++ libraries that act as a bridge between WinRT and the underlying operating system. On top of the WinRT core is a rich set of specific libraries and types by which languages can interact with the various tools and devices available in any Windows 8 app. For example, there is a library to work with the network, another to read and write from storage (local or remote), a set of pickers to select items (files, pictures, and so on), a bunch of classes to leverage media services, and so on. All these types and libraries are defined in a structured set of namespaces and described by a set of metadata called Windows Metadata (WinMD). The metadata information is based on a new file format, which is built upon the Common Language Infrastructure (CLI) metadata definition language (ECMA-335).

As already stated, the WinRT core engine is written in C++. Internally, it leverages a proprietary set of data types. For example, there is the notion of HSTRING, which is the name of the type that represents a text value in WinRT. Further, there are various numeric types such as INT32 and UINT64, enumerable collections represented by *IVector<T>*, enums, structures, runtime classes, and so forth.

So that developers can consume all these libraries from any supported programming language, WinRT provides a projection layer that translates types and data backward and forward from WinRT to the target language. For example, the HSTRING type in WinRT gets translated into a *Platform::String* for C++, or to a *System.String* for .NET.

Next to this layered architecture is the Runtime Broker, which bridges from the operating system to the hosts executing Windows 8 apps, whether those are the CLR, HTML5/WinJS, or C++ apps.

To better understand the architecture and philosophy behind WinRT, in the following procedure you will consume WinRT from a C# Windows 8 app and then from a C++ Windows 8 app.

Use WinRT from a C# Windows 8 app

In this procedure, you will use the WinRT Camera APIs to capture an image from a Windows 8 app written in C#.

1. Create a new application project. To do so, open Microsoft Visual Studio 2012 and select New Project from the File menu (the sequence can be File | New | Project for full-featured versions of Visual Studio). Choose Visual C# in the Templates tree and then Windows Store from the list of installed templates. Then select Blank App (XAML) from the list of available projects.

2. Select version 4.5 as the Microsoft .NET Framework target version for your new project.

3. Name the new project **WinRTFromCS**, and then choose a location on your file system and accept the default solution name. When you've finished, click OK.

   As you saw in Chapter 3, "My first Windows 8 app," the Windows Store application template provides a default page (MainPage.xaml), an application entry point in the *App* class (App.xaml.cs), a default application description, and a declaration in the Package.appxmanifest file, as well as four default images representing logos and a splash screen.

4. In Solution Explorer, double-click MainPage.xaml.

5. This file contains the layout for the user interface. The window, named Designer, shows two different views of this file: the Design view and the XAML view.

6. Scroll down through the MainPage.xaml source code and insert a *Button* control inside a *StackPanel* control, as illustrated in the bold lines of the following code excerpt.

```
<Page x:Class="WinRTFromCS.MainPage"
    xmlns="http://schemas.microsoft.com/winfx/2006/xaml/presentation"
    xmlns:x="http://schemas.microsoft.com/winfx/2006/xaml"
    xmlns:local="using:WinRTFromCS"
    xmlns:d="http://schemas.microsoft.com/expression/blend/2008"
    xmlns:mc="http://schemas.openxmlformats.org/markup-compatibility/2006"
    mc:Ignorable="d">
  <Grid Background="{StaticResource ApplicationPageBackgroundThemeBrush}">
    <StackPanel>
        <Button Click="UseCamera_Click" Content="Use Camera" />
    </StackPanel>
  </Grid>
</Page>
```

7. Right-click the *UseCamera_Click* attribute of the *Button* element and select the menu item Navigate to Event Handler.

8. Replace the event handler code with the following:

```
private async void UseCamera_Click(object sender, RoutedEventArgs e)
{
    var camera = new Windows.Media.Capture.CameraCaptureUI();
    var photo = await camera.CaptureFileAsync(
        Windows.Media.Capture.CameraCaptureUIMode.Photo);
}
```

Notice the two lines of code inside the event handler, which first instantiate an object of type *CameraCaptureUI* and then invoke its *CaptureFileAsync* method.

9. Insert a breakpoint at the first line of code (the one starting with *var camera = ...*) and start debugging the app. As the next image shows, when execution reaches the breakpoint, the call stack windows illustrate that the app was called by external code, which is native code.

```
Call Stack
   Name
 ⊙ WinRTFromCS.exe!WinRTFromCS.MainPage.ChooseFiles_Click(object sender, Windows.UI.Xaml.RoutedEventArgs e) Line 40
   [External Code]
```

10. If you try to step into the code for the constructor of the *CameraCaptureUI* type, you will see that you can't do that in managed code, because the type is defined in WinRT, which is unmanaged.

11. Stop the app from executing by stopping the debugger or pressing Alt+F4 to close the app.

Next, you'll write equivalent code to use WinRT from a C++ app.

Use WinRT from a C++ Windows 8 app

In this procedure, you will use the WinRT Camera APIs to capture an image from a C++ Windows 8 app.

1. Create a new application project. To do so, open Visual Studio 2012 and select New Project from the File menu (the sequence can be File | New | Project for full-featured versions of Visual Studio). Choose Visual C++ from the Templates tree and then Windows Store from the list of installed templates. Then choose Blank App (XAML) from the list of available projects.

2. Name the new project **WinRTFromCPP**, and then choose a location on your file system, without changing the default solution name. When you have finished, click OK.

3. Repeat steps 4–7 of the previous C# example.

4. Replace the event handler code with the following code:

```
void WinRTFromCPP::MainPage::UseCamera_Click(Platform::Object^ sender,
    Windows::UI::Xaml::RoutedEventArgs^ e) {
    auto camera = ref new Windows::Media::Capture::CameraCaptureUI();
    camera->CaptureFileAsync(Windows::Media::Capture::CameraCaptureUIMode::Photo);
}
```

5. Insert a breakpoint at the first line of code (the one starting with *auto camera* = ...) and begin debugging the app. This time, you will be able to step into the native code for the *CameraCaptureUI* constructor, as well as into the code of the *CaptureFileAsync* method.

6. Stop the app from executing by stopping the debugger or pressing Alt+F4 to close the app.

By playing with this exercise, you will likely also notice that the names of the types, as well as the names of the methods and enums, are almost the same in C++ and C#. Nevertheless, each single language has its own syntax, code casing, and style. By this point, you have had a hands-on example of the true nature of WinRT: a multilanguage API that adapts its syntax and style to the host language, while maintaining a common behavior and set of capabilities under the covers. What you have just seen is the result of the language projection layer defined in the architecture of WinRT.

As an additional exercise, you could create the equivalent example using HTML5/WinJS, just as you have done here using C# and C++. If you do so, you will see that the code casing will adapt to the JavaScript style.

WinRT under the hood

The language projection feature of WinRT is based on a set of new metadata files, called Windows Metadata (WinMD). Those files are by default stored in the *<OS Root Path>*\System32\WinMetadata folder, where you should replace *<OS Root Path>* with the Windows 8 root installation folder, which is normally C:\Windows. The following list names the default contents of the WinMetadata folder:

- Windows.ApplicationModel.winmd

- Windows.Data.winmd

- Windows.Devices.winmd

- Windows.Foundation.winmd

- Windows.Globalization.winmd

- Windows.Graphics.winmd

- Windows.Management.winmd

- Windows.Media.winmd

- Windows.Networking.winmd

- Windows.Security.winmd

- Windows.Storage.winmd

- Windows.System.winmd

- Windows.UI.winmd

- Windows.UI.Xaml.winmd

- Windows.Web.winmd

Each contains the definition for a grouped set of functionality. For example, the Windows.Media. winmd file contains the definition of the *CameraCaptureUI* type you used in the previous exercise.

You can inspect any WinMD file using the ILDASM tool available in the Microsoft .NET SDK, which is distributed with Visual Studio 2012. For example, Figure 5-2 shows ILDASM displaying the content outline of the Windows.Media.winmd file and the *CameraCaptureUI* type.

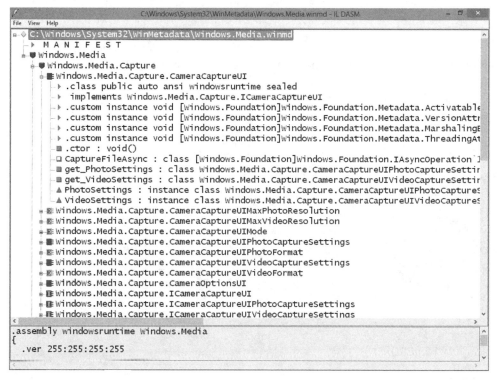

FIGURE 5-2 The ILDASM tool showing part of the Windows.Media.winmd file, which contains the definition of the *CameraCaptureUI* type.

In Figure 5-2, you can see a file manifest near the top of the file, which defines the name, version, signature, and dependencies of the current WinMD file. In addition, there is a hierarchy of namespaces that group various types. Each individual type defines a class from the WinRT perspective. For example, you can clearly identify the *CaptureFileAsync* method used in the previous procedures. Double-clicking a method in the outline reveals its definition. Note that the definition is not the source code of the method; instead, it describes the metadata that maps the method to the native library that will be leveraged under the hood. The following code excerpt shows the metadata definition of the *CaptureFileAsync* method defined for the *CameraCaptureUI* type:

```
.method public hidebysig newslot virtual final
        instance class [Windows.Foundation]Windows.Foundation.IAsyncOperation`1<class
[Windows.Storage]Windows.Storage.StorageFile>
        CaptureFileAsync([in] valuetype Windows.Media.Capture.CameraCaptureUIMode mode)
runtime managed {
  .override Windows.Media.Capture.ICameraCaptureUI::CaptureFileAsync
} // end of method CameraCaptureUI::CaptureFileAsync
```

The language projection infrastructure will translate this neutral definition into the proper format for the target language.

Whenever a language needs to access a WinRT type, it will inspect its definition through the corresponding WinMD file and will use the *IInspectable* interface, which is implemented by any single WinRT type. The *IInspectable* interface is an evolution of the already well-known *IUnknown* interface declared many years ago in the COM world.

Figure 5-3 shows a graphical schema of the structure of every single WinRT object.

Windows Runtime Object

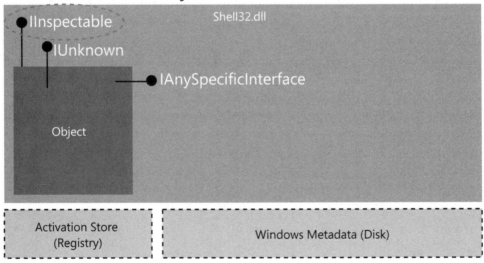

FIGURE 5-3 Windows Runtime object.

First, there is a type declaration inside the registry of the operating system. All the WinRT types are registered under the following path: HKEY_LOCAL_MACHINE\SOFTWARE\Microsoft\ WindowsRuntime\ActivatableClassId. For example, the *CameraCaptureUI* type is defined under this path: HKEY_LOCAL_MACHINE\SOFTWARE\Microsoft\WindowsRuntime\ActivatableClassId\ Windows.Media.Capture.CameraCaptureUI.

The registry key contains basic information, including the activation type (in process or out of process), as well as the full path of the native DLL file containing the implementation of the target type.

The type itself implements the *IInspectable* interface, which provides the following three methods:

- **GetIids** Gets the interfaces that are implemented by the current WinRT class

- **GetRuntimeClassName** Gets the fully qualified name of the current WinRT object

- **GetTrustLevel** Gets the trust level of the current WinRT object

By querying the *IInspectable* interface, the language projection infrastructure of WinRT can translate the type from its original declaration into the target language that will consume the type.

As shown in Figure 5-4, the projection occurs at compile time for a C++ app consuming WinRT. For a CLR app (C#/Visual Basic), it produces native code that may not need any more access to the metadata—this can happen during compilation into IL code or at run time through a runtime callable wrapper (RCW). The cost of communication between the CLR and the WinRT metadata is not much different from the cost of talking to the CLR metadata in general. Lastly, for an HTML5/WinJS app, the projection occurs at run time through the Chakra engine.

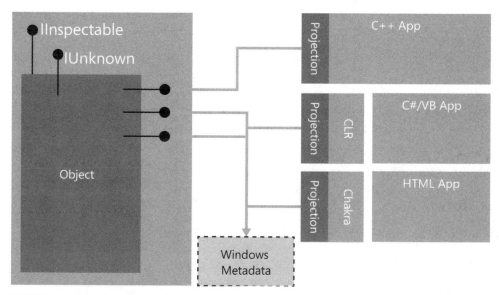

FIGURE 5-4 Projection engine schema.

The overall architecture of WinRT is versioning compliant; in fact, every WinRT type will be capable of supporting future versions of the operating system and/or the WinRT engine, simply by extending the list of available implemented interfaces and by providing information about the new extensions through the *IInspectable* interface.

WinRT design requirements

To support the architecture of WinRT and the language projection infrastructure, every Windows 8 app—regardless of the programming language used to write it—runs in a standard code execution profile that is based on a limited set of capabilities. To accomplish this goal, the WinRT product team defined the minimum set of APIs needed to implement a Windows 8 app. For example, the entire set of console APIs, which are not needed in a Windows 8 app, has been removed from the Windows 8 app profile. The same is true of ASP.NET, as another example. The list of removed .NET types is fairly long. Moreover, the WinRT product team decided to remove all the old-style, complex, and/or dangerous APIs in order to give developers a safer and simpler working environment. As an example, if you want to access XML nodes from a classic .NET application, you have a rich set of APIs to choose from (XML Document Object Model, Simple API for XML, LINQ to XML in .NET, and so on). This set also depends on the programming language that you are using. In contrast, from a Windows 8 app written in the CLR (C#/Visual Basic), the only available way to read XML nodes is to use the LINQ to XML support; the XML Document Object Model has been removed.

Furthermore, because Microsoft began thinking about a Windows 8 app as an application that can be executed on multiple devices (desktop PCs, tablets, ARM-based devices, and Windows Phone 8 mobile phones), all the APIs specific to a particular operating system or hardware platform were also removed.

The final result is a set of APIs that is clear, simple, well designed, and portable across multiple devices. From a C++ developer perspective, Windows 8 offers a single uniform set of APIs to access many of the features available through standard C/C++/COM APIs, whereas from a .NET developer perspective, the Windows 8 app profile is a .NET 4.5 profile containing a simple set of types and capabilities—the minimum set useful to implement a real Windows 8 app.

For the sake of clarity, here's another comparison. The standard .NET 4.5 profile is composed of more than 120 assemblies containing 400 namespaces, which group more than 14,000 types. The Windows 8 app profile is composed of about 15 assemblies containing 70 namespaces, which group only about 1,000 types.

The main goals in the profile design for WinRT were as follows:

- Avoid duplication of types and/or functionalities.

- Remove APIs not applicable to Windows 8 apps.

- Remove badly designed or legacy APIs.

- Make it easy to port existing .NET applications to Windows 8 apps.

- Keep .NET developers comfortable with the Windows 8 app profile.

Figure 5-5 shows the main .NET APIs available in a Windows 8 app.

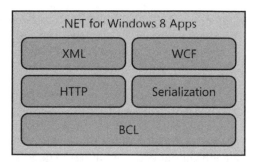

FIGURE 5-5 .NET APIs available to a Windows 8 app

For example, you can see that a Windows Communication Foundation (WCF) API is available, but you can use it only to consume services, leveraging a reduced set of communication bindings. You cannot use WCF in a Windows 8 app to host a service, for security and portability reasons.

Creating a WinMD library

In the previous sections, you learned some basic information about the WinRT architecture and the WinMD infrastructure, which allows the language projection of WinRT to make a set of APIs available to multiple programming languages. In this section, you will learn how to create a custom library of APIs and make it available to all the other Windows 8 apps through the same projection environment that WinRT itself uses.

Internally, the WinRT types in your component can use any functionality that's allowed in a Windows 8 app. However, externally your types need to adhere to a simple and strict set of requirements:

- The fields, parameters, and return values of all the public types and members in your component must be WinRT types.

- Public structures cannot have any members other than public fields, and those fields must be value types or strings.

- Public classes must be sealed. If your programming model requires polymorphism, you can create a public interface and implement that interface on the classes that must be polymorphic. The only exceptions are XAML controls.

- All public types must have a root namespace that matches the assembly name, and the assembly name must not begin with *Windows*.

In the following exercise, you will create a WinMD library and share it across the languages supported by Windows 8 apps.

1. Create a new Windows Runtime component project. To do so, open Visual Studio 2012 and select New Project from the File menu. Choose Visual C++ from the Templates tree and then Windows Store from the list of installed templates. Then choose Windows Runtime Component from the list of available projects.

2. Name the new project **WinMDCPPLibrary**, and then choose a location on your file system, without changing the default solution name. When you've finished, click OK.

3. Right-click the project icon in Solution Explorer and choose Properties. As you can see in the following screen shot of the Manifest Tool Input and Output page, Visual Studio generates a manifest file, which means that the project will create not only a DLL, but also a WinRT metadata file suitable for sharing the library with any Windows 8 app written in any language that can create Windows 8 apps.

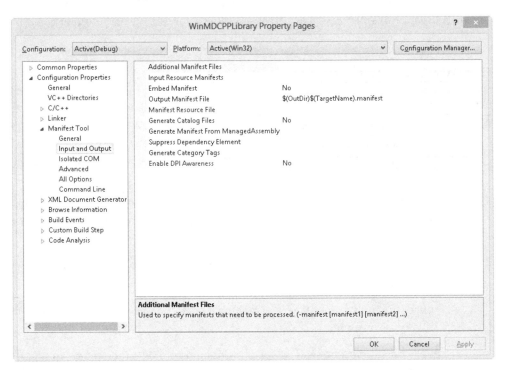

4. Close the project properties window.

5. In Solution Explorer, right-click the Class1.cpp file and select Rename. Provide the new name **SampleUtility.cpp**. Using the same technique, rename the file Class1.h to **SampleUtility.h**.

6. Double-click the SampleUtility.h node and rename all occurrences of Class1 to **SampleUtility**.

7. Add the declaration for an *IsMailAddress* function as follows. The resulting code should look like this:

```
#pragma once

namespace WinMDCPPLibrary
{
    public ref class SampleUtility sealed
    {
    public:
        SampleUtility();
        Platform::Boolean IsMailAddress( Platform::String^ email );
    };
}
```

8. Double-click the SampleUtility.cpp node and rename all occurrences of Class1 to **SampleUtility**. Add the following #*include* statement at the beginning of the file, before any existing *include* statements:

   ```
   #include <regex>
   ```

9. Insert the following code into the class file:

   ```
   Platform::Boolean SampleUtility::IsMailAddress( Platform::String^ email )
   {
       std::tr1::wregex rx(L"(\\w+)(\\.|_)?(\\w*)@(\\w+)(\\.(\\w+))+");
       return std::tr1::regex_match<const wchar_t*>( email->Begin(), email->End(), rx );
   }
   ```

10. Build the project by right-clicking the project icon in Solution Explorer and choosing Build.

11. Check the output by right-clicking the project icon in the Solution Explorer and choosing the Open Folder in File Explorer menu item.

12. Browse to the Debug\WinMDCPPLibrary subfolder (you might have to navigate to the parent folder first to find the right Debug output folder).

13. The output folder will contain a WinMDCSLibrary.winmd file.

14. Open the file with ILDASM, just to check its contents and to verify that the file defines the *WinMDCSLibrary.SampleUtility* class.

Next, you will consume the WinRT component you just created from C#.

Consume a WinMD library created with C++ from C#

1. Open the solution defined in the previous exercise, if it's not already open.

2. Add a new application project. To do so, select Add New Project from the File menu. Choose Visual C# from the Templates tree and then Windows Store from the list of installed templates. Finally, choose Blank App (XAML) from the list of available projects.

3. Name the new project **WinMDCSConsumer**, and then choose a location on your file system. When you've finished, click OK.

4. In Solution Explorer, right-click the WinMDCSConsumer project and select Set as Startup Project.

5. In Solution Explorer, right-click the WinMDCSConsumer project and select the References menu item.

6. In the WinMDCPPConsumer Property Pages window, select Add Reference.

7. In the left pane of the Add Reference window, select Solution, and then select Projects.

8. In the right pane, select the WinMDCPPLibrary project and click OK.

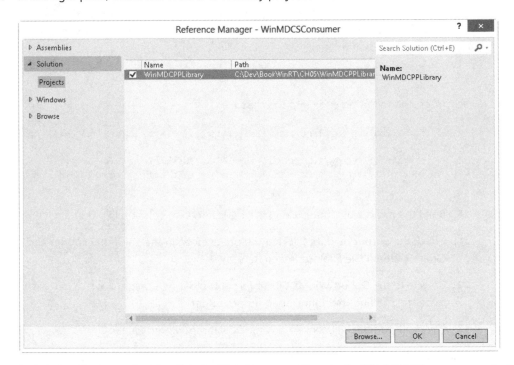

9. In Solution Explorer, double-click the MainPage.xaml item in the WinMDCSConsumer project.

This file contains the user interface layout. The window, named Designer, shows two different views of this file: a Design view and a XAML view.

10. Scroll down through the MainPage.xaml source code and insert a *Button* control inside a *StackPanel* control, as shown in the bold lines of the following code excerpt.

```
<Page x:Class="WinRTFromCS.MainPage"
    xmlns="http://schemas.microsoft.com/winfx/2006/xaml/presentation"
    xmlns:x="http://schemas.microsoft.com/winfx/2006/xaml"
    xmlns:local="using:WinRTFromCS"
    xmlns:d="http://schemas.microsoft.com/expression/blend/2008"
    xmlns:mc="http://schemas.openxmlformats.org/markup-compatibility/2006"
```

```
    mc:Ignorable="d">
    <Grid Background="{StaticResource ApplicationPageBackgroundThemeBrush}">
        <StackPanel>
            <Button Click="ConsumeWinMD_Click" Content="Consume WinMD Library" />
        </StackPanel>
    </Grid>
</Page>
```

11. Right-click the *ConsumeWinMD_Click* attribute of the *Button* element and select Navigate to Event Handler.

12. Replace the event handler code with the following:

```
private void ConsumeWinMD_Click(object sender, RoutedEventArgs e) {
    var utility = new WinMDCPPLibrary.SampleUtility();
    bool result = utility.IsMailAddress("paolo@devleap.com");
}
```

13. Build the entire solution (Ctrl+Shift+B).

14. Place a breakpoint in the *IsMailAddress* method of the WinMDCPPLibrary project, and launch the C# project in debug mode, configuring Mixed (Managed and Native) in the debugging properties of the WinMDCSConsumer project, as shown in the following image.

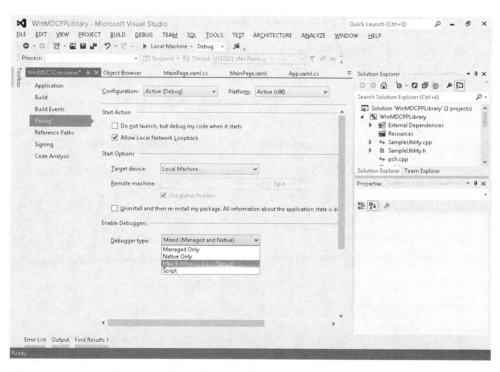

15. When you execute the code, the debugger will step into the C++ code starting from the C# code.

16. After debugging, close the sample C# app by pressing Alt+F4 or by stopping the execution in Visual Studio.

17. Do not close Visual Studio.

In the next procedure, you'll consume the same WinMD library you created with C++ from HTML5/WinJS.

Consume a WinMD library created with C++ in HTML5/WinJS

1. Open the solution used in the previous two exercises if it is not already open.

2. Add a new HTML5/WinJS application project. To do so, select Add New Project from the File menu. Choose JavaScript from the Templates tree and then Windows Store from the list of installed templates. Finally, choose Blank App from the list of available projects.

3. Name the new project **WinMDJSConsumer**, and then choose a location on your file system. When you've finished, click OK.

4. In Solution Explorer, right-click the References folder of the WinMDJSConsumer project and select Add Reference.

5. In the left pane of the Reference Manager window, select Solution and then choose Projects.

6. In the right pane of the Reference Manager window, select the WinMDCPPLibrary project and click OK.

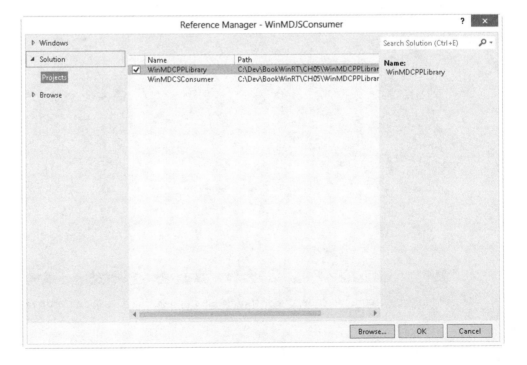

7. In Solution Explorer, double-click the default.html item in the WinMDJSConsumer project.

This file contains the user interface layout.

8. Replace the HTML body of the default.html page with the following code:

```
<body>
    <p><button id="consumeWinMDLibrary">Consume WinMD Library</button></p>
</body>
```

9. Open the default.js file and place the following event handler inside the file, just before the *app.start()* method invocation:

```
function consumeWinMD(eventInfo) {
    var utility = new WinMDCPPLibrary.SampleUtility();
    var result = utility.isMailAddress("paolo@devleap.com");
}
```

Notice that the casing of the *IsMailAddress* method, which you defined in C++, has been translated into the *isMailAddress* casing typical of JavaScript, thanks to the language projection infrastructure provided by WinRT.

10. In addition, insert the following lines of code into the function associated with the *app.onactivated* event, just before the end of the function.

```
// Retrieve the button and register the event handler.
var consumeWinMDLibrary = document.getElementById("consumeWinMDLibrary");
consumeWinMDLibrary.addEventListener("click", consumeWinMD, false);
```

Here's the complete code for the edited default.js file:

```
// For an introduction to the Blank template, see the following documentation:
// http://go.microsoft.com/fwlink/?LinkId=232509
(function () {
    "use strict";

    WinJS.Binding.optimizeBindingReferences = true;

    var app = WinJS.Application;
    var activation = Windows.ApplicationModel.Activation;

    app.onactivated = function (args) {
        if (args.detail.kind === activation.ActivationKind.launch) {
            if (args.detail.previousExecutionState !==
                activation.ApplicationExecutionState.terminated) {
                // TODO: This application has been newly launched. Initialize
                // your application here.
            } else {
                // TODO: This application has been reactivated from suspension.
                // Restore application state here.
            }
            args.setPromise(WinJS.UI.processAll());
```

```
            // Retrieve the button and register our event handler.
            var consumeWinMDLibrary = document.getElementById("consumeWinMDLibrary");
            consumeWinMDLibrary.addEventListener("click", consumeWinMD, false);
        }
    };

    app.oncheckpoint = function (args) {
        // TODO: This application is about to be suspended. Save any state
        // that needs to persist across suspensions here. You might use the
        // WinJS.Application.sessionState object, which is automatically
        // saved and restored across suspension. If you need to complete an
        // asynchronous operation before your application is suspended, call
        // args.setPromise().
    };

    function consumeWinMD(eventInfo) {
        var utility = new WinMDCSLibrary.SampleUtility();
        var result = utility.isMailAddress("paolo@devleap.com");
    }

    app.start();
})();
```

11. Build the solution.

12. Place a breakpoint in the *IsMailAddress* method of the WinMDCPPLibrary project and start the HTML5/WinJS project in debug mode, configuring Mixed (Managed and Native) in the debugging properties of the WinMDJSConsumer project, as shown in the following image.

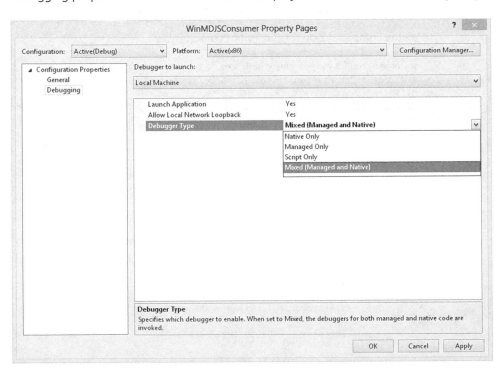

13. When executing the code, you will see the debugger step into the C++ code from the JavaScript code.

14. After debugging, close the sample HTML5/WinJS app by pressing Alt+F4 or by stopping the execution in Visual Studio.

WinRT app registration

Whenever you create a Windows 8 app and you walk through it in the Visual Studio 2012 debugger, you will see that your app gets placed as a tile on the Windows 8 Start screen. For example, if you experimented with all the previous exercises, your Windows 8 start menu will contain the tiles shown in Figure 5-6.

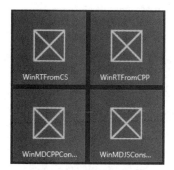

FIGURE 5-6 Tiles for the sample project on the Windows 8 Start screen.

In fact, every single time you execute a project from Visual Studio 2012, the IDE automatically registers your app so it appears on the Start screen. Under the covers, what happens is that your app is registered into the Windows Registry, using information defined in the Package.appxmanifest file available in your project. If you double-click that file (for example, in the WinMDJSConsumer project you defined in the last exercise), you will see a graphical editor/designer like the one in Figure 5-7, which shows the packaging tab of the designer.

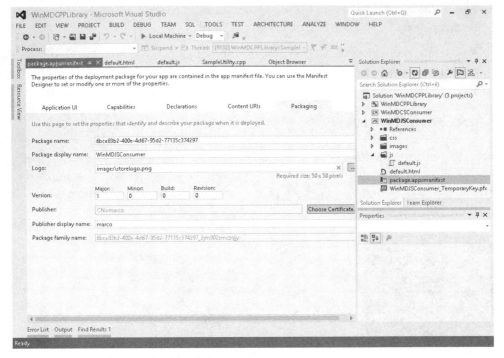

FIGURE 5-7 The packaging tab of the designer.

The Package Name property defines a unique name that will be used to identify the package on any target device. It is recommended that you provide a friendly name for this property instead of accepting the default GUID generated by Visual Studio 2012. The Package Display Name is the name that displays on the app's tile on the Start screen. The Logo, the Version, and the Publisher Display Name are additional information used to better describe the package and the app.

When you register (execute for the first time in Visual Studio 2012) a Windows 8 app, some of the packaging information is written into the Windows Registry. You can execute the following procedure to better understand what happens under the covers.

1. In the WinMDJSConsumer project in the Package.appxmanifest file, change the Package Name property to **WinMDJSConsumer**.

2. Execute the sample WinMDJSConsumer Windows 8 app.

3. Close the app by pressing Alt+F4.

4. Open the Registry Editor by pressing Windows+Q and then typing **Regedit**. Select the Registry Editor tool from the search results page and, when prompted, agree to let it execute it with elevated privileges.

Under the HKEY_CLASSES_ROOT\Extensions\ContractId\Windows.Launch key, you will find a subkey named PackageId. Inside that key is a subkey called WinMDJSConsumer_1.0.0.0_x86__2jm902zmczqjy, which is the name of the package, followed by its build version, the target platform, and an alphanumeric code describing the publisher.

The key will contain a subkey named ActivatableClassId, which defines the subkey App (for CLR and C++ apps) or App.wwa (for HTML5/WinJS apps).

Under HKEY_CURRENT_USER\Software\Classes\ActivatableClasses\Package, you will find corresponding ActivatableClasses that define the packages, under the Package subkey. Figure 5-8 shows the registry outline for this section if you registered the apps built in the preceding exercises.

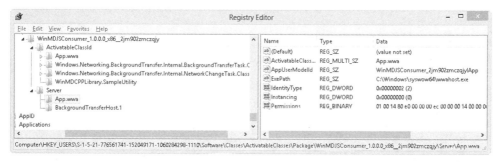

FIGURE 5-8 The Registry editor showing entries made by registering the example apps in this chapter.

When you start a new app instance or resume an already executing instance by clicking or tapping its tile on the Start screen, Windows 8 reads the Server subkey of the package defined in the ActivatableClasses and retrieves the path of the process to execute from the ExePath key. Notice that the WinMDJSConsumer app has an ExePath that corresponds to the standard HTML5 app host, which is C:\Windows\syswow64\wwahost.exe. In contrast, the WinMDCSConsumer app will have an ExePath value of *<Path of your exercise>*\AppX\WinMDCSConsumer.exe. Moreover, both apps will have a registry key named CustomAttributes, under the app key that is a child of the ActivatableClassId subkey of each package.

The CustomAttributes key will define the AppObject.EntryPoint string value, which defines the entry point of the app. The C# app will have a value of WinMDCSConsumer.App (that is, the main class), while the HTML5/WinJS app will have the value default.html (the default HTML page).

Summary

In this chapter, you learned what the Windows Runtime (WinRT) is, how it works, and its architecture. You also discovered what the Windows 8 app profile is and how to create a custom WinRT component library that you can consume from multiple languages, leveraging the language projection features of WinRT.

Quick reference

To	Do this
Get a picture from the camera of a Windows 8 device	Using C++ code, instantiate the *CameraCaptureUI* class and invoke the *CaptureFileAsync* method.
Inspect the content of a WinMD file	Use the ILDASM tool available in the .NET Framework SDK.
Debug a solution based on a mixture of CLR and C++ code	Configure the debugging options to support Mixed (Managed and Native).
Understand what apps are registered on the Windows 8 Start screen	Inspect the Windows Registry under the key HKEY_CLASSES_ ROOT\Extensions\ContractId\Windows.Launch.

CHAPTER 6

Windows Runtime APIs

After completing this chapter, you will be able to

- Understand how to interact with Windows Runtime application programming interfaces from a Windows 8 application.

- Use some of the available pickers.

- Interact with the webcam to take photos and videos.

- Implement the Share contract to share information between applications.

The preceding chapter covered the Windows Runtime (WinRT) architecture and the basic types, how to write code using the multilanguage features, and the concept of language projection. This chapter shows you how to interact with the user-related WinRT application programming interfaces (APIs) such as FilePicker and Webcam, and the APIs that you need to implement the Share contract.

Using pickers

Microsoft Windows 8 has two types of pickers. One has been in common use since the 1990s; it lets users choose something such as a date, a file, or a printer. This type of picker normally corresponds to user controls that are part of the framework or the programming environment. For example, ASP. NET provides the DatePicker Calendar control, Windows Presentation Foundation (WPF) exposes a *DatePicker* control, and Microsoft Foundation Classes (MFC) provided common dialog box controls that let users pick files or printers from the operating system.

In Windows 8, you can find these kinds of controls as part of the Extensible Application Markup Language (XAML) framework and as part of the Windows Library for JavaScript (WinJS) library for HTML Windows 8 apps. You can use them simply by dragging the controls from the toolbox to the window editor surface in Microsoft Visual Studio, or by coding their definition declaratively in XAML or HTML code.

The other types of pickers in Windows 8 are provided not by user controls, but via APIs exposed by WinRT. You can use them directly in your Windows 8 UI style applications or Windows 8 UI style class libraries without having to add any reference because they are part of the environment. For example, you can invoke these APIs to retrieve a file path for a document directly from code. It's important to realize that the WinRT APIs are accessible from any Windows 8 UI style application, so you can access them using Microsoft C++ from a Windows 8 UI style app, from Microsoft C# or Microsoft Visual Basic code from a .NET Windows 8 UI style app, or from JavaScript code in an HTML Windows 8 UI style app.

The picker has its own user interface that adheres to the Windows 8 UI design language that you learned about in Chapter 2, "Windows 8 user interface style," and neither the layout nor the appearance can be modified from code; instead, your applications can customize only some settings.

To get a feel for how this works, in the next exercise you'll start by coding the file picker.

Use the file picker

In this procedure, you will use the *FileOpenPicker* class, which allows a user to choose a file from the document library.

1. Create a new application project. To do so, open Visual Studio 2012 and select New Project from the File menu (the sequence can be File | New | Project for full-featured versions of Visual Studio). Choose Visual C++ from the Templates tree, and then choose Windows Store from the list of installed templates. Finally, choose the Blank App (XAML) project type from the list of available projects.

2. Name the new project **FilePicker**, and then choose a location on your file system without changing the default solution name. When you've finished, click OK.

   As you saw in Chapter 3, "My first Windows 8 app," the Windows Store application template provides a default page (MainPage.xaml), an application entry point in the *App* class (App. xaml.cpp), a default application description and a declaration in the Package.appxmanifest file, and four default images representing logos and a splash screen.

   The following screen shot shows the project at this stage.

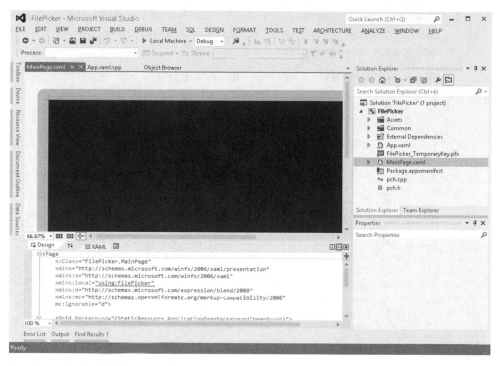

3. Scroll down the MainPage.xaml source code and insert a *ListBox* control and a *Button* control inside a *StackPanel* control, as illustrated in the bold lines of the following code excerpt:

```
<Page x:Class="FilePicker.MainPage"
    xmlns="http://schemas.microsoft.com/winfx/2006/xaml/presentation"
    xmlns:x="http://schemas.microsoft.com/winfx/2006/xaml"
    xmlns:local="using:FilePicker"
    xmlns:d="http://schemas.microsoft.com/expression/blend/2008"
    xmlns:mc="http://schemas.openxmlformats.org/markup-compatibility/2006"
    mc:Ignorable="d">

    <Grid Background="{StaticResource ApplicationPageBackgroundThemeBrush}">
        <StackPanel>
            <Button Click="ChooseFiles_Click" Content="Choose Files" />
            <ListBox x:Name="filesList"  />
        </StackPanel>
    </Grid>
</Page>
```

The *ListBox* control will be filled with the file names chosen by the user through the *FileOpenPicker* picker. The button will simply fire the code to start the picker and bind the selected files in the *ListBox*.

4. Open the MainPage.xaml.cpp file and add the method *ChooseFiles_Click*, which implements the event handler for the button. You can also double-click the button in the integrated development environment (IDE) designer.

   The code here represents the complete method definition:

   ```
   void FilePicker::MainPage::ChooseFiles_Click(Platform::Object^ sender,
       Windows::UI::Xaml::RoutedEventArgs^ e)
   {
   }
   ```

5. Add the following code to the method to open the file picker and retrieve the selected files:

   ```
   auto picker = ref new Windows::Storage::Pickers::FileOpenPicker();
   picker->FileTypeFilter->Append("*");

   concurrency::create_task(picker->PickMultipleFilesAsync())
       .then([this]( concurrency::task<IVectorView<Windows::Storage::StorageFile^>^> files )
       {
           this->filesList->Items->Clear();
           for each (auto file in files.get() )
           {
               this->filesList->Items->Append( file->Name );
           }
       });
   ```

   The first line of code creates an instance of the *FileOpenPicker* class and assigns it to the local variable named *picker*. Then the code adds a filter on the file type that the picker will show to the user.

   The third line of code is the most important: it asks the *FileOpenPicker* class to let the user choose multiple files. The result of the *PickMultipleFilesAsync* call is used by *create_task* to wait for method completion in an asynchronous way, without blocking the current thread. This pattern enables the developer to write code that resembles synchronous code, simplifying coding and debugging. It also eliminates the need to define callbacks and use the *IAsyncResult* interface.

   After a user has chosen some files (or has clicked the Cancel button on the picker), the application flow continues executing the code passed to the *then* method, which is invoked on the task returned by the *create_task* method. The code simply clears and then fills the *ListBox* with the selected files.

   The complete code for MainPage.xaml.cpp should look like the following listing:

```cpp
#include "pch.h"
#include "MainPage.xaml.h"
#include <ppltasks.h>

using namespace FilePicker;
using namespace Platform;
using namespace Windows::Foundation;
using namespace Windows::Foundation::Collections;
using namespace Windows::UI::Xaml;
using namespace Windows::UI::Xaml::Controls;
using namespace Windows::UI::Xaml::Controls::Primitives;
using namespace Windows::UI::Xaml::Data;
using namespace Windows::UI::Xaml::Input;
using namespace Windows::UI::Xaml::Media;
using namespace Windows::UI::Xaml::Navigation;

// The Blank Page item template is documented at
// http://go.microsoft.com/fwlink/?LinkId=234238

MainPage::MainPage()
{
    InitializeComponent();
}

/// <summary>
/// Invoked when this page is about to be displayed in a Frame.
/// </summary>
/// <param name="e">Event data that describes how this page was reached.
/// The Parameter property is typically used to configure the page.
/// </param>
void MainPage::OnNavigatedTo(NavigationEventArgs^ e)
{
    (void) e; // Unused parameter
}


void FilePicker::MainPage::ChooseFiles_Click(Platform::Object^ sender,
    Windows::UI::Xaml::RoutedEventArgs^ e)
{
    auto picker = ref new Windows::Storage::Pickers::FileOpenPicker();
    picker->FileTypeFilter->Append("*");

    concurrency::create_task(picker->PickMultipleFilesAsync())
        .then( [this](
            concurrency::task<IVectorView<Windows::Storage::StorageFile^>^> files )
        {
            this->filesList->Items->Clear();
            for each (auto file in files.get() )
            {
                this->filesList->Items->Append( file->Name );
            }
        });

}
```

6. Before running the application, remember that Microsoft Visual Studio first deploys the application to Windows 8 and then starts it. Then you can find the default application tile on the Start screen. As you learned in Chapter 3, the default value for the Show Name property in the application manifest is All Logos. Before moving on, choose the behavior you want for your App tile by opening the Package.appxmanifest file in the designer and choosing the property Show Name.

 Note Please refer to Chapter 3 and Chapter 4, "Application life-cycle management," for a description of the structure of the manifest.

The following screen shot shows the user interface for the main page of the application.

7. Click Choose Files and use the Windows 8 file picker to select some files.

You can simply click or tap a file to select or clear it. The following screen shot shows the file picker on the desktop with the Logo.png and SmallLogo.png files selected.

The top of the picker shows the user the selected directory, the applied sorting, and a link to select all the files in that folder. The content pane shows the available files, where you enter selections by simply clicking or tapping them.

The bottom line of the picker shows the selected files, the Open button, and the Cancel button.

8. Select some files and then click Open. A typical result is shown in the following screen shot.

As you have seen so far, the steps and the code to use picker controls such as the file picker are quite simple.

You can define the text for the Open button using the *CommitButtonText* property, provide a default start location using the *SuggestedStartLocation* property, and use the *PickSingleFileAysnc* property if the user has to select a single file.

You also can change the viewing mode from list to thumbnail; this is the only allowed customization for the user interface. Add the following line of code just before the *PickMultipleFileAsync* call to modify the view mode:

```
void FilePicker::MainPage::ChooseFiles_Click(Platform::Object^ sender,
    Windows::UI::Xaml::RoutedEventArgs^ e)
{
    auto picker = ref new Windows::Storage::Pickers::FileOpenPicker();
    picker->FileTypeFilter->Append("*");
    picker->ViewMode = Windows::Storage::Pickers::PickerViewMode::Thumbnail;
```

```
concurrency::create_task(picker->PickMultipleFilesAsync())
    .then( [this]( concurrency::task<IVectorView<Windows::Storage::StorageFile^>^> files )
{
    this->filesList->Items->Clear();
    for each (auto file in files.get() )
    {
        this->filesList->Items->Append( file->Name );
    }
});
```

The last thing to notice before moving to the Webcam API is that you haven't modified the manifest file to allow the access to the library. When you opened the Capabilities tab on the Package.appxmanifest designer, while in step 6, you may have noticed a Document Library property. It is not necessary to grant this capability, the Music Library property, or the Picture Library property, because they are not related to *FileOpenPicker*.

Webcam

WinRT provides a very simple API to interact with the webcam from C++, .NET, or JavaScript code. As with other WinRT APIs, you do not need any reference to additional class libraries to use the Webcam API.

Use the Webcam API

In this procedure, you will start using the Webcam API to let the user take a photo (or a video) and return it to the Windows 8 UI style application.

1. Create a new application project. To do so, open Visual Studio 2012 and select New Project from the File menu. Choose Windows Store from the list of installed templates, and then choose Blank App (XAML) from the list of available projects.

2. Name the new project **Webcam**, and then choose a location on your file system and a solution name. When you've finished, click OK.

3. Open the MainPage.xaml page and add a *Button* and an *Image* control. The button will fire the code to start the webcam, and the image will display the photo that the user will take. The following listing shows the complete XAML code for MainPage.xaml. The lines in bold are those you have to add to the page:

```
<Page x:Class="Webcam.MainPage"
    xmlns="http://schemas.microsoft.com/winfx/2006/xaml/presentation"
    xmlns:x="http://schemas.microsoft.com/winfx/2006/xaml"
    xmlns:local="using:Webcam"
    xmlns:d="http://schemas.microsoft.com/expression/blend/2008"
    xmlns:mc="http://schemas.openxmlformats.org/markup-compatibility/2006"
    mc:Ignorable="d">
```

```
<Grid Background="{StaticResource ApplicationPageBackgroundThemeBrush}">
    <StackPanel>
        <Button Click="TakePhoto_Click" Content="Take Photo"/>
        <Image x:Name="image" Height="800" />
    </StackPanel>
</Grid>
</Page>
```

4. Add the following *using* statements to the code of the *MainPage* class:

```
using namespace Webcam;
using namespace Platform;
using namespace Windows::Foundation;
using namespace Windows::Foundation::Collections;
using namespace Windows::Media::Capture;
using namespace Windows::Storage;
using namespace Windows::UI::Xaml;
using namespace Windows::UI::Xaml::Controls;
using namespace Windows::UI::Xaml::Controls::Primitives;
using namespace Windows::UI::Xaml::Data;
using namespace Windows::UI::Xaml::Input;
using namespace Windows::UI::Xaml::Media;
using namespace Windows::UI::Xaml::Media::Imaging;
using namespace Windows::UI::Xaml::Navigation;
```

5. Implement the *TakePhoto_Click* method, which is the event handler for the button click event, using the following code as a reference:

```
void Webcam::MainPage::TakePhoto_Click(Platform::Object^ sender,
    Windows::UI::Xaml::RoutedEventArgs^ e)
{
    CameraCaptureUI^ dialog = ref new CameraCaptureUI();

    concurrency::create_task(
        dialog->CaptureFileAsync(CameraCaptureUIMode::Video)).then(
            [this] (StorageFile^ file)
    {
        if (nullptr != file)
        {
            concurrency::create_task(
                file->OpenAsync(FileAccessMode::Read)).then(
                    [this] (Streams::IRandomAccessStream^ stream)
            {
                BitmapImage^ bitmapImage = ref new BitmapImage();
                bitmapImage->SetSource(stream);
                image->Source = bitmapImage;
            });
        }
    });
}
```

The first line of code in the *TakePhoto_Click* method creates an instance of the *CameraCaptureUI* class, and the second line waits for the completion of its method, *CaptureFileAsync*, which, as you can imagine, captures the stream using the asynchronous pattern, which prevents the UI thread from blocking. The method accepts the *CameraCaptureUIMode* parameter, which can assume the value of *Photo*, *Video*, or *PhotoOrVideo*. In the example, the webcam will be activated to take a photo.

The *CaptureFileAsync* method returns an instance of the *StorageFile* WinRT class representing the captured stream as a file. This file can be opened as a stream using the *OpenAsync* method: the method returns an instance of the *IRandomAccessStream* interface that can be used to set the source for a *BitmapImage* instance. Finally, the instance of the bitmap can be assigned to the *Source* property of the XAML *Image* control.

6. Modify the application manifest to set the Show Name property according to your preferences, just as you did in the previous procedure, and then press F5.

If you click Take Photo, the webcam screen will occupy the entire screen, but no photo can be taken—in fact, the default message is very clear and informs you that this app needs the user's permission to use the camera. The reason is very simple: the Webcam API cannot be used without declaring the Webcam capability in the application manifest. Obviously, if you have no camera attached to your PC, the application will ask you first to connect the device.

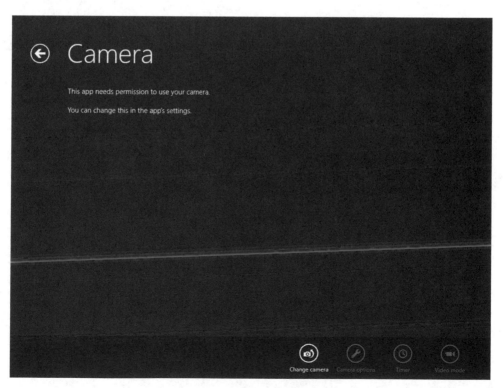

7. Stop the application, open the Package.appxmanifest file, go to the Capabilities tab, and select Webcam from the Capabilities list, as shown in the following screen shot.

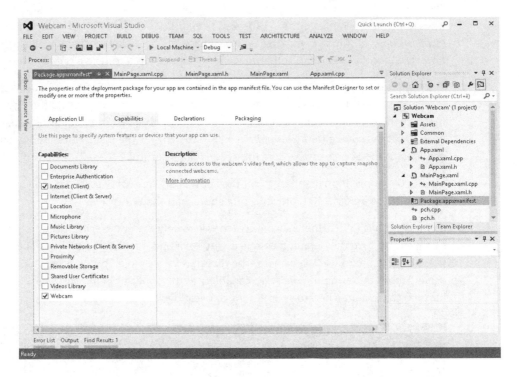

8. Run the application again, and then click or tap the Take Photo button. A message box (displayed in Windows 8 UI style) will ask you if this application can use the webcam, as illustrated in the following screen shot.

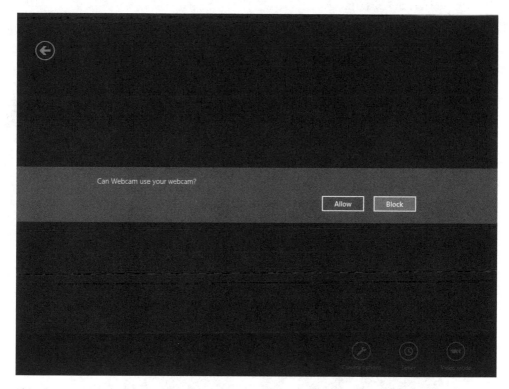

This request is the standard mechanism through which Windows 8 asks the user for permission to use a specific application capability. In practice, the application declares its capabilities in the manifest and the user provides permission to the application explicitly for each capability. If the user blocks a capability, the corresponding feature cannot be used; in the application you are building, the webcam shows a black screen in which the user cannot do anything but click Back to return to the application.

The system retains the user choice indefinitely. Users can remove a specific permission at any time for every application and, obviously, restore a permission at any time, as you will see in the following steps.

9. Tap the Block button in the screen represented in the previous image. The user can do nothing with the camera in this app.

10. Move the mouse to the lower-right corner to open the charms bar and select Settings. A panel appears on the right of the screen with some settings in the lower section, such as the network joined by the system, the volume level, the language, and a button to turn off/sleep/restart the system.

11. In the upper section of the panel, you can see the application name, the user currently using the application, the version of the application, and the text *Permissions* for the webcam. The following screen shot shows the permissions for the Webcam application.

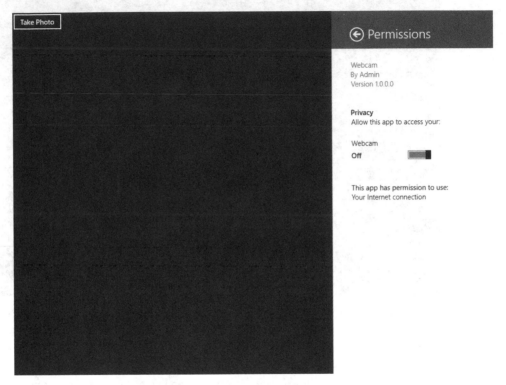

As you can see, the pane presents in its lower section the two capabilities requested in the application manifest: Internet Connection and Webcam.

12. Using the slider next to Webcam, you can enable the permission to use the webcam. Immediately, you will be able to preview the image taken from the webcam in the remaining part of the screen, as shown in the following screen shot.

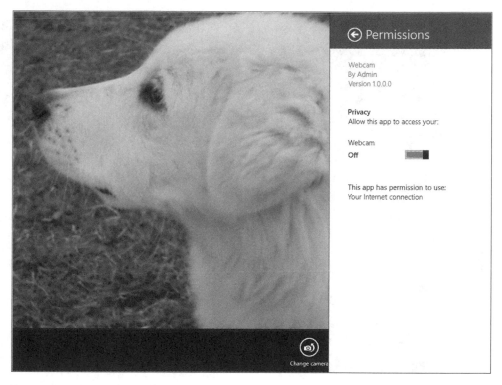

You can try to turn the Webcam permission on and off at any time to verify how the permission mechanism works.

13. Tap or click the screen to take the photo and go to the confirmation screen, where you can crop the photo, accept it, or take a new one.

14. Accept the photo by clicking OK. The webcam dialog box will return the photo to the application, which, in turn, will display it on the main page, as you can see in the following screen shot.

The *CameraCaptureUI* class exposes some properties to define the settings to take photos and some properties to adjust the settings for taking videos. For instance, with the first, you can set the *AllowCropping* property to *True* or *False*, and you can set the format and the resolution for the image; with the latter, you can set the resolution for the video, the maximum duration, and the format.

If you want to record audio as well, specify the Microphone capability in the application manifest.

Sharing contracts

In Chapter 3, you implemented the Search contract feature to allow the user to search data inside your application.

A contract regulates the interaction between an application and the operating system. Every application that implements a Windows 8 contract can use the corresponding operating system feature.

The Share contract regulates data exchange between applications. Chapter 1, "Introduction to Windows Store apps," introduced and demonstrated the use of the Share contract to show how data can be passed from one application to another without direct communication. The operating system acts as a bridge between the source application and the target application, invoking the necessary APIs on both of them.

The source app needs to do the following:

- Register itself with the Data Transfer Manager, which is the operating system component that manages the information exchange between the application and the target application.

- Implement an event handler to reply to sharing requests. When the user chooses to share something, he or she activates the Share pane by using the Share charm. The operating system asks the source application to prepare the data package, invoking an event on the source application—this corresponding event handler is the place where you prepare the data package. The source application can request a sharing operation directly from code without the user needing to use the Share charm.

The package specifies the type of resources it contains. The operating system lists all the target applications that can receive the same type of resources. For instance, if the source application shares images, the operating system will enumerate all the possible target applications that can receive images.

The target app needs to do the following:

- Define the Share Target declaration inside the application manifest.

- Declare the type of resources that it can receive. This information is used by the operating system to create the list of applications that can receive the content shared by the source application.

- Implement the sharing target activation, a special kind of application activation that receives the data package. This activation is requested by the operating system when the user chooses the application as the target for sharing operations.

- Provide the page to be displayed in the pane filled with the information about the received data. For instance, a social media application can display the received image and ask the user for a description and a tag before posting it to the social network.

- Implement the logic to process the data. Following the preceding example, the application can post the image to the social media application. This process can be done in an asynchronous way if the operations are time consuming.

- Report the completion of the operation.

As you learned in Chapter 1, some native Windows 8 applications can be used as sources and others can be used as targets. For instance, the Windows 8 UI style version of Microsoft Internet Explorer can act as a source application, sharing the text the user has selected on a page with Mail, the preinstalled email application, which can receive the text and send it to a recipient.

Next, you'll see an example of using the native applications, and then you'll implement a source application from scratch by using a very simple but effective application.

In this procedure, you'll start using the Windows 8 UI style version of Internet Explorer to share some information with Mail.

1. Open Internet Explorer from the Start screen. Be careful—do not use the classic Win32 version of Internet Explorer (which you can find on the classic taskbar, just in case you have activated the "old desktop" of Windows 8 from the Desktop tile).

2. Open any website (for example, *http://www.devleap.com/*) in the address bar.

3. Select some text on the home page.

4. Move the mouse to the lower-right corner of the screen (or press Windows+C) to open the charm (or flip your finger from the right corner toward the center of the screen).

5. Choose Share from the menu or the charm. The following screen shot shows the result of these operations.

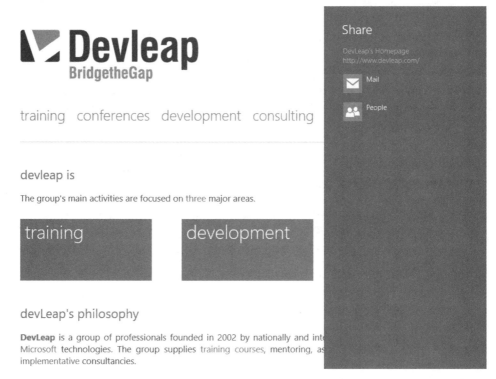

As you can see, the Windows 8 version of Internet Explorer does not have a window at all, or a menu item or an address bar—it fills the entire surface of the screen. The Share pane appears on the right side of the screen.

The Share pane cannot be customized because it is an operating system component. On the top, it displays the information that comes from the source application, and immediately below it, all the applications that are capable to receive the content are listed.

6. Select Mail to open the target application. The target application will receive the data package sent from Internet Explorer via the Data Transfer Manager. As you can see in the following screen shot, Mail will present the shared text with the hyperlink and show the Send Mail button. The target application page is presented in the foreground, letting the user see the source application in the background.

The target application is responsible for presenting the content on the Share pane and informing the user about the available operations on that content. This is a good example of a target application because Mail receives the data package and processes it, sending the resulting email to the target recipients.

Now that you have seen the complete flow, you'll implement a sharing source application of your own from scratch.

Implement a source application

In this procedure, you will implement a simple source application that shares textual content.

1. Create a new application project. To do so, open Visual Studio 2012 and select New Project from the File menu. Choose Windows Store from the list of installed templates, and then choose Blank App (XAML) from the list of available projects.

2. Name the new project **SharingSource**, and then choose a location on your file system. Click OK.

3. Open the MainPage.xaml page and add a *ListView* control using the following code as a guide:

```
<Page x:Class="SharingSource.MainPage"
    xmlns="http://schemas.microsoft.com/winfx/2006/xaml/presentation"
    xmlns:x="http://schemas.microsoft.com/winfx/2006/xaml"
    xmlns:local="using:SharingSource"
    xmlns:d="http://schemas.microsoft.com/expression/blend/2008"
    xmlns:mc="http://schemas.openxmlformats.org/markup-compatibility/2006"
    mc:Ignorable="d">

    <Grid Background="{StaticResource ApplicationPageBackgroundThemeBrush}">
        <ListView x:Name="list" DisplayMemberPath="FullName"
                    SelectedValuePath="FullName" />
    </Grid>
</Page>
```

4. Right-click the SharingSource project node in the Solution Explorer pane, select Add | New Item, and then choose Header File (.h) from the list of available files. Name the new file **Person.h** and click Add.

5. The new Person.h file should have the following content, which defines a *Person* class:

```
namespace SharingSource
{
    [Windows::UI::Xaml::Data::Bindable]
    public ref class Person sealed
        {
        public:
                Person() {}
                Person( Platform::String^ name ) { FullName = name; }
                property Platform::String^ FullName;
        };
}
```

6. Fill the *ListView* control with some people's names using the following code in the constructor of the *MainPage* class in the MainPage.xaml.cpp file:

```cpp
#include "pch.h"
#include "MainPage.xaml.h"
#include <collection.h>

using namespace SharingSource;
using namespace Platform;
using namespace Platform::Collections;
using namespace Windows::Foundation;
using namespace Windows::Foundation::Collections;
using namespace Windows::UI::Xaml;
using namespace Windows::UI::Xaml::Controls;
using namespace Windows::UI::Xaml::Controls::Primitives;
using namespace Windows::UI::Xaml::Data;
using namespace Windows::UI::Xaml::Input;
using namespace Windows::UI::Xaml::Media;
using namespace Windows::UI::Xaml::Navigation;

// The Blank Page item template is documented at
// http://go.microsoft.com/fwlink/?LinkId=234238

MainPage::MainPage()
{
    InitializeComponent();

    Vector<Person^>^ vec = ref new Vector<Person^>();
    vec->Append( ref new Person("Roberto Brunetti") );
    vec->Append( ref new Person("Paolo Pialorsi") );
    vec->Append( ref new Person("Marco Russo") );
    vec->Append( ref new Person("Luca Regnicoli") );
    vec->Append( ref new Person("Vanni Boncinelli") );
    vec->Append( ref new Person("Guido Zambarda") );
    vec->Append( ref new Person("Katia Egiziano") );
    vec->Append( ref new Person("Jessica Faustinelli") );
    list->ItemsSource = vec;
}

/// <summary>
/// Invoked when this page is about to be displayed in a Frame.
/// </summary>
/// <param name="e">Event data that describes how this page was reached.
/// The Parameter property is typically used to configure the page.
/// </param>///
void MainPage::OnNavigatedTo(NavigationEventArgs^ e)
{
    (void) e;// Unused parameter
}
```

Try the application to verify that you can see the names on the page and you can select one of them.

7. Add the code to respond to the sharing event that the operating system will fire on the applications using the *DataTransferManager* WinRT class. Use this code inside the constructor of the class, just below the *InitializeComponent* method call:

```
DataTransferManager::GetForCurrentView()->DataRequested +=
    ref new TypedEventHandler<DataTransferManager^,
        DataRequestedEventArgs^>(this, &MainPage::DataRequested);
```

8. Add the *using* statement to the namespace that provides the *DataTransferManager* class in both the MainPage.xaml.cpp and MainPage.xaml.h files as follows:

```
using namespace Windows::ApplicationModel::DataTransfer;
```

9. Add the declaration of the *DataRequested* method in the *MainPage* class in the MainPage.xaml.h file, so the complete declaration is as follows:

```
namespace SharingSource
{
    /// <summary>
    /// An empty page that can be used on its own or navigated to within a Frame.
    /// </summary>
    public ref class MainPage sealed
    {
    public:
            MainPage();

    protected:
        virtual void OnNavigatedTo(Windows::UI::Xaml::Navigation::NavigationEventArgs^ e)
                    override;
        void MainPage::DataRequested(DataTransferManager^ sender,
            DataRequestedEventArgs^ args);
    };
}
```

10. Implement the *MainPage::DataRequested* method, adding the following code to the MainPage.xaml.cpp file:

```
void MainPage::DataRequested(DataTransferManager^ sender, DataRequestedEventArgs^ args)
{
    args->Request->Data->Properties->Title = "DevLeap Sharing";
    if (list->SelectedItem != NULL)
    {
        args->Request->Data->Properties->Description =
            "DevLeap is sharing his crew member " + list->SelectedValue->ToString();
        args->Request->Data->SetText(list->SelectedValue->ToString());
    }
    else
    {
        args->Request->FailWithDisplayText("You have selected no one");
    }
```

The method sets the *Request* property of the received event arguments. It represents the data package to pass to the Data Transfer Manager, which, in turn, sends it to the target application.

The first line sets the *Title* property of the data package. If no item was selected in the list, then the package shows text indicating a failure in data sharing because there is nothing to share.

If a name is selected, the source application sets the description of the data package and, more important, uses the *SetText* method to indicate that the package contains a set of characters and defines the desired text. The first one is very important because the Share pane will list all the registered applications that can receive text.

You can use *SetBitmap*, *SetHtml*, *SetStorageItems*, *SetUri*, *SetRtf*, and some other self-explanatory methods.

11. Run the application, open the charm, and choose Share. You will end up with the result shown in the following screen shot.

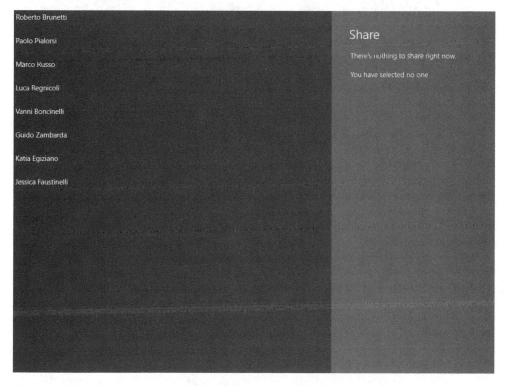

The message "There's nothing to share right now." is the default text that the Share pane shows the user when the source application uses the *FailWithDisplayText* method. The text provided by the source application is shown immediately below the default error message.

12. Select the first name from the list and share the content again. Now the Share pane shows several applications and presents the text provided by the code you implemented—see the top of the Share pane in the following screen shot.

13. Select Mail and you will see the result shown in the following screen shot.

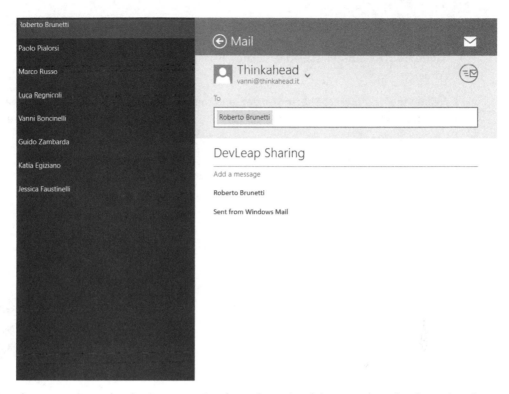

You also can activate the sharing operation from the code of the source application using the *ShowSendUI* or *ShowShareUI* static method of the *DataTransferManager* class.

Implement a target application

In this procedure, you will implement a simple target application that displays textual content shared by some other application. Remember that any app that can share textual content will be able to share it with the application you are about to implement in this procedure; this is because the Share contract regulates the data exchange between applications that don't need to know each other in advance. You will implement an HTML Windows 8 UI style application to see how to interact with WinRT APIs from JavaScript and how to create a simple HTML page to show the text shared by some other applications. You can do the same thing using XAML and C# or Visual Basic.

1. Create a new application project. To do so, open Visual Studio 2012 and select New Project from the File menu. Choose JavaScript from the Templates tree, and then choose Windows Store from the list of installed templates. Finally, choose Blank App from the list of available projects.

2. Name the new project **SharingTarget**, and then choose a location on your file system and a solution name. When you've finished, click OK. Use the following image as a reference.

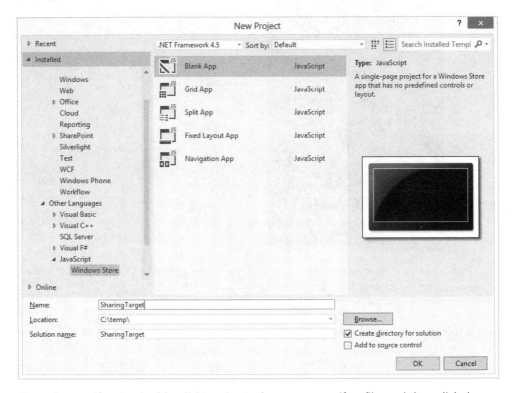

3. Open the manifest by double-clicking the Package.appxmanifest file, and then click the Declaration tab.

4. Select Share Target from the list of Available Declarations and click Add. This setting is necessary for this application to be considered a share target.

5. Click the Add New button in the Data Formats pane and type **Text** in the Data Format text box. This setting tells the Share pane that this application supports only text.

6. Leave the other settings at their default values and save the manifest. You will have a manifest configured like the one shown in the following screen shot.

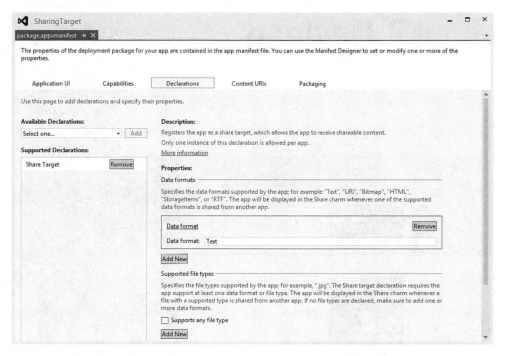

7. Deploy the application to test it. You have not provided a user interface yet, but the steps you have completed so far will suffice for the application to be listed as a target when you try to share text from other applications.

8. Open Windows 8 Internet Explorer from the Start screen. You may see the home page of the site used in the previous procedure. If not, type an address (such as *http://www.devleap.com/*) in the address bar.

9. Select the first line of text and activate the Share pane.

10. Verify that the application (SharingTarget, if you have carefully followed this procedure) appears in the list, as shown in the following screen shot.

If you select your application in the Share pane, you will see a blank page (with the default "content goes here" text) because you have not implemented the page yet. It's time to do that.

Implement a result page

In this procedure, you will develop an HTML Windows 8 UI style application. The page that displays when the user selects this application as the target for the sharing operation will be implemented in HTML5, using the WinRT APIs from JavaScript.

It is beyond the scope of this book to analyze or explain how to build an HTML Windows 8 app. For further details about developing an HTML Windows 8 app, refer to the book *Programming Windows 8 Apps with HTML, CSS, and JavaScript* by Kraig Brockschmidt, published by Microsoft Press. You will use the easiest way to build this page.

1. Replace the default body content (the paragraph) with *H1, H2,* and *H3* HTML tags inside the body of the default page as follows:

```
<body>
    <h1 />
    <h2 />
    <h3 />
</body>
```

The default page is referenced by the manifest and represents the starting point.

2. Open the default.js file, which is available in the js folder of the project, and add the following variable declaration, just after the *app* variable declaration:

```
var shareOperation;
```

3. This variable will be used in the next steps to hold information about the data shared.

4. Within the same default.js file, add a script excerpt in the *app.onactivated* event handler. The code excerpt implements the activation of the application by using the WinRT environment, in case of a request for sharing content. The following code illustrates how the *app.onactivated* event handler should appear after modification:

```
app.onactivated = function (args) {
if (args.detail.kind === activation.ActivationKind.launch) {
    if (args.detail.previousExecutionState !==
        activation.ApplicationExecutionState.terminated) {
        // TODO: This application has been newly launched. Initialize
        // your application here.
    } else {
        // TODO: This application has been reactivated from suspension.
        // Restore application state here.
    }
    args.setPromise(WinJS.UI.processAll());
} else if (args.detail.kind ==
        Windows.ApplicationModel.Activation.ActivationKind.shareTarget) {
    shareOperation = args.detail.shareOperation;
    if (shareOperation.data.contains(
        Windows.ApplicationModel.DataTransfer.StandardDataFormats.text)) {
        document.querySelector('h1').textContent =
            shareOperation.data.properties.title;
        document.querySelector('h2').textContent =
            shareOperation.data.properties.description;
        shareOperation.data.getTextAsync().then(function (text) {
            if (text !== null) {
                document.querySelector('h3').textContent = text;
            }
        });
    }
}
};
```

The inserted code appears in bold. The activation of an application can be done via the application tile on the Start screen or, as with the page you are building, when the user selects the application as a search target. The recently added *else if* statement in the *onactivated* event handler tests this condition by analyzing the *kind* property of the *detail* of the received event arguments.

If the condition is met, the code fills the HTML header elements with the properties of the received data package. In the source application that you built in the previous procedures, you filled the same properties during the share operation.

5. Deploy the application again and test it as a share target from Internet Explorer, as you did in steps 8–10 of the preceding procedure.

6. Open the share application that you built in this chapter from the Start screen, select a name from the list, and activate the sharing operation. When the Share pane opens, choose SharingTarget as the target for the sharing operation, and you will see the page that you built filled with the shared information. The following screen shot shows the result.

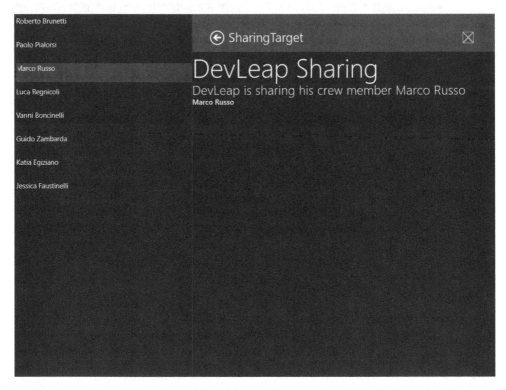

Sharing is a powerful technique for sending information to and receiving information from applications using a common contract defined by WinRT.

Summary

In this chapter, you saw some WinRT APIs at work. You started with the *FileOpenPicker* class, which enables the user to choose and send file information to the calling application. Next, you implemented a simple application using the *CameraCaptureUI* class to take and retrieve photos from the webcam. The last example featured two different applications: the first allows the user to choose a person from a list and share the person's full name with other applications, and the second represents the target application and was built using HTML and JavaScript. Every WinRT API can be called from any language.

Quick reference

To	Do this
Use APIs that access the system	Specify the corresponding capabilities in the application manifest.
Block or allow capabilities for one application	Open the settings pane for the application and set the slider for every capability accordingly.
Interact with the webcam	Specify the Web capability and use the *CameraCaptureUI* class settings, the video and photo attributes, and then the *CaptureFileAsync* method.
Create a source application for sharing content	Use the *DataTransferManager* class to create the data package and respond to the sharing event.
Receive content from other applications	Use the Share Target declaration in the application manifest and intercept the activation for the sharing operation.

CHAPTER 7

Enhance the user experience

After completing this chapter, you will be able to

- Draw an application using Microsoft Visual Studio 2012 visual tools.

- Create an application layout.

- Customize the appearance of controls.

Understanding the XAML layout system is fundamental to position and arrange elements in a Windows Store app. The base class for all elements that provide layout support is *Panel*, and the platform includes a suite of derived *Panel* classes that enable many complex layouts. This chapter provides an introduction to the available *Panel* layout elements.

Styling and templating refer to a suite of features that allow developers and designers to create visually compelling effects and to create a consistent appearance for their applications. Another feature of the XAML styling model is the separation of presentation and logic. Designers can work on the appearance of an application by using only XAML at the same time that developers work on the programming logic using C++. This chapter focuses on the styling and templating aspects of the application.

Draw an application using Visual Studio 2012

Microsoft Visual Studio 2012 contains many different tools for creating Windows Store apps both graphically and interactively.

In this section, you will learn how to use the Microsoft Visual Studio 2012 designer to add controls to the page structure and customize the properties using the appropriate graphics palettes.

Create a graphical application in Visual Studio 2012

1. Create a new application project. To do so, open Visual Studio 2012 and select New Project from the File menu (the sequence can be File | New | Project for full-featured versions of Visual Studio). Choose Visual C++ from the Templates tree, and then choose Windows Store from the list of installed templates. Finally, choose the Blank App (XAML) project type from the list of available projects.

2. Name the new project **Panels**, and then choose a location on your file system without changing the default solution name. When you've finished, click OK.

As you saw in Chapter 3, "My first Windows 8 app," the Windows Store application template provides a default page (MainPage.xaml), an application entry point in the *App* class (App.xaml.cpp), a default application description and a declaration in the Package.appxmanifest file, and four default images representing logos and a splash screen.

3. In Solution Explorer, double-click MainPage.xaml.

This file contains the layout of the user interface. The window, named Designer, shows two different views of this file. The result is shown in the following screen shot.

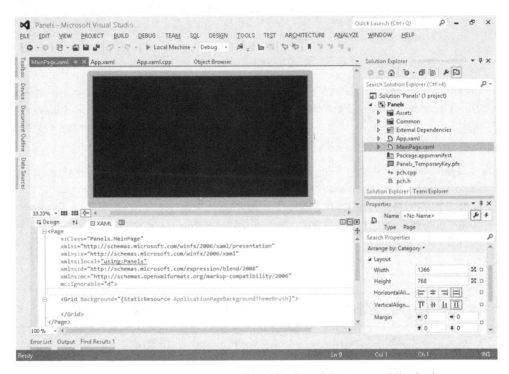

The top pane, named Design, shows a graphical display of the page, while the bottom pane, named XAML, shows the XAML code for the same page.

In the following procedure, you will use the Designer window to add a control to the user interface of an application and customize some of its properties using the designer and the Properties window.

Create the user interface

1. Click the Toolbox tab that appears to the left of the form in the Designer window.

2. Expand the Common XAML Controls section.

    This section contains the most common controls. You can click the All XAML Controls section to see the full list of controls provided by the platform.

3. In the Common XAML Controls section, drag the *TextBlock* control onto the page.

> **Tip** If you dragged a different control, you can delete it from the page by selecting the item within the design area and pressing Delete.

This operation creates a *TextBlock* control on the page and the Toolbox disappears temporarily. If you want the Toolbox to be always visible, just click Auto Hide on the right side of the title bar.

> **Tip** The thumbtack (pushpin) provides a visual cue as to whether the Toolbox (or any other window, for that matter) will automatically hide itself when not in use.

4. Click the *TextBlock* control in the form and drag it wherever you prefer. Notice that you may need to click away from the control and then click it again before you can move it in Design view.

    The bottom panel of the Designer window contains the markup code of the layout you have just created. It includes a description of a *TextBlock* control with its properties: *Margin*, *Text*, *HorizontalAlignment*, and *VerticalAlignment*.

    The XAML code of the *TextBlock* control should look like the following:

    ```
    <TextBlock HorizontalAlignment="Left" Height="54" Width="250" Margin="216,171,0,0"
            TextWrapping="Wrap" Text="TextBlock" VerticalAlignment="Top"/>
    ```

    The *Margin* property may be different depending on where you placed the control on the page, such as the *Height* and *Width* properties that depend on your actions on the designer. XAML view and Design view have a two-way relationship with each other. You can edit the XAML code from XAML view and see the changes reflected in Design view, and vice versa. Practice changing the *Margin* property in the XAML pane. You will notice a visual change in the position of the control in the Design pane.

5. On the View menu, select Properties Window.

It is possible to set any property by using XAML code, but it is definitely easier to use the Properties window for this task.

The Properties window shows the properties of the currently selected control; in fact, if you click the *TextBlock* control in Design view, you'll see the properties of that control. However, if you click outside the *TextBlock*, you will notice the Properties window displaying the properties of the parent *Grid*.

6. Click the *TextBlock* control in Design view. The Properties window will display the properties for the *TextBlock* control again.

7. In the Properties window, expand the Text property and change the FontSize property to **16px**. This property is located next to the drop-down list box containing the name of the font.

8. In XAML view, examine the text that defines the *TextBlock* control. If you scroll to the end of the line, you should see the text *FontSize="16"*. Changes performed using the Properties window will be reflected in the XAML source code automatically and, consequently, also in Design view.

9. Set the value of the *FontSize* property in the XAML pane to *24*. You will notice a visual change in Design view, as well as a change in the drop-down list box of the Properties window.

10. Open the Common section of the Properties window and change the value of the Text property from TextBlock to **Hello Windows 8 App!**

> **Note** If you choose to organize the property names in alphabetical order, you will not find the Common section or any other categories, so you have to find the property in the list (the *Text* property, in this case) and change its value as described in the procedure.

11. On the Build menu, select Build Solution and verify that the project builds successfully.

12. On the Debug menu, click Start Debugging.

The result should look similar to the following image.

13. Return to Visual Studio 2012 by pressing Alt+Tab. On the Debug menu, click Stop Debugging.

Create the layout of a Windows 8 application

The objects deriving from the *Panel* class are responsible for the placement of controls on a screen. These objects act as containers for user interface elements, and each has specific characteristics and behaviors. In this section, you will explore and use these objects from a Windows 8 application.

Use the *Canvas* control

The goal of the *Canvas* control is to place its child elements using coordinates relative to the parent *Canvas*.

1. Create a new application project. To do so, open Visual Studio 2012 and select New Project from the File menu. Choose Windows Store from the list of installed templates, and then choose Blank App (XAML) from the list of available projects.

2. Name the new project **Canvas**, and then choose a location on your file system and a solution name. When you've finished, click OK.

3. Click the Toolbox tab that appears on the left side of the form in the Designer window.

4. Expand the All XAML Controls section.

5. Click the *Canvas* control and drag it onto the form.

6. Using the designer surface, modify the dimensions and position of the *Canvas* control until you get something that resembles the following screen shot.

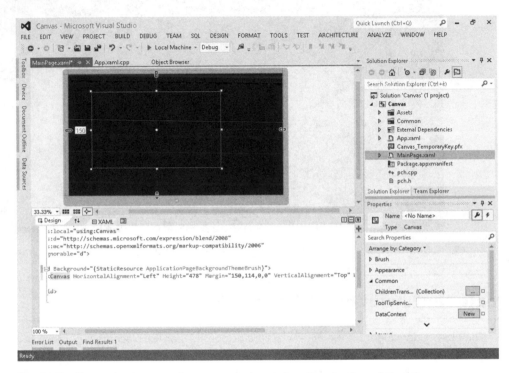

7. On the Toolbox tab, choose a *Button* control and drag it onto the existing *Canvas*.

8. Modify the *Margin*, *Height*, and *Width* properties as you like.

9. Repeat steps 7 and 8 two more times until you have a total of three *Button* controls on the *Canvas* panel. The following image shows one possible composition of the previously mentioned controls, but feel free to express your creativity by arranging them in a different order or by modifying their dimensions.

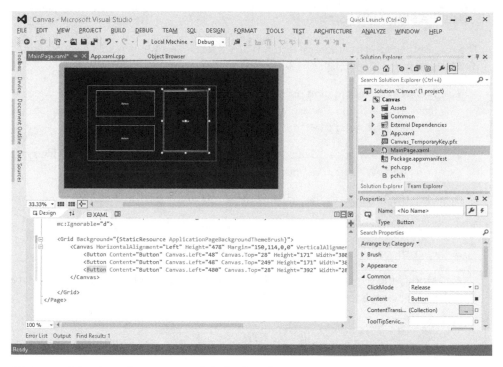

10. Click any of the three *Button* controls in Design view.

11. In the Properties window, expand the Layout category and modify the Left property by setting a higher value. You will notice a change in the placement of the selected control.

12. In the XAML pane, look at the source code of the *Button* controls. In addition to the classic properties, you can see the new properties *Canvas.Left* and *Canvas.Top*.

    These properties are called *attached properties*, since they do not belong to the object model of the target element, but are instead "attached" to the control itself by the parent control. Their purpose is to provide an indication to the parent panel about the position of the control. In this scenario, the *Canvas* panel exposes the attached properties *Canvas.Left* and *Canvas. Top*; their role is to allow the absolute positioning of the child controls.

> **Note** The *Canvas.Left* and *Canvas.Top* properties represent the distance between the top-left corner of the *Canvas* parent and the top-left corner of the control. By modifying the Left property in the Properties window, you act on the *Canvas.Left* property, and by modifying the Top property in the Properties window, you operate on the *Canvas.Top* property.

Use the *StackPanel* control

The role of the *StackPanel* control is to position the child elements below each other or side by side depending on the *Orientation* property.

1. Create a new application project. To do so, open Visual Studio 2012 and select New Project from the File menu. Choose Windows Store from the list of installed templates, and then choose Blank App (XAML) from the list of available projects.

2. Name the new project **StackPanel**, and then choose a location on your file system and a solution name. When you've finished, click OK.

3. Click the Toolbox tab that appears to the left of the form in the Designer window.

4. Expand the Common XAML Controls section.

5. Click the *StackPanel* control and drag it onto the form.

6. Modify the dimensions and position of the *StackPanel* control until you get something that resembles the following screen shot.

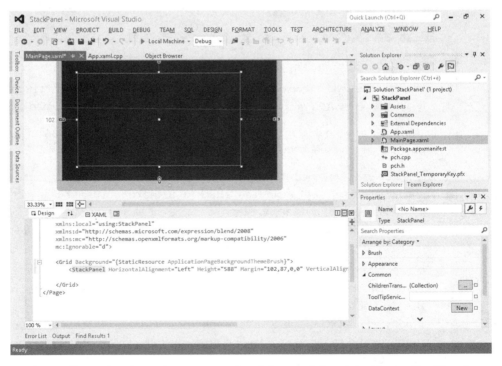

7. On the Toolbox tab, select a *Button* control and drag and drop it inside the *StackPanel*.

8. Modify the *Margin*, *Height*, and *Width* properties as you like. For a somewhat better result, set the *Height* property to a value about one quarter of the *StackPanel* height (about 150 pixels).

9. Click the *Button* control in Design view.

10. Press Ctrl+C to copy the control, and then press Ctrl+V. A new *Button* control will be placed right under the preceding button.

11. Press Ctrl+V two more times to add two more *Button* controls placed according to the default *StackPanel* behavior.

12. In Design view, select the *StackPanel* control by clicking inside the area defined by the control—but not on any of the buttons. Press Delete.

13. Click the Toolbox tab that appears on the left side of the form in the Designer window.

14. Expand the All XAML Controls section.

15. Click the *StackPanel* control and drag it onto the form.

16. Modify the dimensions and position of the *StackPanel* control until you get something similar to the preview image.

17. In the Properties window, set the Orientation property to Horizontal.

18. On the Toolbox tab, select a *Button* control and drag it onto the preceding *StackPanel*.

19. Modify the *Margin, Height*, and *Width* properties as you like. For a better result, set the *Width* property to a value about one quarter of the *StackPanel* height (about 250 pixels).

20. Click the *Button* control in Design view and press Ctrl+C to copy the control.

21. Press Ctrl+V. You will notice a new *Button* control positioned next to the preceding button.

22. Press Ctrl+V two more times to paste two more *Button* controls positioned according to the default *StackPanel* behavior. You will find the result of these steps in the *StackPanelHorizontal* sample project.

23. On the Debug menu, click Start Debugging.

Use the *ScrollViewer* control

The role of the *ScrollViewer* control is to enable scrolling (both vertical and horizontal) in the case of overflow of the content (that is, when the content exceeds the size of the *ScrollViewer* control).

1. Create a new application project. To do so, open Visual Studio 2012 and select New Project from the File menu. Choose Windows Store from the list of installed templates, and then choose Blank App (XAML) from the list of available projects.

2. Name the new project **ScrollViewer**, and then choose a location on your file system and a solution name. When you've finished, click OK.

3. Click the Toolbox tab that appears on the left side of the form in the Designer window.

4. Expand the All XAML Controls section.

5. Click the *StackPanel* control and drag it onto the form.

6. Modify the dimensions and position of the *StackPanel* control until you get something that resembles the following screen shot.

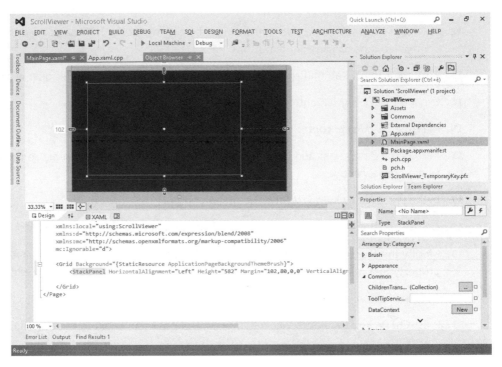

7. On the Toolbox tab, select a *Button* control and drag it onto the preceding *StackPanel*.

8. Modify the *Margin*, *Height*, and *Width* properties as you like. For a better result, set the *Height* property to about 215 pixels.

9. Click the *Button* control in Design view and press Ctrl+C to copy the control.

10. Press Ctrl+V. You will notice a new *Button* control is placed below the preceding button.

11. Press Ctrl+V two more times until you get something similar to the following screen shot.

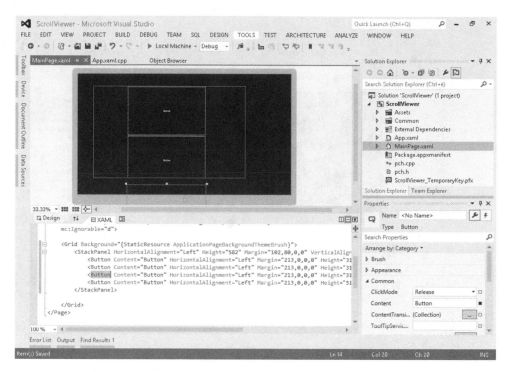

Do not worry if the second button is only partially visible and the others are completely invisible.

12. On the Debug menu, click Start Debugging.

13. You will also notice that at run time the second button is partially visible (but still clickable), while the other buttons are completely invisible and therefore not usable.

14. Return to Visual Studio 2012. On the Debug menu, click Stop Debugging.

15. Right-click the *StackPanel* control in Design view, and then select Group Into | ScrollViewer.

16. Click the *StackPanel* node in the XAML pane.

17. In the Properties window, expand the Layout property and click Set to Auto next to the Width property, as shown in the following screen shot.

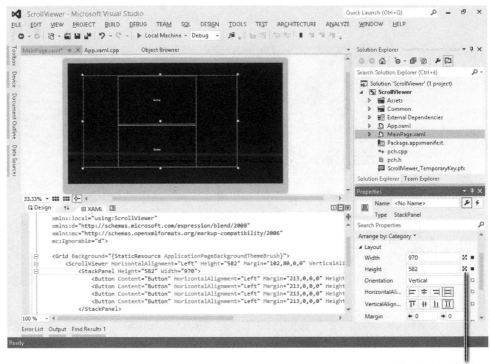

Set to Auto button

18. Click the Set to Auto button next to the Height property.

19. On the Debug menu, click Start Debugging.

20. Place the mouse over a button and scroll between the various *Button* controls.

 Note The controls of the platform have been designed to natively support different types of input; therefore, it is possible to scroll through touch gestures, a digital pen, a mouse, and a keyboard (in the latter case, using the arrow keys or the Page Up and Page Down keys).

21. Return to Visual Studio 2012 by pressing Alt+Tab. On the Debug menu, click Stop Debugging.

The purpose of the *Grid* control is to place its child elements in rows and columns.

1. Create a new application project. To do so, open Visual Studio 2012 and select New Project from the File menu. Choose Windows Store from the list of installed templates, and then choose Blank App (XAML) from the list of available projects.

2. Name the new project **Grid**, and then choose a location on your file system and a solution name. When you've finished, click OK.

3. Click the Toolbox tab that appears on the left side of the form in the Designer window, expand the Common XAML Controls section, click the *Grid* control, and drag it onto the form.

   Modify the dimensions and position of the *Grid* control until you get something similar to the following screen shot.

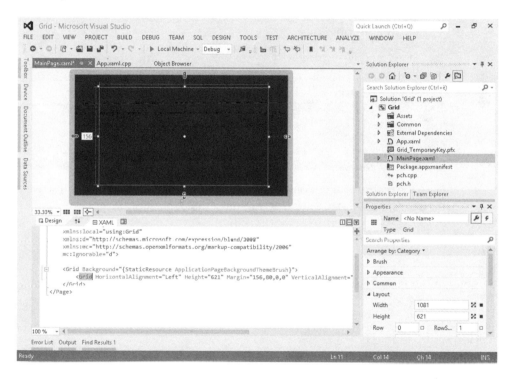

In Design view, place the mouse pointer in the area between the top margin of the *Grid* control and the dotted border positioned a few pixels above the *Grid* control. You will notice that the pointer changes to a column delimiter, as in the following screen shot.

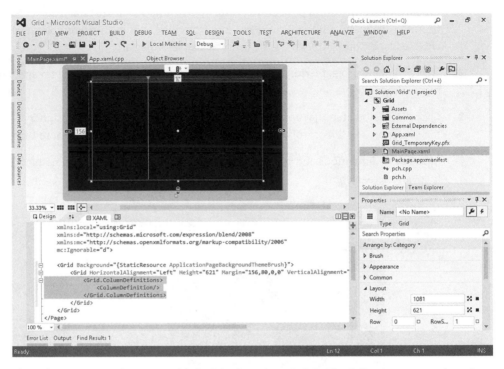

Place the mouse at about one third of the length and click. The following screen shot shows the appearance of Design view at the end of this operation.

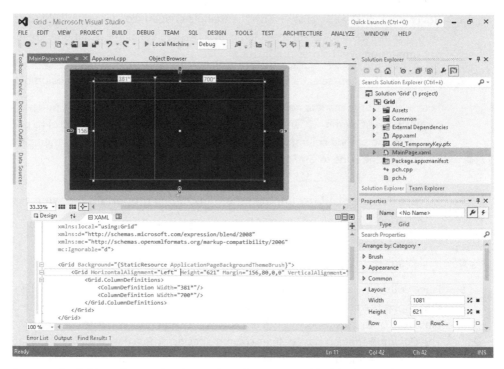

As a result of this action, two columns have been created inside the *Grid* control. The first column has a width equal (in this case) to *381** and the second column to *700**. Do not worry if your numerical values are different. By observing XAML view, you will find that the XAML code is similar to the following:

```xaml
<Grid HorizontalAlignment="Left" Height="621" Margin="156,80,0,0" VerticalAlignment="Top"
      Width="1081">
    <Grid.ColumnDefinitions>
        <ColumnDefinition Width="381*"/>
        <ColumnDefinition Width="700*"/>
    </Grid.ColumnDefinitions>
</Grid>
```

The *Grid* control uses the *ColumnDefinitions* property to define the number of columns and their properties.

4. In Design view, you can add more columns at your will.

5. Hover the mouse a few pixels below the triangle-shaped icon that represents the boundary of a column. You will see the pointer of the mouse assuming the shape of two arrows pointing, respectively, to the left and right. While holding the left mouse button, move the mouse left or right to resize the column. Release the left button to confirm the position.

6. Hover the mouse a few pixels below the triangle-shaped icon (as you would to resize a column), double-click to delete the column, and then delete all the additional columns until you get something like the previous image.

7. On the Toolbox tab, select a *Button* control and drag it into the second column of the *Grid*.

Take a look at the markup code of the *Button* control in XAML view and notice the attached property *Grid.Column="1"*; this property is used by the parent *Grid* control to position the button in the second column. If you want to place the *Button* control in the first column, simply change the code to *Grid.Column="0"*.

> **Note** For the platform, omitting the *Grid.Column* property is the same as writing *Grid.Column="0"*.

8. In Design view, drag the *Button* control inside the first column.

9. Place your mouse over the label that represents the width of the column (in this case, the label that shows the number *381**), and you'll notice a new drop-down list above the column. The main role of this drop-down list is to allow you to edit the properties of a *ColumnDefinition*. The *ColumnDefinition* class defines column-specific properties, like *Width*, that apply to *Grid* controls. Opening the drop-down list will reveal a view similar to that shown in the following screen shot.

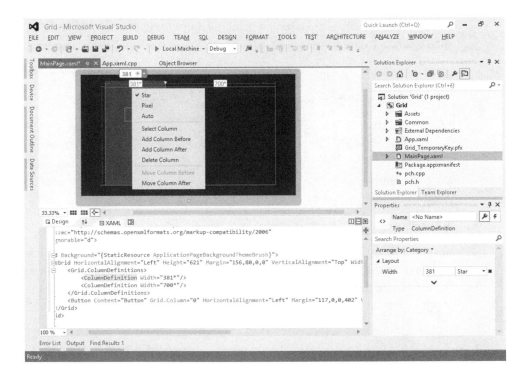

10. In the drop-down list, select Pixel. The underlying label will show a value without the * character (in this case, the value is *381*).

This operation results in the creation of a *ColumnDefinition* with a fixed width of 381 pixels.

11. From the drop-down list, select Auto to set the column width to the width of its child controls automatically. In this scenario, the actual width of the column will be the sum of the width of the button and its margins.

12. From the drop-down list, select Star to return to the initial situation. Do not worry if the numerical values are different—just make sure that both *ColumnDefinition* elements have their *Width* property set to Star (that is, the value contains the * character).

The Star option allows you to create columns with proportional width; this ratio will be maintained even at run time. This option is very useful if you want to create user interfaces capable of adapting to different client screen resolutions.

This procedure created two columns with the values *381** and *700** (your actual values might be different). From the runtime perspective, the creation of columns with these values means that if the first column is 381 times a "logical unit," the second column will be 700 times that same unit, thus maintaining an identical ratio.

13. In XAML view, modify the *Width* property of the two *ColumnDefinition* elements as follows (the property to edit is highlighted in bold):

```
<Grid.ColumnDefinitions>
    <ColumnDefinition Width="1*"/>
    <ColumnDefinition Width="2*"/>
</Grid.ColumnDefinitions>
```

This way, you can be sure that the width of the second column will always be double the width of the first column.

14. In Design view, place the mouse pointer into the area between the left edge of the *Grid* control and the dotted line that is just a few pixels from the left of the *Grid* control. Notice that the pointer changes its shape into a row delimiter, as shown in the following screen shot.

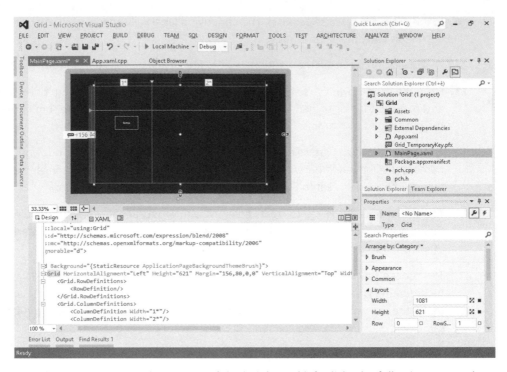

Stop the mouse at around a quarter of the height and left-click. The following screen shot shows Design view at the end of the operation.

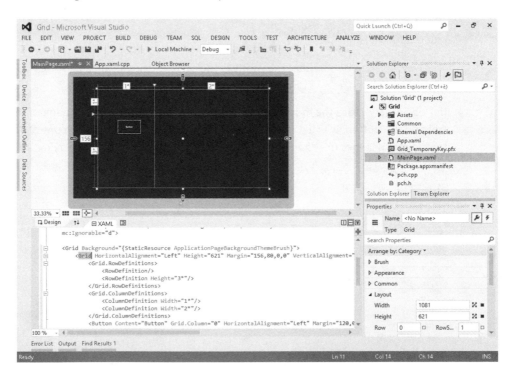

This operation led to the creation of two rows inside the *Grid* control: the first one with a height (in this example) of *1**, and the second row with a height of *3**. If you look at XAML view, you will notice that the XAML code of the *Grid* control is similar to the following code (the code produced by the last operation is highlighted in bold):

```
<Grid HorizontalAlignment="Left" Height="621" Margin="156,80,0,0" VerticalAlignment="Top"
    Width="1081">
    <Grid.RowDefinitions>
        <RowDefinition/>
        <RowDefinition Height="3*"/>
    </Grid.RowDefinitions>
    <Grid.ColumnDefinitions>
        <ColumnDefinition Width="1*"/>
        <ColumnDefinition Width="2*"/>
    </Grid.ColumnDefinitions>
    <Button Content="Button" HorizontalAlignment="Left" Height="84"
        Margin="57,18.556,0,0" VerticalAlignment="Top" Width="217" Grid.Row="1"/>
</Grid>
```

The *Grid* control uses the *RowDefinitions* property to define the rows and their properties.

Notice that the first *RowDefinition* does not have any *Height* property defined. In that case, the platform assumes *Height="*"* or *Height="1*"*, which is the same.

> **Note** A *ColumnDefinition* with no *Width* property is the same as a *ColumnDefinition* with *Width="*"* or, if you prefer, *Width="1*"*.

If you look at the markup code of the *Button* control in XAML view, you can see the attached property *Grid.Row = "1"*; this property is used by the parent *Grid* control to position the child control in the specified row. If you need to place the *Button* control in the first line, you should specify *Grid.Row = "0"*.

> **Note** From the platform perspective, omitting the *Grid.Row* property equates to *Grid.Row = "0"*.

15. In Design view, add as many rows as you like.

Position the mouse a few pixels to the right of the triangle-shaped icon that represents the demarcation of a row and you'll see that the pointer of the mouse takes the shape of two arrows pointing upward and downward. Pressing the left mouse button, drag the mouse up or down to resize the affected row. Release the left mouse button to confirm the position.

16. Place the mouse few pixels to the right of the triangle-shaped icon (as you would to resize the row), double-click to delete the row, and then delete all the additional rows until you obtain something that resembles the previous screen shot.

17. Place your mouse over the label that represents the height of the first line (in this scenario, it's the label with the value of *1**) and you'll notice a new drop-down list next to the row. The main purpose of this drop-down list is to allow you to modify the *Height* property of a *RowDefinition*. Opening the drop-down list reveals a view similar to that shown the following screen shot.

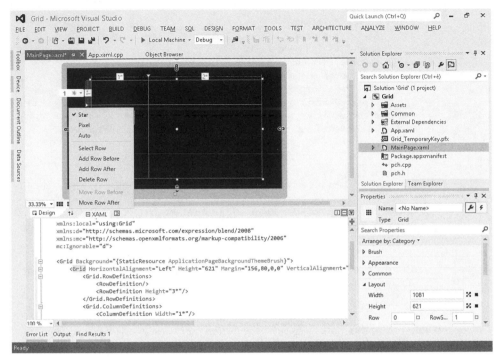

18. In the drop-down list, select Pixel, and the underlying label will show a value without the * character (for instance, the value could be 155).

This operation allows you to create a *RowDefinition* with fixed width of (again, in this case) 155 pixels.

19. From the drop-down list, select Auto to automatically set the row height; it will be the height of its child controls to determine the actual height of the *RowDefinition*. In this sample scenario, there aren't any children controls yet; therefore, it seems that the row has been deleted, so just look at XAML view to ensure the presence of both rows. Press Ctrl+Z to undo the last operation.

20. In the drop-down list, select Star to step back to the initial situation. Do not worry if the numerical values are different—just make sure that the *Height* property of both *RowDefinition* elements is set to Star (that is, the value contains the * character).

The Star option allows you to create rows with proportional height, and this ratio will be maintained at run time as well. This option is extremely important to design user interfaces capable of adapting to different client screen resolutions.

In this procedure, you created two rows with values of *1** and *3**. At run time, if the height of the first row is one "logical unit" high, the second row is four times higher, thus preserving the same fixed ratio.

21. On the Toolbox tab, select a *Button* control and drag it in the second column and second row of the *Grid* control.

22. Modify the *Margin*, *Height*, and *Width* properties as you like. The XAML code of the new *Button* control should look like the following:

```
<Button Content="Button" HorizontalAlignment="Left" Height="84" Margin="241,198,0,0"
        VerticalAlignment="Top" Width="217" Grid.Row="1" Grid.Column="1"/>
```

Notice that the two attached properties, *Grid.Row* and *Grid.Column*, will be used by the parent *Grid* control to position the control properly.

23. On the Debug menu, click Start Debugging.

Use the *Border* control

The *Border* class is not derived from the *Panel* base class—it cannot contain a list of user interface controls, but it can contain a single child element. The purpose of the *Border* control is to draw a frame around a single child control. *Border* is mostly useful for creating an appealing graphic effect around elements, such as round corners.

1. Create a new application project. To do so, open Visual Studio 2012 and select New Project from the File menu. Choose Windows Store from the list of installed templates, and then choose Blank App (XAML) from the list of available projects.

2. Name the new project **Border**, and then choose a location on your file system and a solution name. When you've finished, click OK.

3. Click the Toolbox tab that appears on the left side of the form in the Designer window.

4. Click the *Border* control and drag it inside the form.

5. Modify the dimensions and position of the *Border* control until you get something that resembles the following screen shot.

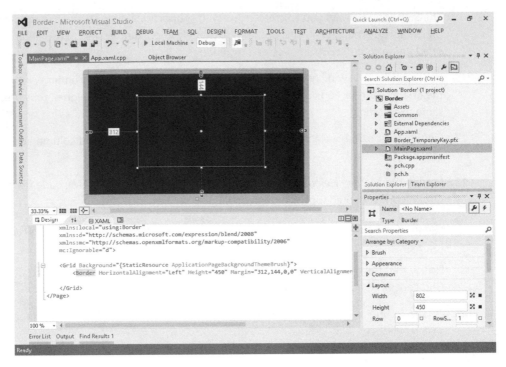

6. In Design view, click the *Border* control.

7. In the Properties window, expand Brush and select BorderBrush | Solid Color Brush. The underlying palette will display a color picker, as shown in the following screen shot.

8. Click and drag the mouse inside the color picker, stopping on whatever color you like (a light color, such as white, will look better).

9. After you have finished, the palette will show a preview of the selected color within the rectangle next to the BorderBrush property, the color code (in this case, #FFFFFFFF), and various shades of red, green, blue, and alpha (the alpha is the transparency of the color). If you choose white, the palette will look like the following screen shot.

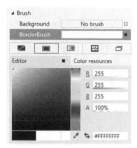

> **Note** A higher transparency value produces an opaque color, while a lower transparency value produces a more transparent color (one where the background can show through).

10. In the Properties window, expand the Appearance property group and set the BorderThickness property by assigning the value **10** to Left and Right, **20** to Top, and **40** to Bottom.

11. In the Properties window, set the CornerRadius property to **20,20,40,40**.

    The *CornerRadius* property represents the radii of a border's corners: the first value (*20*, in this example) specifies the radius of the top-left corner, the second value (*20*) specifies the radius of the top-right corner, the third value (*40*) specifies the radius of the bottom-right corner, and the fourth value (*40*) specifies the radius of the bottom-left corner.

> **Note** If you specify only a single value, that value is applied to *all* the *TopLeft*, *TopRight*, *BottomRight*, and *BottomLeft* corners of the *CornerRadius* property.

The result is shown in the following screen shot.

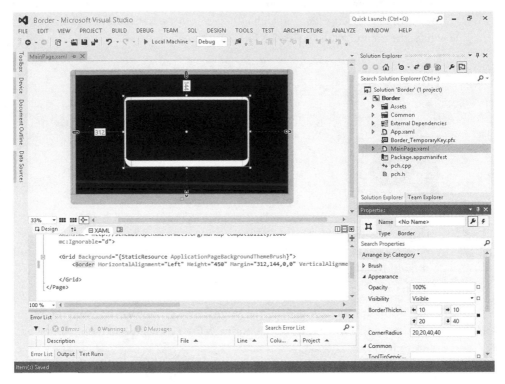

12. On the Debug menu, click Start Debugging. The application will look like the designer surface shown in the previous screen shot.

Use the *Margin* property

The *Margin* property describes the distance between an element and its child or peers. The use of this property enables very fine control of an element's rendering position.

1. Create a new application project. To do so, open Visual Studio 2012 and select New Project from the File menu. Choose Windows Store from the list of installed templates, and then choose Blank App (XAML) from the list of available projects.

2. Name the new project **Margin**, and then choose a location on your file system and a solution name. When you've finished, click OK.

3. Click the Toolbox tab that appears on the left side of the form in the Designer window.

4. Expand the Common XAML Controls section.

5. Click the *Button* control and drag it within the form.

6. In XAML view, set the *Height* property with a value of *200*. Set the *Width* property with a value of *450*. Set the *Margin* property with a value of *300,200,0,0*. The result is shown in the following screen shot.

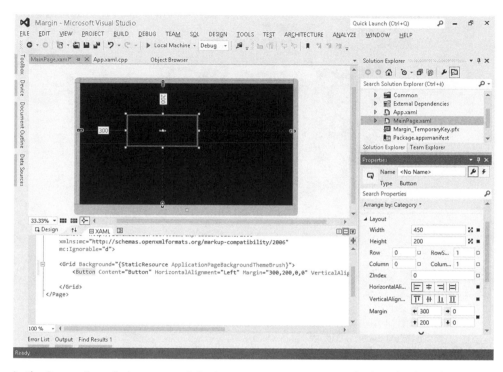

7. In the Properties window, expand the Layout property group and take a look at the Margin property, where the value 300 represents the left margin, the subsequent value 200 defines the top margin, and the other two values represent the right and bottom margin, respectively. A value of 0 means that the margins have not been defined.

8. In Design view, follow the dashed line that starts from the right side of the button to the right side of the parent *Grid* control to find an icon shaped like an anchor. Click the icon.

    By doing this, you set a fixed margin with a specific value (616 in the current example, but in your application the value might be different).

9. In the Properties window, expand the Layout property group and make sure that the Width property is set to Auto; if it is not, click Set to Auto next to the Width property.

    Attributing a value of *Auto* to the *Width* property (or omitting that property from the XAML code) shifts the task of assigning a width to the control onto the *Margin* property. In other words, at run time the *Button* control will expand and collapse in compliance with the "contract" imposed by the *Margin* property—that is, a left margin of 300 pixels and a right margin of 616 pixels.

10. In the Visual Studio 2012 toolbar, click the drop-down list by the Local Machine button to open the menu shown in the following screen shot.

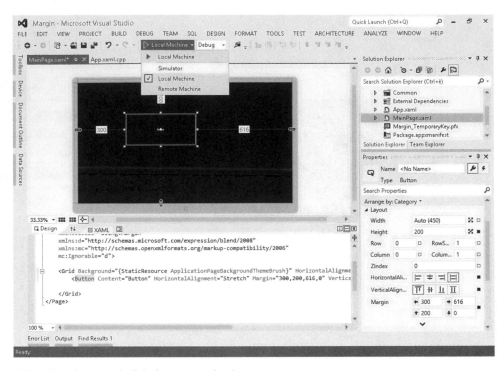

11. Select Simulator and click the green play icon.

Visual Studio 2012 will start the Windows 8 Simulator and then run the application within that virtual environment.

12. In the simulator, click Change Resolution (positioned in the right toolbar of the simulator) and select the first entry, 10.6″ 1024 × 768, as shown in the following image.

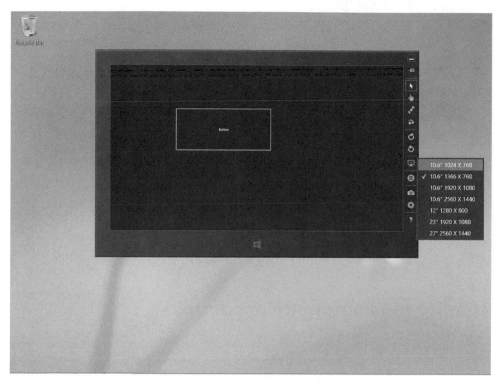

Notice that the button width varies according to the screen resolution.

13. Try other resolutions and notice the changes in the button width.

14. Return to Visual Studio 2012. On the Debug menu, click Stop Debugging.

15. In Design view, follow the dotted line running from the underside of the button to the lower edge of the parent *Grid* control, and you will find an icon with the shape of an anchor. Click that icon.

By doing this, you set a fixed bottom margin with a specific value, which is 368 in the current example, but in your environment it might be different.

16. Drag the *Button* control toward the bottom-right margin of the parent *Grid* control.

Notice how the *Margin* property varies while you are dragging the control.

17. Click the anchor-shaped icon that represents the top margin.

Notice how the solid line changes its shape into a dashed line, which indicates that the margin value has been set to zero.

18. Click the anchor-shaped icon that represents the left margin.

   Notice how the solid line changes its shape into a dashed line, which indicates that the margin value has been set to zero.

19. Set the *Margin* property through XAML view to the value *0,0,80,80*.

20. Make sure that the *Width* property of the *Button* control is set to any value other than zero (for example, 450).

21. On the Debug menu, click Start Debugging.

22. In the simulator, click Change Resolution and select whatever resolution you prefer.

23. Try other resolutions and observe the button. Its dimensions, as well as its right and bottom margins, remain constant.

24. Return to Visual Studio 2012. On the Debug menu, click Stop Debugging.

Customize the appearance of controls

In the previous examples, you set various properties in a control-by-control fashion; however, by leveraging a powerful feature of the XAML platform, it is possible to centralize the layout definition of the various controls to improve the maintainability of the solution and create a consistent appearance for the product.

Another feature of the XAML styling model is that it supports clean separation between presentation and logic, meaning that designers can focus on the appearance of the application, while developers can take care of the application logic.

You will start this section by reusing a style that is already included in the Visual Studio 2012 project. Then you will customize that style. Lastly, you will create a new style from scratch and use templates to redefine the structure of a control.

Use a predefined style

A *Style* element is a container of property values. In this procedure, you will use a *Style* element already included in the Visual Studio 2012 project template.

1. Create a new application project. To do so, open Visual Studio 2012 and select New Project from the File menu. Choose Windows Store from the list of installed templates, and then choose Blank App (XAML) from the list of available projects.

2. Name the new project **UsingStyles**, and then choose a location on your file system and a solution name. When you've finished, click OK.

3. Click the Toolbox tab that appears on the left side of the form in the Designer window.

4. Expand the Common XAML Controls section.

5. Click the *TextBlock* control and drag it onto the form.

6. In XAML view, set the *Margin* property to *200,100,0,0*.

7. In Design view, select the *TextBlock* control and open the context menu by right-clicking, as shown in the following screen shot.

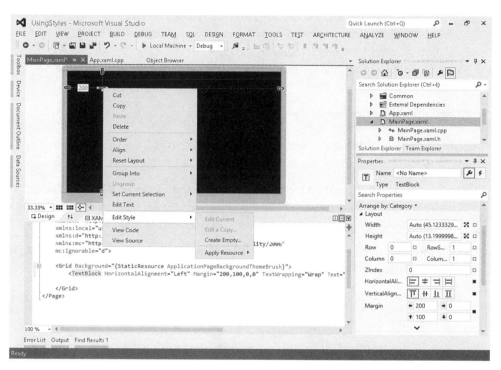

8. Select Edit Style | Apply Resource. Then select PageHeaderTextStyle from the inner menu.

   In XAML view, the XAML code of the *TextBlock* control should look like the following:

   ```
   <TextBlock HorizontalAlignment="Left" Margin="200,100,0,0" TextWrapping="Wrap"
              Text="TextBlock" VerticalAlignment="Top"
              Style="{StaticResource PageHeaderTextStyle}"/>
   ```

   The previous operation set the *Style* property with a reference to a shared resource called *PageHeaderTextStyle*.

9. In Solution Explorer, expand the Common directory and double-click the StandardStyles.xaml file.

10. Press Ctrl+F, and in the text box type **PageHeader**. Visual Studio 2012 will shift the focus to the definition of the style named *PageHeaderTextStyle*; the markup code should look like the following:

    ```
    <Style x:Key="PageHeaderTextStyle" TargetType="TextBlock"
    ```

```
        BasedOn="{StaticResource HeaderTextStyle}">
    <Setter Property="TextWrapping" Value="NoWrap"/>
    <Setter Property="VerticalAlignment" Value="Bottom"/>
    <Setter Property="Margin" Value="0,0,30,40"/>
</Style>
```

As you can see, a style is just a container of property settings, as the properties *TextWrapping*, *VerticalAlignment*, and *Margin* illustrate.

Starting from the first line of code of the style, you can find its name, expressed by the *x:Key* attribute, then the kind of controls that can use it (*TextBlock*, in this case), and finally the *BasedOn* attribute, which indicates the style from which it derives (the *PageHeaderTextStyle* style will inherit all the settings of the base style, plus its own personal settings).

Customize a predefined style

A *Style* element is a container of property values. In this procedure, you will customize a *Style* element that is already included in the Visual Studio 2012 project template.

1. Create a new application project. To do so, open Visual Studio 2012 and select New Project from the File menu. Choose Windows Store from the list of installed templates, and then choose Blank App (XAML) from the list of available projects.

2. Name the new project **CustomStyles**, and then choose a location on your file system and a solution name. When you've finished, click OK.

3. Click the Toolbox tab that appears on the left side of the form in the Designer window.

4. Expand the Common XAML Controls section.

5. Click the *TextBlock* control and drag it within the form.

6. In XAML view, set the *Margin* property to *200,100,0,0*.

7. In Design view, click the *TextBlock* control and right-click to open the context menu. From the menu, select Edit Style | Apply Resource | PageHeaderTextStyle.

8. In Design view, click the *TextBlock* control and right-click to open the context menu. From that menu, select Edit Style | Edit Current.

Replace the following *PageHeaderTextStyle* style definition:

```xml
<Style x:Key="PageHeaderTextStyle" TargetType="TextBlock"
       BasedOn="{StaticResource HeaderTextStyle}">
    <Setter Property="TextWrapping" Value="NoWrap"/>
    <Setter Property="VerticalAlignment" Value="Bottom"/>
    <Setter Property="Margin" Value="0,0,30,40"/>
</Style>
```

with this code:

```xml
<Style x:Key="PageHeaderTextStyle" TargetType="TextBlock"
       BasedOn="{StaticResource HeaderTextStyle}">
    <Setter Property="Foreground" Value="Red"/>
    <Setter Property="TextWrapping" Value="NoWrap"/>
    <Setter Property="VerticalAlignment" Value="Bottom"/>
    <Setter Property="Margin" Value="0,0,30,40"/>
</Style>
```

The new line of code that will customize the control's foreground color is highlighted in bold.

9. In Solution Explorer, double-click MainPage.xaml.

10. Notice that the foreground color of the *TextBlock* control is now red.

11. Click the Toolbox tab.

12. Expand the Common XAML Controls section.

13. Click the *TextBlock* control and drag it within the form, and then move it under the previously added control.

14. Click the new *TextBlock* control and right-click to open the context menu. From the menu, select Edit Style | Apply Resource | PageHeaderTextStyle.

15. Observe the new control again. The foreground color is red, meaning that it uses the custom definition of a predefined style.

16. On the Debug menu, click Start Debugging. The result is shown in the following screen shot.

Customize a copy of a predefined style

A *Style* element is a container of property values. In this procedure, you will customize a copy of a *Style* element that is already included in the Visual Studio 2012 project template.

1. Create a new application project. To do so, open Visual Studio 2012 and select New Project from the File menu. Choose Windows Store from the list of installed templates, and then choose Blank App (XAML) from the list of available projects.

2. Name the new project **CopyStyles**, and then choose a location on your file system and a solution name. When you've finished, click OK.

3. Click the Toolbox tab that appears on the left side of the form in the Designer window.

4. Expand the Common XAML Controls section.

5. Click the *TextBlock* control and drag it within the form.

6. In XAML view, set the *Margin* property to *200,100,0,0*.

7. In Design view, click the *TextBlock* control and right-click to open the context menu. From the menu, select Edit Style | Apply Resource | PageHeaderTextStyle.

8. In Design view, click the *TextBlock* control and right-click the mouse to open the context menu. From that menu, select Edit Style | Edit a Copy to open the Create Style Resource modal dialog box, shown in the following screen shot.

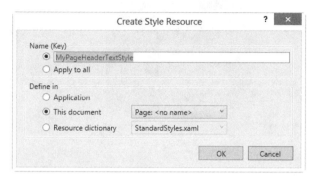

9. In the Name property field, type **MyPageHeaderTextStyle** and make sure that This Document is selected. Click OK.

10. Replace the *PageHeaderTextStyle* style definition that follows:

```
<Style x:Key="MyPageHeaderTextStyle" TargetType="TextBlock"
       BasedOn="{StaticResource HeaderTextStyle}">
    <Setter Property="TextWrapping" Value="NoWrap"/>
    <Setter Property="VerticalAlignment" Value="Bottom"/>
    <Setter Property="Margin" Value="0,0,30,40"/>
</Style>
```

with this code:

```
<Style x:Key="MyPageHeaderTextStyle" TargetType="TextBlock"
       BasedOn="{StaticResource HeaderTextStyle}">
    <Setter Property="Foreground" Value="Red"/>
    <Setter Property="TextWrapping" Value="NoWrap"/>
    <Setter Property="VerticalAlignment" Value="Bottom"/>
    <Setter Property="Margin" Value="0,0,30,40"/>
</Style>
```

The new line of code that will customize the control's foreground color is highlighted in bold.

11. Notice that the foreground color of the *TextBlock* control is now red.

12. Click the Document Outline tab.

13. Click the Return Scope to [Page] button positioned near the style name (MyPageHeaderTextStyle). The following graphic shows the Document Outline tab.

Return scope to [Page] button

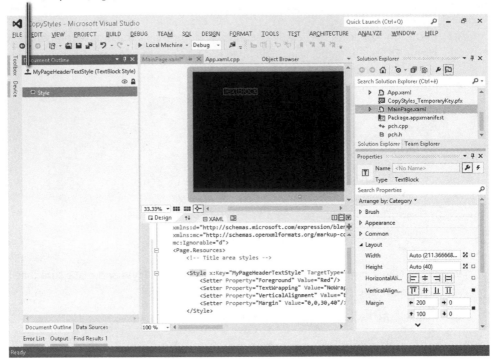

This operation is quite important, since it allows you to leave the style editing mode and go back to the design layout mode.

14. Click the Toolbox tab.

15. Expand the Common XAML Controls section.

16. Click the *TextBlock* control and drag it within the form, and then move it below the previously added control.

17. Click the *TextBlock* control you just added, and then right-click to open the context menu. Select Edit Style | Apply Resource | MyPageHeaderTextStyle. Your new style has been created by starting from a predefined one.

18. On the Debug menu, click Start Debugging. The result will look similar to the final screen shot in the previous procedure.

Create a new style

A *Style* element is a container of property values. In this procedure, you will create a new style from scratch.

1. Create a new application project. To do so, open Visual Studio 2012 and select New Project from the File menu. Choose Windows Store from the list of installed templates, and then choose Blank App (XAML) from the list of available projects.

2. Name the new project **NewStyles**, and then choose a location on your file system and a solution name. When you've finished, click OK.

3. Click the Toolbox tab that appears on the left side of the form in the Designer window.

4. Expand the Common XAML Controls section.

5. Click the *TextBlock* control and drag it within the form.

6. In XAML view, set the *Margin* property to *200,100,0,0*.

7. In Design view, click the *TextBlock* control, and right-click to open the context menu. Select Edit Style | Create Empty to open the Create Style Resource modal dialog box.

8. In the Name text box, type **MyTextBlockStyle** and make sure that This Document is selected. Click OK.

9. In the Properties window, expand the Brush property group, click the Foreground property, and choose whatever color you like from the color picker.

10. Take a look at XAML view. Every operation you execute in the Properties window is recorded as a *Setter* of the style object.

 Note There is a two-way synchronization between the Properties window values and the XAML values, so you can set the *Setters* of a *Style* object through XAML view either by directly typing the corresponding XAML code or by using the visual tools exposed by the Properties window in Visual Studio 2012.

11. In the Properties window, expand the Text property and set the FontSize property to **48px**. This property is located next to the drop-down list box containing the name of the font.

12. Expand Show Advanced Properties in the Text section, as shown in the following screen shot.

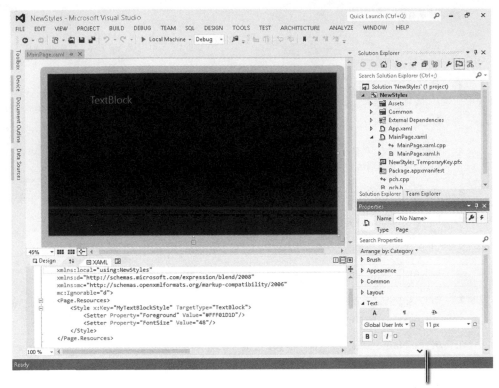

Show Advanced Properties button

13. Set the FontWeight property to Light.

14. Click the Document Outline tab.

15. Click the Return Scope to [Page] button located at the left of the style name (MyTextBlockStyle).

16. Click the Toolbox tab.

17. Expand the Common XAML Controls section.

18. Click the *TextBlock* control and drag it within the form, and then move it below the previously added control.

19. Click the *TextBlock* control just added and right-click to open the context menu. Select Edit Style | Apply Resource and then select the new MyTextBlockStyle style you just created.

Create a new template

The *ControlTemplate* of a control defines the appearance of the control. In this procedure, you will create a new template from scratch.

1. Create a new application project. To do so, open Visual Studio 2012 and select New Project from the File menu. Choose Windows Store from the list of installed templates, and then choose Blank App (XAML) from the list of available projects.

2. Name the new project **NewTemplate**, and then choose a location on your file system and a solution name. When you've finished, click OK.

3. Click the Toolbox tab that appears on the left side of the form in the Designer window, expand the Common XAML Controls section, and click the *Button* control and drag it within the form.

4. In the Properties window, expand the Layout property group and set the Width property to **400** and the Height property to **400**.

5. In Design view, drag the *Button* control to roughly the center of the page, right-click the button to open the context menu, and select Edit Template | Create Empty to open the Create ControlTemplate Resource modal dialog box.

6. In the Name text box, type **MyButtonControlTemplate** and make sure that This Document is selected. Click OK.

   Visual Studio 2012 will enter the editing mode of the *ControlTemplate* of the *Button*. A *ControlTemplate* is a fragment of XAML code capable of representing the structure of a user interface control.

7. Click the Document Outline tab.

 Note If you want to keep the Document Outline tab always visible, click Auto Hide, positioned to the right of the title bar.

   Notice the default structure of a *ControlTemplate*. Visual Studio 2012 has inserted a *Grid* control as the root element of the template.

8. Click the Toolbox tab, expand the All XAML Controls section, click the *Ellipse* control, and drag the *Ellipse* control inside the *Grid* control.

9. In Design view, click the *Ellipse* control and right-click to open the context menu. Select Reset Layout | All. The *Ellipse* control will fill the whole parent element.

10. In the Properties window, expand the Brush property, click the Fill property, and then click the Local button positioned to the right of the rectangle showing the preview, as illustrated in the following screen shot.

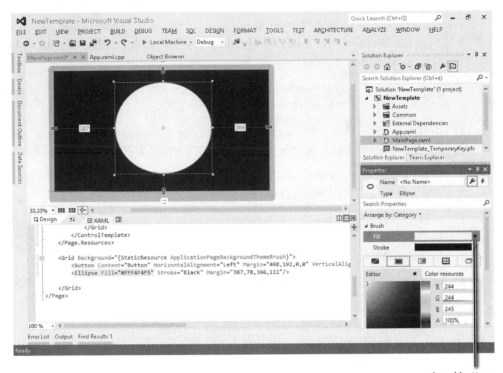

Local button

11. In the context menu of the Local button of the Fill property, select Reset.

Make sure that the background of the *Ellipse* control is set to transparent.

12. In the Properties window, click Stroke and, in the color picker, choose the white color (#FFFFFFFF).

13. Expand the Appearance property and set the StrokeThickness property to **10**.

Note The *StrokeThickness* property represents the width of the object outline.

14. Click the Toolbox tab, expand the All XAML Controls section, and then click the *TextBlock* control and drag it within the form, inside the *Grid* control.

15. In the Properties window, expand the Layout property group.

16. In the context menu of the Local button of the Margin property, select Reset.

17. In the Properties window, set both HorizontalAlignment and VerticalAlignment to Center.

Observe how the *TextBlock* control is being centered within the parent *Grid* control.

18. Expand the Miscellaneous property group, click the Default button next to the Style property, and from the context menu select Local Resources | PageHeaderTextStyle.

19. Expand the Layout property group (if it is not already expanded) and set both the right and bottom margins to **0**.

20. Expand the Common property group, click the Local button next to the Text property, and from the context menu select Template Binding | Content.

With this operation, you have bound the *Content* property of the button, which is going to use this template with the *Text* property of the *TextBlock* control.

21. Click the Document Outline tab and click the Return Scope to [Page] button, which is located next to the name of the template (MyButtonControlTemplate).

22. In Design view, click the *Button* control.

In the Properties window, expand the Common property group, and in the Content property type **Save**.

23. Click the Toolbox tab, expand the Common XAML Controls section, and click the *Button* control and drag it within the form, so it is side by side with the previously added control.

In the Properties window, expand the Layout property and set both the Width and the Height properties to **400**.

24. Expand the Common property group, and then in the Content property type **Cancel**.

25. In Design view, click the *Button* control you just added and right-click to open the context menu. Select Edit Template | Apply Resource, and then choose the new MyButtonControlTemplate template that you just created.

The result is shown in the next screen shot.

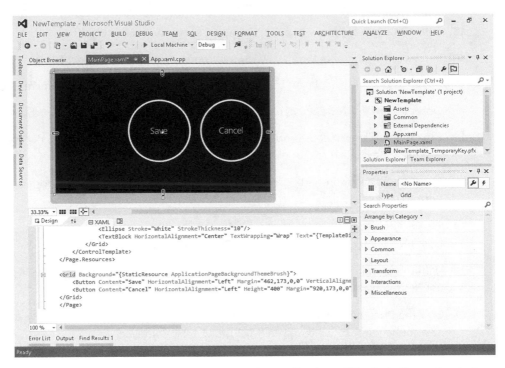

26. On the Debug menu, click Start Debugging. The application will look similar to the designer surface shown in the previous screen shot.

   If the right side of the Cancel button is cut off, return to Visual Studio 2012 and move the two buttons to the left side of the screen.

Use a predefined template

The *ControlTemplate* of a control defines the appearance of the control. In this procedure, you will reuse a *ControlTemplate* element included in the Visual Studio 2012 project template.

1. Create a new application project. To do so, open Visual Studio 2012 and select New Project from the File menu. Choose Windows Store from the list of installed templates, and then choose Blank App (XAML) from the list of available projects.

2. Name the new project **UsingTemplate**, and then choose a location on your file system and a solution name. When you've finished, click OK.

3. Click the Toolbox tab that appears on the left side of the form in the Designer window.

4. Expand the Common XAML Controls section.

5. Click the *Button* control and drag it within the form.

6. In the Properties window, expand the Layout property group, and set both the Width and the Height properties to **400**.

7. In Design view, drag the *Button* control to roughly the center of the page.

8. In Design view, click the *Button* control, and right-click to open the context menu. Select Edit Template | Apply Resource | TextButtonStyle.

This *ControlTemplate* will make the button very similar to a *TextBlock* control visually, but without affecting its behavior. The ability to manage the common events of the *Button* class, such as the *Click* event, will not be affected.

Customize a predefined template

The *ControlTemplate* of a control defines the appearance of the control. In this procedure, you will customize a *ControlTemplate* element included in the Visual Studio 2012 project template

1. Create a new application project. To do so, open Visual Studio 2012 and select New Project from the File menu. Choose Windows Store from the list of installed templates, and then choose Blank App (XAML) from the list of available projects.

2. Name the new project **CustomTemplate**, and then choose a location on your file system and a solution name. When you've finished, click OK.

3. Click the Toolbox tab that appears on the left side of the form in the Designer window.

4. Expand the Common XAML Controls section.

5. Click the *Button* control and drag it within the form.

6. In the Properties window, expand the Layout property group and set both the Width and the Height properties to **400**.

7. In Design view, drag the *Button* control to roughly the center of the page.

8. In Design view, click the *Button* control and right-click to open the context menu. Select Edit Template | Apply Resource | TextButtonStyle.

9. In Design view, click the *Button* control again and right-click to open the context menu. Select Edit Template | Edit Current.

10. Click the Document Outline tab.

11. On the Document Outline tab, expand the Template node (if it is not already expanded), then the Grid node, and finally click the Text node.

   Thanks to this operation, you have selected the *TextBlock* control inside the template.

 Note You can select a control of the *ControlTemplate* by clicking it in Design view.

12. In the Properties window, expand the Brush property group and click the Default button next to the Foreground property. Select Template Binding | Foreground.

13. Expand the Layout property, click the Default button next to the Margin property, select Template Binding, and then click Padding.

 Note The *Padding* property represents the distance between the child elements of a control.

14. On the Document Outline tab, click the Return Scope to [Page] button next to the template name (TextButtonStyle).

15. In Design view, click the *Button* control.

16. In the Properties window, expand the Brush property, and choose whatever color you like for the Foreground property.

17. Expand the Text property and set the FontSize property to **72px**.

18. Click the Show Advanced Properties button and set the FontWeight property to Light.

19. Expand the Layout property group, click the Show Advanced Properties button, and set both the left and top padding to **80**.

Summary

In this chapter, you learned how to use Visual Studio 2012 to create an application by using visual tools; how to define the layout of a Windows 8 application through the *Canvas*, *Grid*, *StackPanel*, and *ScrollViewer* panels; and finally, how to customize the appearance of a visual control through the *Style* and *ControlTemplate* objects.

Quick reference

To	Do this
Add a *Grid* control to the layout	Click the Toolbox tab, expand All XAML Controls, and click the *Grid* control and drag it within the form.
Add a *StackPanel* control to the layout	Click the Toolbox tab, expand All XAML Controls, and click the *StackPanel* control and drag it within the form.
Add a *Canvas* control to the layout	Click the Toolbox tab, expand All XAML Controls, and click the *Canvas* control and drag it within the form.
Use a predefined style	In Design view, click the desired control, right-click and select Edit Style | Apply Resource, and select the style.
Use a predefined template	In Design view, click the desired control, right-click and select Edit Template | Apply Resource, and select the template.

CHAPTER 8

Asynchronous patterns

After completing this chapter, you will be able to

- Write code using the asynchronous pattern in WinRT.

- Call asynchronous methods with the Parallel Patterns Library in C++.

- Choose the right synchronization context in your code.

The preceding chapters have shown you how to write a Windows Store application, and you have already seen and written asynchronous code related to Windows Runtime (WinRT) methods and events. This chapter explains how asynchronous calls work in WinRT and how to write your own asynchronous code correctly in application and library code.

Asynchronous calls with the Parallel Patterns Library in C++

In previous versions of Microsoft Windows, many APIs were exposed mainly through synchronous methods. Asynchronous methods were not always available, making it the programmer's job to choose when to use an asynchronous call and also implement the asynchronous pattern by wrapping the synchronous method when an asynchronous one was not available.

For example, to read the content of a text file in a string variable, you might have written sequential code like this:

```
void Operation() {
    String^ content;
    StorageFile^ file = GetFile();
    content = FileIO::ReadText( file );
    DisplayContent( content );
}
```

However, the *FileIO* class in WinRT does not have a *ReadText* function; instead, it has a *ReadTextAsync* method that you will see shortly. If *ReadText* existed, it would have been synchronous, and if the time required to access the file was too long—and this code was embedded in an event connected to the click of a button or a menu selection event—the user interface of the whole application would have been blocked for the entire time required to read the content from the file.

To avoid this UI-blocking issue, code must read the file in an asynchronous way, returning control to the operating system that handles the user interface. To do that, the method attached to the user interface event must return as soon as possible. Performing an operation in an asynchronous manner means that the caller of a function does not wait for its completion, but will obtain the result of a completed operation later, after that operation has finished execution.

If the function *ReadTextAsync* did not exist, it would be necessary to wrap the *ReadText* call in a task executed in a separate thread. However, WinRT offers an asynchronous call named *ReadTextAsync* that returns a task object representing the asynchronous activity. You must call such a function by using the *create_task* method available in the *concurrency::task* class that is part of the Parallel Patterns Library (PPL) and defined in ppltasks.h.

The *create_task* function accepts an argument of a lambda or function object, an *IAsyncInfo* interface, a *task_completion_event* object, or a different task. The asynchronous methods available in WinRT usually return an *IAsyncOperation* interface, which is inherited from *IAsyncInfo*, so it can be used as a *create_task* argument. The call is embedded in a task executed asynchronously, so the method can return without waiting for the complete execution the operation. If you need to write code that must execute when the asynchronous operation completes, you use the *then* method on the task returned by *create_task*, specifying in a lambda expression the code that must be executed next.

```
void Operation() {
    String^ content;
    StorageFile^ file = GetFile();
    concurrency::create_task(
        FileIO::ReadTextAsync( file )
        ).then([this, file](task<String^> t)
    {
        String^ content = t.get();
        DisplayContent( content );
    });
}
```

The result returned by the *ReadTextAsync* call is a *String* object that becomes a template parameter of the task class. By calling the *get* method, you obtain the value returned by the *ReadTextAsync* function, and you can also manipulate and control the task object by using the *t* parameter of the lambda expression. However, you can simplify such code by replacing the task parameter with the template argument, so you do not have to call the *get* method, as shown in the following example:

```
void Operation() {
    String^ content;
    StorageFile^ file = GetFile();
    concurrency::create_task(
        FileIO::ReadTextAsync( file )
        ).then([this, file](String^ content)
    {
        DisplayContent( content );
    });
}
```

Understanding how to handle asynchronous methods is now fundamental to Windows programming, because the WinRT APIs offer only asynchronous versions of the API for each method that might have a response time higher than 50 milliseconds. In practice, any API that performs an I/O operation, in either an explicit or implicit way, will belong to this category, because the response time of an I/O operation is not always predictable.

Call asynchronous methods

In this procedure, you will write the code to perform asynchronous operations that call the WinRT APIs to choose a file from the document library and then display its contents.

1. Create a new application project. To do so, open Visual Studio 2012 and select New Project from the File menu (the sequence can be File | New | Project for full-featured versions of Visual Studio). Choose Visual C++ in the Templates tree, and then choose Windows Store from the list of installed templates. Choose Blank App (XAML) from the list of available projects.

2. Name the new project **DisplayFile**, and then choose a location on your file system, without changing the default solution name. When you've finished, click OK.

As you saw in Chapter 3, "My first Windows 8 app," the Windows Store application template provides a default page (MainPage.xaml), an application entry point in the *App* class (App. xaml.cpp), a default application description and a declaration in the Package.appxmanifest file, and four default images representing logos and a splash screen.

The following screen shot shows the project at this stage.

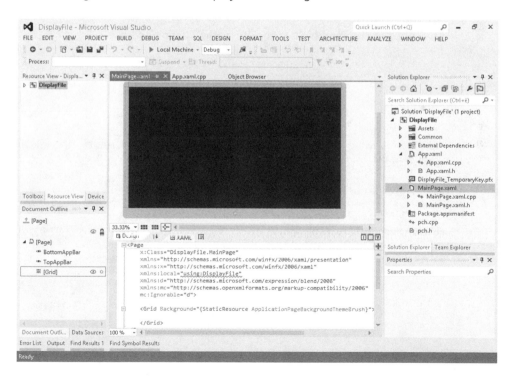

3. Scroll down the MainPage.xaml source code and insert a *TextBlock* control and a *Button* control inside a *StackPanel* control, as illustrated in the bold lines of the following code excerpt:

```
<Page
    x:Class="DisplayFile.MainPage"
    xmlns="http://schemas.microsoft.com/winfx/2006/xaml/presentation"
    xmlns:x="http://schemas.microsoft.com/winfx/2006/xaml"
    xmlns:local="using:DisplayFile"
    xmlns:d="http://schemas.microsoft.com/expression/blend/2008"
    xmlns:mc="http://schemas.openxmlformats.org/markup-compatibility/2006"
    mc:Ignorable="d">

    <Grid Background="{StaticResource ApplicationPageBackgroundThemeBrush}">
        <StackPanel>
            <Button Click="ChooseFile_Click" Content="Choose File" />
            <TextBlock x:Name="Result" Height="600" />
        </StackPanel>
    </Grid>
</Page>
```

The *TextBlock* control will be filled with the contents of the file selected by the user through the *FileOpenPicker* picker. The button will simply fire the code to start the picker, read the file in a string, and put it in the *TextBlock*.

4. Double-click the Choose File button in the integrated development environment (IDE) designer, and then open the MainPage.xaml.cpp file and edit the method *ChooseFile_Click*, which implements the event handler for the button.

The code here represents the complete method definition:

```
void DisplayFile::MainPage::ChooseFile_Click(Platform::Object^ sender,
    Windows::UI::Xaml::RoutedEventArgs^ e)
{

}
```

5. Add the following code to the method to open the file picker, retrieve the selected file, and display the file's content in the *TextBlock*:

```
auto picker = ref new Pickers::FileOpenPicker();
picker->FileTypeFilter->Append("*");

concurrency::create_task(
    picker->PickSingleFileAsync() ).then([this](StorageFile^ file) {
        concurrency::create_task(
            FileIO::ReadTextAsync( file )
            ).then([this, file](String^ text)
        {
            String^ content = text;
            this->Result->Text = content;
        });
});
```

The code creates an instance of the *FileOpenPicker* class as you saw in Chapter 6, "Windows Runtime APIs." In this case, the *PickSingleFileAsync* method is used to select just one file. This call is passed as an argument to a *create_task* call, and the following operations are included in the code of the lambda expression passed as an argument to the following *then* method call of the task returned by *create_task*. The code in the lambda expression will execute after the *PickSingleFileAsync* call completes, and this will be coordinated by the message pump. In this way, the *ChooseFile_Click* method immediately returns control to its caller, which is the Windows message pump, so that any other user interaction with this application will be handled correctly.

The value returned by *PickSingleFileAsync* is of type *IAsyncOperation<Windows::Storage::StorageFile^>*, but because it has been passed as an argument to *create_task*, the following *then* method can use the *StorageFile^* argument directly.

After a user has chosen one file, the code continues by reading the file's content, calling the static method *Windows::Storage::FileIO::ReadTextAsync*, which internally handles the required opening and closing of the file. The asynchronous pattern is also used in this case, by wrapping the asynchronous call in a *call_task* statement and including the following code in a lambda expression passed to a *then* call. The complete code for MainPage.xaml.cpp should look like the following listing:

```
#include "pch.h"
#include "MainPage.xaml.h"
#include <ppltasks.h>

using namespace DisplayFile;
using namespace Platform;
using namespace concurrency;
using namespace Windows::Foundation;
using namespace Windows::Foundation::Collections;
using namespace Windows::Storage;
using namespace Windows::UI::Xaml;
using namespace Windows::UI::Xaml::Controls;
using namespace Windows::UI::Xaml::Controls::Primitives;
using namespace Windows::UI::Xaml::Data;
using namespace Windows::UI::Xaml::Input;
using namespace Windows::UI::Xaml::Media;
using namespace Windows::UI::Xaml::Navigation;
```

```
// The Blank Page item template is documented at
// http://go.microsoft.com/fwlink/?LinkId=234238

MainPage::MainPage()
{
    InitializeComponent();
}


/// <summary>
/// Invoked when this page is about to be displayed in a Frame.
/// </summary>
/// <param name="e">Event data that describes how this page was reached.  The Parameter
/// property is typically used to configure the page.</param>
void MainPage::OnNavigatedTo(NavigationEventArgs^ e)
{
    (void) e;    // Unused parameter
}



void DisplayFile::MainPage::ChooseFile_Click(Platform::Object^ sender,
    Windows::UI::Xaml::RoutedEventArgs^ e)
{
    auto picker = ref new Pickers::FileOpenPicker();
    picker->FileTypeFilter->Append("*");

    concurrency::create_task(
        picker->PickSingleFileAsync() ).then([this](StorageFile^ file) {
            //StorageFile^ file = p.get();
            concurrency::create_task(
                FileIO::ReadTextAsync( file )
                ).then([this, file](String^ text)
            {
                String^ content = text;
                this->Result->Text = content;
            });
    });
}
```

6. Run the application, and then choose a text file from your Documents folder. You will see the file's content on the screen. The following screen shot shows the user interface for the main page of the application after reading a sample text document containing three lines.

Writing asynchronous methods

Handling an event in an asynchronous manner requires using the *concurrency::task* class that is part of the PPL and defined in ppltasks.h. To expose a method so that you can call it in an asynchronous way, you can implement the asynchronous pattern by using the *create_async* function.

It is important to understand that the method for an event is always called in a synchronous way and does not release control to the message pump until it ends. By calling *create_async*, you execute the asynchronous operation later, after control has returned to the message pump (a parallel operation in another thread could also be executed according to the type of synchronization context chosen). Thus, you must evaluate whether you are executing code that could require a significant amount of time to be executed. You could consider adopting the same metric used for WinRT APIs: using asynchronous calls for any operations that might require more than 50 milliseconds to complete.

For example, imagine that you have a calculation that might require a few seconds, such as the following *LongCalculation* method that simulates a long calculation by looping for the number of seconds specified in the parameter:

```
void MainPage::LongCalculation(int seconds)
{
    Windows::Globalization::Calendar^ stop = ref new Windows::Globalization::Calendar;
    Windows::Globalization::Calendar^ current = ref new Windows::Globalization::Calendar;
    stop->SetToNow();
    stop->AddSeconds(seconds);
    do {
        current->SetToNow();
    } while (current->GetDateTime().UniversalTime < stop->GetDateTime().UniversalTime);
}
```

If you call this method before any other asynchronous call in a method handling an event, the application will become unresponsive until the method completes, and the asynchronous calls will not be made until the *LongCalculation* method completes. For instance, consider what would happen if you call *LongCalculation* in the first line of the *ChooseFile_Click* method of the previous example, resulting in the following version:

```
void DisplayFile::MainPage::ChooseFile_Click(Platform::Object^ sender,
        Windows::UI::Xaml::RoutedEventArgs^ e)
{
    LongCalculation(5);
    auto picker = ref new Pickers::FileOpenPicker();
    picker->FileTypeFilter->Append("*");

    concurrency::create_task(
        picker->PickSingleFileAsync() ).then([this](StorageFile^ file) {
            //StorageFile^ file = p.get();
            concurrency::create_task(
                FileIO::ReadTextAsync( file )
                ).then([this, file](String^ text)
            {
                String^ content = text;
                this->Result->Text = content;
            });
    });
}
```

By running this code, you can observe that when a user clicks the Choose File button, the application becomes unresponsive for about five seconds (the value passed as parameter to *LongCalculation*). Only after that period will the user interface that lets the user choose a file display. This delay occurs because the call to *ChooseFile_Click* is synchronous; only the code passed to *create_task* will be executed asynchronously later.

To avoid the delay, you would need to write the *LongCalculation* method using the asynchronous pattern, returning an interface derived by *IAsyncInfo* that controls the asynchronous execution. After that, you can call it with a *create_task* function in the *ChooseFile_Click* method. You can also call *create_task*, embedding the call to *LongCalculation* in the lambda expression passed as a parameter, but that makes it less explicit that *LongCalculation* must be called in an asynchronous way, because the operation could require more than 50 milliseconds to execute—as is true for every possible long-running operation in the WinRT APIs.

To identify a method that developers should call in an asynchronous way, add the *Async* suffix to the name of the method itself. The asynchronous pattern has these characteristics:

- If the method is void, the asynchronous method returns *IAsyncAction*.

- If the method returns a type *T*, the asynchronous method returns *IAsyncOperation<T>*.

In other words, the following three methods:

```
void Sample1();
int Sample2();
String^ Sample3();
```

would have these corresponding asynchronous signatures:

```
IAsyncAction^ Sample1Async();
IAsyncOperation<int>^ Sample2Async();
IAsyncOperation<String^>^ Sample3Async();
```

A simple way to transform a CPU-intensive function into an asynchronous one is to embed its body within a lambda expression passed as a parameter to a *create_async* call, returning a result of type *IAsyncAction* to the caller:

```
IAsyncAction^ MainPage::LongCalculationAsync(int seconds)
{
    return concurrency::create_async( [seconds]() {
        Windows::Globalization::Calendar^ stop = ref new Windows::Globalization::Calendar;
        Windows::Globalization::Calendar^ current = ref new Windows::Globalization::Calendar;
        stop >SetToNow();
        stop->AddSeconds(seconds);
        do {
            current->SetToNow();
        } while (current->GetDateTime().UniversalTime < stop->GetDateTime().UniversalTime);
    });
}
```

However, remember that executing the code asynchronously might execute code in a different thread, depending on the caller, introducing possible race conditions caused by execution of code in parallel threads. You will see how to synchronize code execution in the proper context later in this chapter.

Implement an asynchronous method

In this procedure, you will implement an asynchronous method that prevents the user interface from becoming unresponsive while the application executes a long-running operation.

1. Open the MainPage.xaml source code and add a *ProgressBar* control inside the existing *StackPanel* control, as illustrated in the bold line of the following code excerpt:

```
<Page
    x:Class="DisplayFile.MainPage"
    xmlns="http://schemas.microsoft.com/winfx/2006/xaml/presentation"
    xmlns:x="http://schemas.microsoft.com/winfx/2006/xaml"
    xmlns:local="using:DisplayFile"
    xmlns:d="http://schemas.microsoft.com/expression/blend/2008"
    xmlns:mc="http://schemas.openxmlformats.org/markup-compatibility/2006"
    mc:Ignorable="d">

    <Grid Background="{StaticResource ApplicationPageBackgroundThemeBrush}">
        <StackPanel>
            <Button Click="ChooseFile_Click" Content="Choose File" />
            <ProgressBar x:Name="Progress" HorizontalAlignment="Left"
                         Height="10" Width="1024"/>
            <TextBlock x:Name="Result" Height="600" />
        </StackPanel>
    </Grid>
</Page>
```

The *ProgressBar* control will be updated through the code you add in the next step.

2. Open the MainPage.xaml.h file and add the declaration of the method *InitializeProgressBar* in the private methods of the *MainPage* class:

```
void InitializeProgressBar();
```

3. Open the MainPage.xaml.cpp file and add the method *InitializeProgressBar*, which implements continuous progress bar updates. The progress bar updates will indicate that the message pump is running and the application is responsive. If the message pump gets blocked, the progress bar will freeze for the duration of the unresponsive state.

The code here represents the complete method definition:

```
void MainPage::InitializeProgressBar()
{
    Windows::Foundation::TimeSpan Period;
    Period.Duration = 100 * 10000; // 100 msec

    auto timerDelegate = [this](Windows::System::Threading::ThreadPoolTimer^ timer)
    {
        auto uiDelegate = [this]()
        {
            this->Progress->Value =
                (this->Progress->Value > 100) ? 0 : this->Progress->Value + 1;
        };
```

```
        Dispatcher->RunAsync(Windows::UI::Core::CoreDispatcherPriority::Normal,
                             ref new Windows::UI::Core::DispatchedHandler(uiDelegate));
    };

    Windows::System::Threading::ThreadPoolTimer::CreatePeriodicTimer(
        ref new Windows::System::Threading::TimerElapsedHandler(timerDelegate),
        Period );
}
```

4. Change the *MainPage* constructor, adding the call to the *InitializeProgressBar* method after the call to *InitializeComponent*. The following code represents the complete method definition:

```
MainPage::MainPage()
{
    InitializeComponent();
    InitializeProgressBar();
}
```

5. Add the following declaration to the private methods of the *MainPage* class in the MainPage. xaml.h file:

```
void LongCalculation(int seconds);
```

6. Add the following method to the MainPage.xaml.cpp file:

```
void MainPage::LongCalculation(int seconds)
{
    Windows::Globalization::Calendar^ stop = ref new Windows::Globalization::Calendar;
    Windows::Globalization::Calendar^ current = ref new Windows::Globalization::Calendar;
    stop->SetToNow();
    stop->AddSeconds(seconds);
    do {
        current->SetToNow();
    } while (current->GetDateTime().UniversalTime < stop->GetDateTime().UniversalTime);
}
```

7. Insert the call to *LongCalculation* as the first line of the *ChooseFile_Click* method:

```
void DisplayFile::MainPage::ChooseFile_Click(Platform::Object^ sender,
    Windows::UI::Xaml::RoutedEventArgs^ e)
{
    LongCalculation(5);

    auto picker = ref new Pickers::FileOpenPicker();
    picker->FileTypeFilter->Append("*");

    concurrency::create_task(
        picker->PickSingleFileAsync() ).then([this](StorageFile^ file) {
            concurrency::create_task(
                FileIO::ReadTextAsync( file )
                ).then([this, file](String^ text)
```

```
            {
                String^ content = text;
                this->Result->Text = content;
            });
        });
    }
```

8. Run the application and you will see that the progress bar continuously changes its state until you click the Choose File button, at which point the application becomes unresponsive for about five seconds, during which time the progress bar freezes, resulting in a state similar to the following image.

9. After five seconds have elapsed, the user interface for selecting a file will appear. At this point, you can close the application and apply the changes required to make an asynchronous call to *LongCalculation*.

10. Change the code as follows. Rename the *LongCalculation* method to **LongCalculationAsync**, embed the code in a lambda expression passed to the *create_async* method, and transform the returning type of the method from *void* to *IAsyncAction^*. Finally, embed the *LongCalculationAsync* call in a *create_task* call and the remaining part of the *ChooseFile_Click* method in a lambda expression passed as an argument to a following *then* call. You can see the changes highlighted in bold in the following code:

```
#include "pch.h"
```

```cpp
#include "MainPage.xaml.h"
#include <ppltasks.h>

using namespace DisplayFile;
using namespace Platform;
using namespace concurrency;
using namespace Windows::Foundation;
using namespace Windows::Foundation::Collections;
using namespace Windows::Storage;
using namespace Windows::UI::Xaml;
using namespace Windows::UI::Xaml::Controls;
using namespace Windows::UI::Xaml::Controls::Primitives;
using namespace Windows::UI::Xaml::Data;
using namespace Windows::UI::Xaml::Input;
using namespace Windows::UI::Xaml::Media;
using namespace Windows::UI::Xaml::Navigation;

// The Blank Page item template is documented at
// http://go.microsoft.com/fwlink/?LinkId=234238

MainPage::MainPage()
{
    InitializeComponent();
    InitializeProgressBar();
}

/// <summary>
/// Invoked when this page is about to be displayed in a Frame.
/// </summary>
/// <param name="e">Event data that describes how this page was reached.  The Parameter
/// property is typically used to configure the page.</param>
void MainPage::OnNavigatedTo(NavigationEventArgs^ e)
{
    (void) e;    // Unused parameter
}


void DisplayFile::MainPage::ChooseFile_Click(Platform::Object^ sender,
    Windows::UI::Xaml::RoutedEventArgs^ e)
{
    concurrency::create_task( LongCalculationAsync(5) ).then([this]()
        {
            auto picker = ref new Pickers::FileOpenPicker();
            picker->FileTypeFilter->Append("*");

            concurrency::create_task(
                picker->PickSingleFileAsync() ).then([this](StorageFile^ file) [
                    concurrency::create_task(
                        FileIO::ReadTextAsync( file )
                        ).then([this, file](String^ text)
                    {
                        String^ content = text;
                        this->Result->Text = content;
                    });
            });
    });
}

void MainPage::InitializeProgressBar()
```

```
{
    Windows::Foundation::TimeSpan Period;
    Period.Duration = 100 * 10000; // 100 msec

    auto timerDelegate = [this](Windows::System::Threading::ThreadPoolTimer^ timer)
    {
        auto uiDelegate = [this]()
        {
            this->Progress->Value =
                (this->Progress->Value > 100) ? 0 : this->Progress->Value + 1;
        };

        Dispatcher->RunAsync(Windows::UI::Core::CoreDispatcherPriority::Normal,
                             ref new Windows::UI::Core::DispatchedHandler(uiDelegate));
    };

    Windows::System::Threading::ThreadPoolTimer::CreatePeriodicTimer(
        ref new Windows::System::Threading::TimerElapsedHandler(timerDelegate),
        Period );
}

IAsyncAction^ MainPage::LongCalculationAsync(int seconds)
{
    return concurrency::create_async( [seconds]() {
        Windows::Globalization::Calendar^ stop =
            ref new Windows::Globalization::Calendar;
        Windows::Globalization::Calendar^ current =
            ref new Windows::Globalization::Calendar;
        stop->SetToNow();
        stop->AddSeconds(seconds);
        do {
            current->SetToNow();
        } while (current->GetDateTime().UniversalTime < stop->GetDateTime().
            UniversalTime);
    });
}
```

11. Run the application again. This time, after you click the Choose File button, the progress bar will continue to update during the five seconds you must wait before the file selection user interface appears. This is because the message pump is not blocked and the application is still responsive—even though it's still executing a lengthy operation before asking the user to select a file.

Waiting for an event in an asynchronous way

In the previous section, you saw how to call a long-running operation without blocking the responsiveness of the user interface of your application. However, this long operation was still called in a synchronous way from the user's viewpoint, because the file picker user interface was displayed only five seconds after the initial click, even though by the end of the section, the user interface was still responsive during that time. The question is, What do you have to do to perform such a long-running operation while letting the user complete the file picker operation without having to wait? To do that, you have to execute the operation itself in an asynchronous way, without moving the remaining code in a *then* call, but directly manipulating the *task* object returned by the asynchronous call you make.

In practice, if you save the result of an asynchronous call into a *task* object, you can wait for the completion of such operation, calling the *then* method for attaching code to be executed next. If you write the following:

```
concurrency::create_task( LongCalculationAsync(5) ).then([this]()
{
    InputData();
    DisplayData();
});
```

the *InputData* call gets made after *LongCalculationAsync* has completed. You use the *create_task/then* pattern to prevent the user interface from becoming unresponsive. However, suppose you move the *then* call after the *InputData* call and put the line calling *DisplayData* in a lambda expression passed to *then*, as shown here:

```
auto t = concurrency::create_task( LongCalculationAsync(5) );
InputData();
t.then([this]()
{
    DisplayData();
});
```

Now the *LongCalculationAsync* call will be executed at the same time as *InputData*, and the *DisplayData* method will be called only after both *LongCalculationAsync* and *InputData* complete.

> **Note** The technique just described is attractive especially when you have long-running calculations that must be performed before showing results to the end user. However, you have to be careful, because executing code in such a way might involve race conditions. For example, if both *LongCalculationAsync* and *InputData* access shared data, you must protect those data structures from possible inconsistencies caused by one method writing data when the other is reading the same memory area. This is a classic problem in multi-threading programming, and it is beyond the scope of this book to discuss these scenarios in more detail (you can find more information about this topic starting with this blog post: *http://msdn.microsoft.com/magazine/cc872852.aspx*).
>
> Just be aware that as soon as you directly manipulate *task* objects in your code, you are no longer using the "safe" synchronous programming paradigm for your code that simply allows you keep the user interface responsive; therefore, you need to apply all the common practices of multithreaded programming to avoid race conditions. Using *create_task* and *then* definitely simplifies the code you write, but it does not avoid race conditions if you're using *task* objects operating in other threads.

Implement asynchronous calls

In this procedure, you will implement an asynchronous call to an asynchronous method in order to execute parallel actions in your user interface without having to wait for a background action to complete.

1. Open the MainPage.xaml.cpp file and locate the following call to *LongCalculationAsync* in the *ChooseFile_Click* method:

```
concurrency::create_task( LongCalculationAsync(5) ).then([this]()
```

2. Remove the *then* call from such a line, increase the parameter from *5* to *40*, and save the result returned from the call in a variable *t* of the type declared as *auto*:

```
auto t = concurrency::create_task( LongCalculationAsync(40) );
```

3. In the *ChooseFile_Click* method, move the remaining code into the method body that was formerly in the lambda expression passed to *then*. Embed the lambda expression passed to *then* of *ReadTextAsync* in a call to *then* of the *t* object. The resulting code for the *ChooseFile_Click* method should look like the following (changes made to the previous example are highlighted in bold):

```
void DisplayFile::MainPage::ChooseFile_Click(Platform::Object^ sender,
    Windows::UI::Xaml::RoutedEventArgs^ e)
{
    auto t = concurrency::create_task( LongCalculationAsync(40) );
    auto picker = ref new Pickers::FileOpenPicker();
    picker->FileTypeFilter->Append("*");

    concurrency::create_task(
        picker->PickSingleFileAsync() ).then([this, t](StorageFile^ file) {
            concurrency::create_task(
                FileIO::ReadTextAsync( file )
                ).then([this, file, t](String^ text)
            {
                t.then([this, file, text]()
                {
                    String^ content = text;
                    this->Result->Text = content;
                });
            });
        });
}
```

4. Run the application, click the Choose File button, and select a file. If you perform the file selection within 40 seconds and click Open within 40 seconds, you will have to wait before seeing the file content on the screen. This is because the content will be displayed only after at least 40 seconds from the Choose File button click, because it's waiting for the *LongCalculationAsync* call to complete.

Cancelling asynchronous operations

When you want to cancel an asynchronous operation, you need to communicate the operational break to code that might be executing in another thread. You could do this by using a simple Boolean flag, having a part of the asynchronously called method poll the flag and exit from the running function when the flag becomes active. However, because such a method could conceivably call other methods that may be running other asynchronous operations, there is a need for a standard pattern that can transfer the request to inner asynchronous methods, so that a cancel request can propagate down to inner asynchronous method calls and keep the latency between cancel request and execution break to the smallest possible duration.

The internal asynchronous interfaces used by WinRT are mapped to the standard PPL, which uses classes such as *cancellation_token* and *cancellation_token_source* to provide a way to cancel an asynchronous operation and propagate the request to any required asynchronous call depth. The basic idea is that you pass a *cancellation_token* object containing the request for cancellation. This way, if an asynchronous method has to call another method asynchronously, it can use the same token, so the cancellation propagates through the call chain automatically.

To be able to provide a *cancellation_token* object to the *PickSingleFileAsync* method, you have to convert this line:

```
concurrency::create_task( picker->PickSingleFileAsync() )
```

to the following line:

```
concurrency::create_task( picker->PickSingleFileAsync(), cancelPickSingleFile.get_token() )
```

where the *cancelPickSingleFile* instance has been declared as follows:

```
cancellation_token_source cancelPickSingleFile;
```

You can use the *cancelPickSingleFile* instance to cancel the asynchronous operation to which the token is assigned. The *cancellation_token_source* class offers a *cancel* method to forward the request for the cancelling operation to the related asynchronous call.

Cancel an operation in asynchronous calls

In this procedure, you will add an automatic cancellation for the file-pick operation if the user did not make a selection within 30 seconds after clicking the Choose File button.

1. Open the MainPage.xaml.cpp file and add the following method:

```cpp
void SetTimeoutOperation( int seconds, cancellation_token_source cts )
{
    Windows::Foundation::TimeSpan Period;
    Period.Duration = seconds * 1000 * 10000;
    Windows::System::Threading::ThreadPoolTimer::CreateTimer(
        ref new Windows::System::Threading::TimerElapsedHandler(
            [cts](Windows::System::Threading::ThreadPoolTimer^ timer)
            {
                cts.cancel();
            }
        ),
        Period );
}
```

2. Locate the *ChooseFile_Click* method and replace its contents with the following code. The code initializes the *cancellation_token_source* object and passes its token as a second parameter to the *create_task* function that calls the File Open Picker dialog box:

```cpp
void DisplayFile::MainPage::ChooseFile_Click(Platform::Object^ sender,
    Windows::UI::Xaml::RoutedEventArgs^ e)
{
    auto t = concurrency::create_task( LongCalculationAsync(40) );
    auto picker = ref new Pickers::FileOpenPicker();
    picker->FileTypeFilter->Append("*");
    cancellation_token_source cancelPickSingleFile;
    SetTimeoutOperation( 30, cancelPickSingleFile );
    concurrency::create_task(
        picker->PickSingleFileAsync(), cancelPickSingleFile.get_token()
    ).then([this, t](task<StorageFile^> file)
    {
        try {
                concurrency::create_task(
                    FileIO::ReadTextAsync( file.get() )
                    ).then([this, file, t](String^ text)
                {
                    t.then([this, file, text]()
                    {
                        String^ content = text;
                        this->Result->Text = content;
                    });
                });
        }
        catch (task_canceled) {
            this->Result->Text = "A task was canceled";
        }
    });
}
```

3. Run the application, click the Choose File button, and then wait until the file-picking user interface disappears and the initial window appears again. It will display the following message:

```
A task was canceled
```

4. The reason is that to cancel the asynchronous operation, a *task_canceled* exception is thrown. That propagates to the *catch* statement in the *ChooseFile_Click* method. Such an exception emerges in the *ChooseFile_Click* method corresponding to the *file.get* call that retrieves the result of the *PickSingleFileAsync* execution. In this way, the following lines in the same *try* block (the call to *ReadTextAsync* and the assignment to the Result text box) are not executed because the control is transferred directly to the *catch* statement. Note that to catch the exception, it is fundamental that the *then* call pass the *task* object as an argument:

```
concurrency::create_task(
    picker->PickSingleFileAsync(), cancelPickSingleFile.get_token()
).then([this, t](task<StorageFile^> file)
```

5. Instead of the *StorageFile* reference, which would not execute the *then* code in case of an exception:

```
concurrency::create_task(
    picker->PickSingleFileAsync(), cancelPickSingleFile.get_token()
).then([this, t]( StorageFile^ file)
```

6. You can cancel an asynchronous operation by passing a *cancellation_token* object to the *task* obtained with the *create_task* method. The best way to generate and interact with a *cancellation_token* is to create an instance of the *cancellation_token_source* class, which exposes methods to request the cancellation of an operation bound to the corresponding *cancellation_token* instance.

Tracking operation progress

During the progress of an asynchronous operation, you might need to display the progress state. You can use the *progress_reporter<T>* type, which standardizes communication of advancement of state of an asynchronous operation in PPL.

By providing an object that implements *IProgress* to an asynchronous operation, it is possible to receive notifications about the state of the operation itself. You can attach all WinRT functions that return an *IAsyncActionWithProgress<TProgress>* object to code that displays operational progress by using the *AsTask* syntax:

```
IProgress<TProgress> progress = ...;
await SomeMethodAsync().AsTask(progress);
```

To easiest way to obtain an object implementing the *IProgress<T>* interface is to create an instance of the *Progress<T>* class. For example, if you have a function that provides progress information through an *int* type, you must pass a lambda function as parameter to the *Progress<int>* constructor that receives an integer as a parameter, such as that shown in the following code:

```
IProgress<int> p = new Progress<int>( (value) =>
{
    // Code that display progress
    // The value parameter is of type int
} );
```

The data type used in the progress interface depends on the asynchronous operation; refer to the WinRT documentation to determine which type to use for a specific method.

Track progress in an asynchronous operation

In this procedure, you will add a method that simulates some work operation, reporting the progress of that ongoing operation through the *IProgress<T>* interface.

1. Open the MainPage.xaml source code and add a *Button* control after the Choose File button, embedding the two buttons in a horizontal *StackPanel*. Next, add a *ProgressBar* named *ProgressSomework* after the *TextBlock* control, as illustrated in the bold lines of the following code excerpt:

    ```
    <Page
        x:Class="DisplayFile.MainPage"
        xmlns="http://schemas.microsoft.com/winfx/2006/xaml/presentation"
        xmlns:x="http://schemas.microsoft.com/winfx/2006/xaml"
        xmlns:local="using:DisplayFile"
        xmlns:d="http://schemas.microsoft.com/expression/blend/2008"
        xmlns:mc="http://schemas.openxmlformats.org/markup-compatibility/2006"
        mc:Ignorable="d">

        <Grid Background="{StaticResource ApplicationPageBackgroundThemeBrush}">
            <StackPanel>
                <StackPanel Orientation="Horizontal">
                    <Button Click="ChooseFile_Click" Content="Choose File" />
                    <Button Click="Start_Click" Content="Run Work" />
                </StackPanel>
                <ProgressBar x:Name="Progress"
                            HorizontalAlignment="Left" Height="10" Width="1024"/>
                <TextBlock x:Name="Result" />
                <ProgressBar x:Name="ProgressSomework"
                            HorizontalAlignment="Left" Height="10" Width="1024"/>
            </StackPanel>
        </Grid>
    </Page>
    ```

    Clicking the Run Work button will call the *Start_Click* method, and the *ProgressSomework* progress bar will display the state of the ongoing operation.

2. Open the MainPage.xaml.h and MainPage.xaml.cpp files and add the method *Start_Click*, which implements the event handler for the Run Work button (you can also double-click the button in the Visual Studio designer to do this).

The following code shows the method definition from the MainPage.xaml.cpp file:

```
void DisplayFile::MainPage::Start_Click(Platform::Object^ sender,
    Windows::UI::Xaml::RoutedEventArgs^ e)
{
}
```

3. Add the following code to the method to display that the loop is running and when it finishes. To do so, call the asynchronous *DoSomeWorkAsync* method after setting the *Progress* property to a lambda expression that updates the value of the *ProgressSomework* progress bar according to the number received as a parameter:

```
this->Result->Text = "Start running...";
auto work = DoSomeWorkAsync();
work->Progress = ref new AsyncActionProgressHandler<int>(
    [this](IAsyncActionWithProgress<int>^ info, int progressValue)
{
    this->ProgressSomework->Value = progressValue;
} );
concurrency::create_task( work ).then([this]()
{
    this->Result->Text = "Loop finished";
} );
```

The code in the lambda expression passed to the *Progress* property of the *work* object will execute every time a progress notification is sent from the asynchronous call. In this case, you're updating the value of the progress bar named *ProgressSomework* every time you receive a notification.

4. Add the method *DoSomeworkAsync*, which implements a dummy loop representing progress with a short pause of 20 milliseconds for each iteration. The code here represents the complete method definition, including the *Delay* function used by *DoSomeWorkAsync*:

```
void Delay(int milliseconds)
{
    Windows::Globalization::Calendar^ stop = ref new Windows::Globalization::Calendar;
    Windows::Globalization::Calendar^ current = ref new Windows::Globalization::Calendar;
    stop->SetToNow();
    stop->AddNanoseconds(milliseconds *1000000);
    do {
        current->SetToNow();
    } while (current->GetDateTime().UniversalTime < stop->GetDateTime().UniversalTime);
}
```

```
Windows::Foundation::IAsyncActionWithProgress<int>^ DoSomeWorkAsync() {
    return concurrency::create_async( [](progress_reporter<int> progress) {
        for (int i = 0; i <= 100; i++) {
            progress.report(i);
            Delay(20);
        }
    });
}
```

The call to the *report* method in the progress object will execute the lambda expression passed as a parameter in the *Progress* property in the previous step.

The complete code for MainPage.xaml.cpp should look like this:

```
#include "pch.h"
#include "MainPage.xaml.h"
#include <ppltasks.h>

using namespace DisplayFile;
using namespace Platform;
using namespace concurrency;
using namespace Windows::Foundation;
using namespace Windows::Foundation::Collections;
using namespace Windows::Storage;
using namespace Windows::UI::Xaml;
using namespace Windows::UI::Xaml::Controls;
using namespace Windows::UI::Xaml::Controls::Primitives;
using namespace Windows::UI::Xaml::Data;
using namespace Windows::UI::Xaml::Input;
using namespace Windows::UI::Xaml::Media;
using namespace Windows::UI::Xaml::Navigation;

// The Blank Page item template is documented at
// http://go.microsoft.com/fwlink/?LinkId=234238

MainPage::MainPage()
{
    InitializeComponent();
    InitializeProgressBar();
}


/// <summary>
/// Invoked when this page is about to be displayed in a Frame.
/// </summary>
/// <param name="e">Event data that describes how this page was reached.  The Parameter
/// property is typically used to configure the page.</param>
void MainPage::OnNavigatedTo(NavigationEventArgs^ e)
{
    (void) e;    // Unused parameter
}
```

```cpp
void SetTimeoutOperation( int seconds, cancellation_token_source cts )
{
    Windows::Foundation::TimeSpan Period;
    Period.Duration = seconds * 1000 * 10000;
    Windows::System::Threading::ThreadPoolTimer::CreateTimer(
        ref new Windows::System::Threading::TimerElapsedHandler(
            [cts](Windows::System::Threading::ThreadPoolTimer^ timer)
            {
                cts.cancel();
            }
        ),
        Period );
}


void DisplayFile::MainPage::ChooseFile_Click(Platform::Object^ sender,
    Windows::UI::Xaml::RoutedEventArgs^ e)
{
    auto t = concurrency::create_task( LongCalculationAsync(40) );
    auto picker = ref new Pickers::FileOpenPicker();
    picker->FileTypeFilter->Append("*");
    cancellation_token_source cancelPickSingleFile;
    SetTimeoutOperation( 10, cancelPickSingleFile );
    concurrency::create_task(
        picker->PickSingleFileAsync(), cancelPickSingleFile.get_token() )
        .then([this, t](task<StorageFile^> file)
    {
        try {
                concurrency::create_task(
                    FileIO::ReadTextAsync( file.get() )
                    ).then([this, file, t](String^ text)
                {
                    t.then([this, file, text]()
                    {
                        String^ content = text;
                        this->Result->Text = content;
                    });
                });
        }
        catch (task_canceled) {
            this->Result->Text = "A task was canceled";
        }
    });
}


void Delay(int milliseconds)
{
    Windows::Globalization::Calendar^ stop = ref new Windows::Globalization::Calendar;
    Windows::Globalization::Calendar^ current = ref new Windows::Globalization::Calendar;
    stop->SetToNow();
    stop->AddNanoseconds(milliseconds *1000000);
    do {
        current->SetToNow();
    } while (current->GetDateTime().UniversalTime < stop->GetDateTime().UniversalTime);
}
```

```cpp
Windows::Foundation::IAsyncActionWithProgress<int>^ DoSomeWorkAsync() {
    return concurrency::create_async( [](progress_reporter<int> progress) {
        for (int i = 0; i <= 100; i++) {
            progress.report(i);
            Delay(20);
        }
    });
}

void DisplayFile::MainPage::Start_Click(Platform::Object^ sender,
    Windows::UI::Xaml::RoutedEventArgs^ e)
{
    this->Result->Text = "Start running...";
    auto work = DoSomeWorkAsync();
    work->Progress = ref new AsyncActionProgressHandler<int>(
        [this](IAsyncActionWithProgress<int>^ info, int progressValue)
    {
        this->ProgressSomework->Value = progressValue;
    } );
    concurrency::create_task( work ).then([this]()
    {
        this->Result->Text = "Loop finished";
    } );
}


void MainPage::InitializeProgressBar()
{
    Windows::Foundation::TimeSpan Period;
    Period.Duration = 100 * 10000; // 100 msec

    auto timerDelegate = [this](Windows::System::Threading::ThreadPoolTimer^ timer)
    {
        auto uiDelegate = [this]()
        {
            this->Progress->Value =
                (this->Progress->Value > 100) ? 0 : this->Progress->Value + 1;
        };

        Dispatcher->RunAsync(Windows::UI::Core::CoreDispatcherPriority::Normal,
                            ref new Windows::UI::Core::DispatchedHandler(uiDelegate));
    };

    Windows::System::Threading::ThreadPoolTimer::CreatePeriodicTimer(
        ref new Windows::System::Threading::TimerElapsedHandler(timerDelegate),
        Period );
}
```

```
IAsyncAction^ MainPage::LongCalculationAsync(int seconds)
{
    return concurrency::create_async( [seconds]() {
        Windows::Globalization::Calendar^ stop =
            ref new Windows::Globalization::Calendar;
        Windows::Globalization::Calendar^ current =
            ref new Windows::Globalization::Calendar;
        stop->SetToNow();
        stop->AddSeconds(seconds);
        do {
            current->SetToNow();
        } while (current->GetDateTime().UniversalTime < stop->GetDateTime().
            UniversalTime);
    });
}
```

5. Run the application. You will see that the first progress bar continuously changes its state. Then click Run Work. You will see a "Start running . . ." message displayed, and the progress bar below this message starts getting updated, rising from 0 to 100% in about two seconds. After that, a "Loop finished" message will appear instead of the "Start running . . ." message displayed before. The resulting state should look similar to the following screen shot.

6. The progress action is always executed in a safe execution context, allowing the user interface to be updated without requiring the use of the *Dispatch* object.

Synchronization with multiple asynchronous calls

When there are multiple asynchronous calls active at the same time, there are useful functions that help programmers write the code that waits for the end of the first or for all of these pending calls to complete. For example, consider the following code:

```
create_task(Operation1Async()).then( [this]()
{
    create_task(Operation2Async()).then ([this]()
    {
        create_task(Operation3Async()).then( [this]()
        {
            this->Result->Text = "Completed";
        });
    });
});
```

The total time required to execute the three operations is equal to the sum of the time required to execute all of them. However, because the three operations are independent, it could be better to use the *when_all* function to execute all three functions at the same time, so that—in the best-case scenario—the time required to execute the *when_all* method corresponds to the time required for the longest operation. You can rewrite the previous code in this way:

```
std::array<concurrency::task<void>,3> tasks =
{
    create_task(Operation1Async()),
    create_task(Operation2Async()),
    create_task(Operation3Async())
};
auto joinTask = when_all( begin(tasks), end(tasks));
joinTask.then([this]() {
    this->Result->Text = "Completed";
});
```

Similarly, it is possible to wait for only the first task in a list of tasks to complete by using the *when_any* function, which returns as soon as any call in the list has completed.

It is important to note that you should use the *when_all* and *when_any* methods instead of the Win32 *WaitForMultipleObjects* method, even when you have a Win32 handle available. The reason is that the Win32 methods ignore the need to using the proper synchronization context (described in the next section) and might block the current thread, resulting in a deadlock situation when such code is mixed with other task-waiting calls.

Wait for multiple asynchronous calls executed in parallel

In this procedure, you will wait for the completion of all of a set of asynchronous calls executed at the same time.

1. Open the MainPage.xaml source code and add a *Button* control after the Run Work button within the same horizontal *StackPanel*, as illustrated in the bold line of the following code excerpt:

```
<Page
    x:Class="DisplayFile.MainPage"
    xmlns="http://schemas.microsoft.com/winfx/2006/xaml/presentation"
    xmlns:x="http://schemas.microsoft.com/winfx/2006/xaml"
    xmlns:local="using:DisplayFile"
    xmlns:d="http://schemas.microsoft.com/expression/blend/2008"
    xmlns:mc="http://schemas.openxmlformats.org/markup-compatibility/2006"
    mc:Ignorable="d">

    <Grid Background="{StaticResource ApplicationPageBackgroundThemeBrush}">
        <StackPanel>
            <StackPanel Orientation="Horizontal">
                <Button Click="ChooseFile_Click" Content="Choose File" />
                <Button Click="Start_Click" Content="Run Work" />
                <Button Click="WhenAll_Click" Content="WhenAll" />
            </StackPanel>
            <ProgressBar x:Name="Progress"
                         HorizontalAlignment="Left" Height="10" Width="1024"/>
            <TextBlock x:Name="Result" />
            <ProgressBar x:Name="ProgressSomework"
                         HorizontalAlignment="Left" Height="10" Width="1024"/>
        </StackPanel>
    </Grid>
</Page>
```

The WhenAll button will call the *WhenAll_Click* method.

2. Open the MainPage.xaml.cpp file and add the following methods, which simulate three operations that have different response times (1, 2, and 3 seconds, respectively):

```
Windows::Foundation::IAsyncAction^ Operation1Async()
{
    return create_async( []() { Delay( 1000 ); });
}

Windows::Foundation::IAsyncAction^ Operation2Async()
{
    return create_async( []() { Delay( 1500 ); });
}

Windows::Foundation::IAsyncAction^ Operation3Async()
{
    return create_async( []() { Delay( 2000 ); });
}
```

3. Add the method *WhenAll_Click*, which implements the event handler for the WhenAll button. You can also double-click the button in the IDE designer.

Here's the method definition:

```
void DisplayFile::MainPage::WhenAll_Click(Platform::Object^ sender,
    Windows::UI::Xaml::RoutedEventArgs^ e)
{
}
```

4. Add the following code to the method *WhenAll_Click* to execute the three asynchronous operations at the same time. This code waits for all three methods to complete and then displays the elapsed time:

```
std::array<concurrency::task<void>,3> tasks =
{
    create_task(Operation1Async()),
    create_task(Operation2Async()),
    create_task(Operation3Async())
};
auto joinTask = when_all( begin(tasks), end(tasks));
joinTask.then([this]() {
    this->Result->Text = "WhenAll Completed";
});
```

5. Run the application, click the WhenAll button, and then wait until the following message is displayed:

```
WhenAll completed
```

6. The total time required for executing the three operations is about two seconds, whereas it would have been almost five seconds if the three functions were executed sequentially (by calling each one in a *then* call).

Synchronizing execution context

The default behavior of the *then* continuation function is to capture the current execution context and use it to synchronize the execution of the completion code (the lambda expression passed as parameter to the *then* function) by using such a context. This is why it is not necessary to write synchronization code when manipulating user interface objects in asynchronous methods using the *then* method to execute a continuation function after an asynchronous operation. However, this behavior is very good in code that directly interacts with the user interface, whereas it may not be such a good idea for a library that might be called by code that does not have to interact with the user interface.

You can control the execution context of a Windows Store app by using the *continuationContext* parameter in the *then* call. For example, the following code executes the *Operation2Async* method in the same thread as the *Test* function:

```
void Test()
{
    concurrency::create_task(
        Operation1Async() ).then(
            []() { concurrency::create_task( Operation2Async() ); }
        );
}
```

By using the *task_continuation_context::use_arbitrary* value as second argument of the *then* call, the *Operation2Async* function is executed in an arbitrary thread, without having to wait for the execution context of the *Test* function.

If you need to synchronize the code that accesses the user interface when the thread cannot be synchronized using the proper *task_continuation_context* parameter, you can rely on the *CoreDispatcher* class, as you saw in the code that updates the progress bar. *InitializeProgressBar* uses the *ThreadPoolTimer* class, which executes code in an arbitrary thread from the thread pool that cannot be easily synchronized with the main thread by using the *task_continuation_context* parameter. In this case, it is simpler to call the *RunAsync* method on the *Dispatcher* instance of the *CoreDispatcher* class, as shown in the bold line of the following code:

```
void MainPage::InitializeProgressBar()
{
    Windows::Foundation::TimeSpan Period;
    Period.Duration = 100 * 10000; // 100 msec

    auto timerDelegate = [this](Windows::System::Threading::ThreadPoolTimer^ timer)
    {
        auto uiDelegate = [this]()
        {
            this->Progress->Value =
                (this->Progress->Value > 100) ? 0 : this->Progress->Value + 1;
        };

        Dispatcher->RunAsync(Windows::UI::Core::CoreDispatcherPriority::Normal,
                            ref new Windows::UI::Core::DispatchedHandler(uiDelegate));
    };

    Windows::System::Threading::ThreadPoolTimer::CreatePeriodicTimer(
        ref new Windows::System::Threading::TimerElapsedHandler(timerDelegate),
        Period );
}
```

You can find more details in the article "Creating Asynchronous Operations in C++ for Windows Store Apps" at *http://msdn.microsoft.com/library/windows/apps/hh750082.aspx*.

Summary

In this chapter, you learned how to use asynchronous patterns in WinRT. The most important functions are *create_task* and *create_async*, which automatically generate much of the required code to implement WinRT interfaces and to handle synchronization, reducing the number of threads required and minimizing the need of synchronization with the user interface. You also implemented an event in an asynchronous way, and you discovered how to cancel pending asynchronous operations safely and efficiently. In addition, you explored how to display the progress of an asynchronous operation and optimized the synchronization with multiple operations executed in parallel. Finally, you saw how to correctly handle synchronization in your code.

Quick reference

To	Do this
Call asynchronous methods	Use the *create_task* method to make asynchronous calls to methods implementing the asynchronous pattern.
Cancel asynchronous operation	Pass a *cancellation_token* object to the asynchronous operation and call the *cancel* method on the *cancellation_token_source* instance.
Track progress of asynchronous operation	Implement an *IAsyncActionWithProgress<TProgress>* interface or an *IAsyncOperationWithProgress<TResult, TProgress>* interface, and implement the *IProgress<TProgress>* interface to execute the code that updates the progress state.
Synchronize execution context	Consider using the *task_continuation_context* parameter of the *then* method, or use the *CoreDispatcher* class.

CHAPTER 9

Rethinking the UI for Windows 8 apps

After completing this chapter, you will be able to

- Use controls that are specific for Windows 8 apps.

- Design flexible layouts.

- Use tiles and toasts.

In Chapter 7, "Enhance the user experience," you analyzed some common XAML controls, which you can also find in other presentation technologies such as Windows Presentation Foundation (WPF) and Windows Phone. In this chapter, you will get acquainted with objects of the XAML platform specific to Microsoft Windows 8, and you will see how to define appropriate application layouts for each Windows 8 UI view state, including portrait, landscape, snapped, filled, and full-screen views. The last part of the chapter is dedicated to tiles and toasts, which are important ways to communicate with your application's users directly from the Windows Start screen. This chapter is dedicated to the user interface and user experience, so you'll focus your attention on specific features and the use of specific controls.

Using Windows 8 UI-specific controls

This section discusses how to use some user interface controls that are specific to Windows 8 apps, such as *AppBar*, *WebView*, *ListView*, *GridView*, *FlipView*, and *SemanticZoom*.

Use the *AppBar* control

The application bar, commonly known as the *app bar*, is a container for custom commands and for options specific to the user's current context. You can create up to two *AppBar* controls for a Windows Store app; usually the bottom app bar is used to manage tasks related to the current context, while the top app bar presents navigation aids to the user. In this procedure, you will add an *AppBar* control to a Windows Store app.

1. Create a new application project. To do so, open Microsoft Visual Studio 2012 and select New Project from the File menu (the sequence can be File | New | Project for full-featured versions of Visual Studio). Choose Visual C++ from the Templates tree and then Windows Store from the list of installed templates. Finally, choose the Blank App (XAML) project type from the list of available projects.

2. Name the new project **AppBar**, and then choose a location on your file system and a solution name. When you've finished, click OK.

   As you saw in Chapter 3, "My first Windows 8 app," the Windows Store application template provides a default page (MainPage.xaml), an application entry point to the *App* class (App.xaml.cpp file), a default application description in the Package.appxmanifest, and four default images representing logos and a splash screen.

3. In Solution Explorer, expand the Common directory and double-click the StandardStyle.xaml file. Uncomment the following styles: *HomeAppBarButtonStyle*, *RefreshAppBarButtonStyle*, and *SaveAppBarButtonStyle*. To uncomment, simply cut the entire definition of the style and paste it above the green code area.

   Note Take a look at Chapter 7 for more details about the *Style* object.

4. From the File menu, select Save All.

5. In Solution Explorer, double-click MainPage.xaml to open the designer.

6. Click the Document Outline tab. If you can't see the Document Outline tab, select View | Other Windows | Document Outline.

   Note To keep the Document Outline tab always visible, click the Auto Hide button on the right side of the title bar.

7. Expand the Page node if it is not already expanded. Click the BottomAppBar node, and then right-click it to open the context menu.

8. Select Pin Active Container.

   By doing this, you have transformed the BottomAppBar node into the active container. This way, any object you drag from or draw using the Toolbox tab will become a child of that container. Note that the BottomAppBar node is boxed in yellow, which indicates it is the active container.

9. Click the Toolbox tab. Expand the All XAML Controls section. Double-click the *AppBar* control.

   The *AppBar* control represents an application toolbar for displaying buttons and other controls.

10. Click the Document Outline tab. Expand the BottomAppBar node if it is not already expanded.

11. Expand the child nodes of the BottomAppBar node. You will see that Visual Studio 2012 has created an *AppBar* control, which in turn contains a *Grid* element; the latter is divided into two columns of the same width, and each column contains a *StackPanel* control.

 Note See Chapter 7 for more details about the *Grid* and *StackPanel* controls.

12. On the Document Outline tab, click the first *StackPanel* control to select it. Right-click the first *StackPanel* control to open the context menu.

13. Select Pin Active Container.

14. Click the Toolbox tab. Expand the Common XAML Controls section. Double-click the *Button* control.

   Note that the *Button* control you just created has become a child of the first *StackPanel* control, (the control you just selected as the active container).

   Repeat this step two more times, until you have created three *Button* controls inside the *StackPanel* control.

15. In Design view, click the first *Button* control and right-click to open the context menu. From that menu, select Edit Template | Apply Resource | HomeAppBarButtonStyle.

16. In the Properties window, expand the Common section.

   In the context menu for the Local button of the Content property, select the Reset option.

17. In Design view, click the second *Button* control and right-click to open its context menu. From the menu, select Edit Template | Apply Resource | RefreshAppBarButtonStyle.

18. In the Properties window, expand the Common section.

   In the context menu for the Local button of the Content property, select Reset.

19. In Design view, click the third *Button* control and right-click to open the context menu. From the menu, select Edit Template | Apply Resource | SaveAppBarButtonStyle.

20. In the Properties window, expand the Common section.

   In the context menu of the Local button of the Content property, select Reset.

21. On the Debug menu, click Start Debugging.

   Right-click to display the application bar, making it possible to interact with the buttons created earlier.

Note The controls of the platform have been designed to support different types of input natively; therefore, it is possible to show the application bar through a digital pen, a mouse, a keyboard, and touch gestures (in the latter case, using a swipe gesture from bottom to top).

The result is shown in the following image.

22. Return to Visual Studio 2012 by pressing Alt+Tab, and on the Debug menu, click Stop Debugging.

Use the *WebView* control

The *WebView* control allows you to visualize HTML content within the application. In this procedure, you will create a simple Windows Store app that includes a *WebView* control.

1. Create a new application project. To do so, open Visual Studio 2012 and select New Project from the File menu. Choose Windows Store from the list of installed templates, and then choose Blank App (XAML) from the list of available projects.

2. Name the new project **WebView**, and then choose a location on your file system and a solution name. When you've finished, click OK.

3. In Solution Explorer, double-click MainPage.xaml.

4. Click the Toolbox tab that appears on the left side of the form in the Designer window.

5. Expand the All XAML Controls section.

6. Click the *WebView* control and drag it within the form.

7. In Design view, click the *WebView* control and right-click to open the context menu. Select Reset Layout and click All. The *WebView* control will fill the whole parent element.

8. In the Properties window, type **WebViewControl** in the Name field.

9. Make sure that in XAML view, the code of the *WebView* control is as follows:

```
<WebView x:Name="WebViewControl"/>
```

10. In Solution Explorer, double-click MainPage.xaml.cpp.

11. Replace the following lines of code:

```
void MainPage::OnNavigatedTo(NavigationEventArgs^ e)
{
    (void) e;// Unused parameter
}
```

with these:

```
void MainPage::OnNavigatedTo(NavigationEventArgs^ e)
{
    (void) e;// Unused parameter
    WebViewControl->Navigate( ref new Uri("http://www.devleap.com") );
}
```

12. On the Debug menu, click Start Debugging.

Click the EN link to see the English language version of the website.

training   conferences   development   consulting   books   clients   contacts

devleap is

The group's main activities are focused on three major areas.

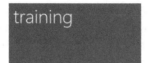
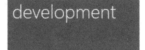

devLeap's philosophy

DevLeap is a group of professionals founded in 2002 by nationally and internationally renowned consultants on Microsoft technologies. The group supplies training courses, mentoring, as well as high-level architectural and implementative consultancies.

13. Return to Visual Studio 2012. On the Debug menu, click Stop Debugging.

Use the *ListView* control

The purpose of the *ListView* control is to represent a collection of data items within a vertical list. In this procedure, you will understand how to bind the *ListView* control to the list of a custom entity.

1. Create a new application project. To do so, open Visual Studio 2012 and select New Project from the File menu. Choose Windows Store from the list of installed templates, and then choose Blank App (XAML) from the list of available projects.

2. Name the new project **ListView**, and then choose a location on your file system and a solution name. When you've finished, click OK.

3. In Solution Explorer, click the project name node (*ListView*, in this case), right-click to open the context menu, and then select the Add option. Click Add New Item and name the new file **DataSource.h**.

4. From the File menu, select Open | File, select the Chapter 09 Demo Files directory, and then click the Code directory. Open the ListView directory and, finally, select the DataSource.h file and click the Open button.

5. Select all the content of the opened DataSource.h file, copy it onto the clipboard, and then double-click the DataSource.h node in Solution Explorer. Paste the content of the clipboard into this window. By doing this, you copy the content of the DataSource.h file into a file that belongs to the project. At this point, you can close both DataSource.h files you opened in Visual Studio.

6. In Solution Explorer, double-click MainPage.xaml.h and add the line highlighted in bold to create an *include* directive for DataSource.h:

```
#pragma once

#include "MainPage.g.h"
#include "DataSource.h"
```

7. On the Build menu, click Build Solution. This step is useful when completing the following steps because it causes Visual Studio to fetch the list of compiled classes and present it in the designer.

8. In Solution Explorer, double-click MainPage.xaml. On the Document Outline tab, select the [Page] node.

   In the Properties window, expand the Common section, and click New next to the DataContext property.

9. In the Select Object dialog box, select the DataSource class of your ListView project and click OK.

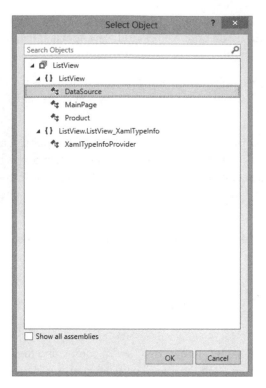

10. In XAML view, take a look at the code produced by the previous operation:

```
<Page.DataContext>
    <local:DataSource/>
</Page.DataContext>
```

Because the *DataContext* property of a control represents the data associated with that control, it is important to understand that such data is visible and usable, not only by the control that you set the *DataContext* property on (in this case, the page), but also by its logical descendant elements (in this case, all the child controls of the *Page* element will be able to see and use the custom object *DataSource*).

11. Click the Toolbox tab. Expand the Common XAML Controls section.

Click the *ListView* control and drag it within the form.

12. In Design view, right-click the *ListView* control to open the context menu, and then select Reset Layout and click All. The *ListView* control fills the entire parent element.

13. In the Properties window, expand the Common property. Click the Default button next to the ItemsSource property.

The *ItemsSource* property represents a collection of objects that will be used to generate the elements of a *ListView*.

14. From the context menu, select Create Data Binding to open the Create Data Binding for [ListView].ItemsSource modal dialog box.

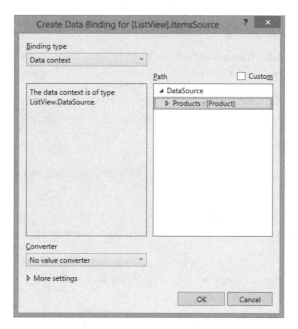

Select the Products node and click OK.

By doing this, you bind the *ItemsSource* property of the *ListView* control to the *Products* property of the *DataSource* custom object.

15. Take a look at the *ListView* control in Design view. You will notice a series of strings with the text *ListView.Product*. Because the class currently in binding does not derive from *Windows. UI.Xaml.UIElement*, the XAML platform is forced to use the *ToString* method of the *Product* class to render the result. In the following steps, you will customize the rendering of the data-bound *Product* object by using *DataTemplate* elements.

16. In Design view, right-click the *ListView* control to open the context menu. To open the Create DataTemplate Resource modal dialog box, select Edit Additional Templates | Edit Generated Items (ItemTemplate) | Create Empty.

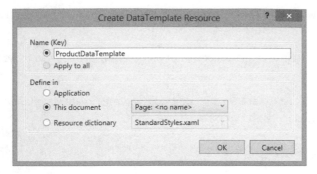

17. In the Name text box, type **ProductDataTemplate**. In the Define In section, make sure the This Document option is selected. Click OK.

Visual Studio 2012 will enter editing mode for the *DataTemplate*. A *DataTemplate* is a fragment of XAML code capable of representing the visual structure of an arbitrary data object.

18. Click the Document Outline tab.

Notice the default structure of a *DataTemplate*: Visual Studio 2012 has inserted a *Grid* control as the root element of the template.

19. Click the [Grid] node. In the Properties window, expand the Layout property and set the Width property to **400**, the Height property to **100**, the Left Margin property to **10**, and the Top Margin property to **10**.

20. Click the Toolbox tab. Expand the Common XAML Controls section. Double-click the *TextBlock* control.

21. In Design view, right-click the *TextBlock* control to open the context menu, and then select Edit Style | Apply Resource | SubheaderTextStyle.

22. In the Properties window, expand the Common section. Click Local (next to the Text property) and select Create Data Binding to open the Create Data Binding for [TextBlock].Text modal dialog box.

23. In the Path tree view, select the Description node and click OK.

The *Description* property of the custom *Product* object is now bound with the *Text* property of the *TextBlock* visual object.

24. Click the Toolbox tab. Expand the Common XAML Controls section, and double-click the *TextBlock* control.

25. In Design view, drag the new *TextBlock* control under the existing *TextBlock* control.

Click the *TextBlock* control and right-click to open the context menu. Select Edit Style | Apply Resource | CaptionTextStyle.

26. In the Properties window, expand the Common section, click the Local button next to the Text property, and select Create Data Binding to open the Create Data Binding for [TextBlock].Text modal dialog box.

27. In the Path tree view, select the Price node and click OK.

    In Design view, you can move around the two *TextBlock* controls as you wish.

28. On the Debug menu, click Start Debugging.

    The result is shown in the following image.

29. Return to Visual Studio 2012. On the Debug menu, click Stop Debugging.

Use the *GridView* control

The purpose of the *GridView* control is to represent a collection of data items within grid visualization. In this procedure, you will bind a list of custom objects to a *GridView* control.

1. Create a new application project. To do so, open Visual Studio 2012 and select New Project from the File menu. Choose Windows Store from the list of installed templates, and then choose Blank App (XAML) from the list of available projects.

2. Name the new project **GridView**, and then choose a location on your file system and a solution name. When you've finished, click OK.

3. In Solution Explorer, right-click the project name node (in this case, GridView) to open the context menu. Then select the Add option, click Add New Item, and name the new file **DataSource.h**.

4. From the File menu, select Open | File, select the Chapter 09 Demo Files directory, click the directory named Code, open the GridView directory and, finally, select the DataSource.h file and click the Open button.

5. Select all the content of the opened DataSource.h file, copy it onto the clipboard, and then double-click the DataSource.h node in Solution Explorer. Paste in this window the content of the clipboard. In this way, you copy the content of the DataSource.h file into a file that belongs to the project. At this point, you can close both DataSource.h files you opened in Visual Studio.

6. In Solution Explorer, double-click MainPage.xaml.h and add the line highlighted in bold to create an *include* directive for DataSource.h:

```
#pragma once

#include "MainPage.g.h"
#include "DataSource.h"
```

7. In Windows Explorer, copy the Photos folder included in the Chapter 09 Demo Files directory into the GridView directory you created for the new Visual Studio 2012 project (it must be the same directory that contains the Assets and Common folders). This directory contains some .jpg files.

8. Right-click the Assets node in Solution Explorer and select Add | Existing Item. Select from the newly added Photos directory all the .jpg files (from 01.jpg to 08.jpg). These files will be deployed with the application in the relative Photos directory.

9. On the Build menu, click Build Solution.

10. In Solution Explorer, double-click MainPage.xaml. On the Document Outline tab, select the [Page] page.

11. In the Properties window, expand the Common section, and then click New next to the DataContext property.

    In the Select Object dialog box, select the DataSource class of your GridView project and click OK.

12. Click the Toolbox tab. Expand the Common XAML Controls section. Click the *GridView* control and drag it within the form.

13. In Design view, right-click the *GridView* control to open the context menu. Select Reset Layout and click All. The *GridView* control will fill the whole parent element.

14. In the Properties window, expand the Common section. Click Default next to the ItemsSource property.

The *ItemsSource* property consists of a collection of objects that will be used to generate the elements of the *GridView*.

15. To open the Create Data Binding for [GridView].ItemsSource modal dialog box, select Create Data Binding from the context menu.

16. Select the Products node and click OK.

The *ItemsSource* property of the *ListView* control is now bound to the *Products* property of the *DataSource* custom object.

17. In Design view, right-click the *GridView* control to open the context menu. To open the Create DataTemplate Resource modal dialog box, select Edit Additional Templates | Edit Generated Items (ItemTemplate) | Create Empty.

18. In the Name text box, type **ProductDataTemplate**. In the Define In section, select This Document and click OK.

Visual Studio 2012 will enter the editing mode of the *DataTemplate*.

19. Click the Document Outline tab. Click the [Grid] node.

20. In the Properties window, expand the Layout property and set the Width property to **300**, the Height property to **300**, and the Left Margin property to **10**.

21. Click the Toolbox tab. Expand the Common XAML Controls section. Double-click the *Image* control.

22. In the Document Outline view, click the [Image] node and right-click to open the context menu. Select Reset Layout and click All. The *Image* control will fill the whole parent element.

23. In the Properties window, expand the Common section. Click the Local button next to the Source property. To open the Create Data Binding for [Image].Source modal dialog box, select Create Data Binding.

24. In the Path tree view, select the Photo node and click OK.

The *Photo* property of the *Product* custom object is now bound to the *Source* property of the *Image* visual object.

25. Click the Toolbox tab. Expand the Common XAML Controls section. Double-click the *TextBlock* control.

26. In Design view, drag the new *TextBlock* control under the *Image* control.

Select the *TextBlock* control and right-click. From the menu, select Edit Style | Apply Resource Option | SubheaderTextStyle.

27. In the Properties window, expand the Common section. Click the Local button next to the Text property. To open the Create Data Binding for [TextBlock].Text modal dialog box, select Create Data Binding.

28. In the Path tree view, select the Description node and click OK.

29. In Design view, you can move the *TextBlock* control as you prefer.

On the Debug menu, click Start Debugging. The result is shown in the following image.

30. Return to Visual Studio 2012. On the Debug menu, click Stop Debugging.

Use the *FlipView* control

A *FlipView* control renders a collection of data items, one item at a time. In this procedure, you will learn how to bind a list of a custom entity type to a *FlipView* control.

1. Create a new application project. To do so, open Visual Studio 2012 and select New Project from the File menu. Choose Windows Store from the list of installed templates, and then choose Blank App (XAML) from the list of available projects.

2. Name the new project **FlipView**, and then choose a location on your file system and a solution name. When you've finished, click OK.

3. In Solution Explorer, right-click the project name node (in this case, FlipView) to open the context menu. Then select the Add option, click Add New Item, and name the new file **DataSource.h**.

4. From the File menu, select Open | File, select the Chapter 09 Demo Files directory, click the Code directory, open the FlipView directory and, finally, select the DataSource.h file and click the Open button.

5. Select all the content of the opened DataSource.h file, copy it onto the clipboard, and then double-click the DataSource.h node in Solution Explorer. Paste in this window the content of the clipboard. In this way, you copy the content of the DataSource.h file into a file that belongs to the project. At this point, you can close both DataSource.h files you opened in Visual Studio.

6. In Solution Explorer, double-click MainPage.xaml.h and add the line highlighted in bold to create an *include* directive for DataSource.h:

```
#pragma once

#include "MainPage.g.h"
#include "DataSource.h"
```

7. In Windows Explorer, copy the Photos folder included in the Chapter 09 Demo Files directory into the GridView directory you created for the new Visual Studio 2012 project (it has to be the same directory containing the Assets and Common folders). This directory contains some .jpg files.

8. Right-click the Assets node in Solution Explorer and select Add | Existing Item. From the newly added Photos directory, select all the .jpg files (from 01.jpg to 08.jpg). These files will be deployed with the application in the relative Photos directory.

9. On the Build menu, click Build Solution.

10. In Solution Explorer, double-click MainPage.xaml. On the Document Outline tab, select the [Page] node.

In the Properties window, expand the Common section, and then click the New button next to the DataContext property.

11. In the Select Object dialog box, select the DataSource class of your FlipView project and click OK.

12. Click the Toolbox tab. Expand the Common XAML Controls section. Select the *FlipView* control and drag it within the form.

13. On the Document Outline tab, select the [FlipView] node and right-click to open the context menu. Select Reset Layout and click All. The *FlipView* control will fill the whole parent element.

14. In the Properties window, expand the Common section. Click the Default button next to the ItemsSource property.

The *ItemsSource* property represents a collection of objects that will be used to generate the elements of *FlipView*.

15. To open the Create Data Binding for [FlipView].ItemsSource modal dialog box, select Create Data Binding. Select the Products node and click OK.

The *ItemsSource* property of the *FlipView* control is now bound to the *Products* property of the *DataSource* custom object.

16. In Design view, select the *FlipView* control and right-click to open the context menu. To open the Create DataTemplate Resource modal dialog box, select Edit Additional Templates | Edit Generated Items (ItemTemplate) | Create Empty.

17. In the Name text box, type **ProductDataTemplate**. In the Define In section, select This Document. Click OK.

Visual Studio 2012 will enter the editing mode of the *DataTemplate*.

18. Click the Document Outline tab. Click the [Grid] node.

19. In the Properties window, expand the Layout section (if it is not expanded already) and make sure that the Width property is set to Auto. If it is not, click Set to Auto next to the Width property.

20. Click the Toolbox tab. Expand the Common XAML Controls section. Double-click the *Image* control.

21. On the Document Outline tab, select the [Image] node and right-click to open the context menu. Select Reset Layout and click All. The *Image* control fills the whole parent element.

22. In the Properties window, expand the Common section. To open the Create Data Binding for [Image].Source modal dialog box, click the Local button next to the Source property and select Create Data Binding.

23. In the Path tree view, select the Photo node and click OK.

The *Photo* property of the *Product* custom object is now bound with the *Source* property of the *Image* visual object.

Set the *Stretch* property to *UniformToFill*.

24. Click the Toolbox tab. Expand the Common XAML Controls section. Double-click the *TextBlock* control.

25. In Design view, drag the new *TextBlock* control on top of the *Image* control.

Select the *TextBlock* control and right-click to open the context menu. Select Edit Style | Apply Resource | SubheaderTextStyle.

26. In the Properties window, expand the Common section. To open the Create Data Binding for [TextBlock].Text modal dialog box, click the Local button next to the Text property, and select Create Data Binding.

27. In the Path tree view, select the Description node and click OK.

28. In Design view, you can move the *TextBlock* control as you prefer.

29. On the Debug menu, click Start Debugging. Click the arrow on the right side of the display. The result is shown in the following image.

30. Click the arrows to navigate among the different elements of the collection.

> **Note** The controls of the platform have been designed to support different types of input natively; therefore, it is possible to navigate among the different elements using a digital pen, a mouse, a keyboard, and touch gestures (in the latter case, using a swipe gesture from left to right or vice versa).

31. Return to Visual Studio 2012. On the Debug menu, click Stop Debugging.

Semantic zoom is a touch-optimized technique used by Windows 8 apps for presenting and navigating large sets of related data or content within a single view (such as a photo album, app list, or address book).

The page that displays all the Windows 8 applications installed on your machine offers an example of semantic zoom. The default view is displayed as "zoomed in"—that is, it presents a complete list of applications. With a simple gesture of pinch/stretch or by scrolling the mouse wheel and pressing the Ctrl button, you can activate the "zoomed out" view that, in this case, will display a series of tiles with the initials of the existing applications.

The *SemanticZoom* control can be used to add the semantic zoom concept into a Windows 8 app. In this procedure, you will learn how to bind a *SemanticZoom* control to a list of a custom data object.

1. Create a new application project. To do so, open Visual Studio 2012 and select New Project from the File menu. Choose Windows Store from the list of installed templates, and then choose Blank App (XAML) from the list of available projects.

2. Name the new project **SemanticZoom**, and then choose a location on your file system and a solution name. When you've finished, click OK.

3. In Solution Explorer, click the project name node (in this case, SemanticZoom) and right-click to open the context menu. Then select the Add option, click Add New Item, and name the new file **DataSource.h**.

4. From the File menu, select Open | File, select the directory named Chapter 09 Demo Files, click the Code directory, open the SemanticZoom directory and, finally, select the DataSource.h file and click the Open button.

5. Select all the content of the opened DataSource.h file, copy it onto the clipboard, and then double-click the DataSource.h node in Solution Explorer. Paste in this window the content of the clipboard. In this way, you copy the content of the DataSource.h file into a file that belongs to the project. At this point, you can close both DataSource.h files you opened in Visual Studio.

6. In Solution Explorer, double-click MainPage.xaml.h and add the line highlighted in bold to create an *include* directive for DataSource.h:

```
#pragma once

#include "MainPage.g.h"
#include "DataSource.h"
```

7. In Windows Explorer, copy the Photos folder included in the Chapter 09 Demo Files directory in the SemanticZoom directory you created for the new Visual Studio 2012 project (it has to be the same directory containing the Assets and Common folders). This directory contains some .jpg files.

8. Right-click the Assets node in Solution Explorer and select Add | Existing Item. Select from the newly added Photos directory all of the .jpg files (from 01.jpg to 08.jpg). These files will be deployed with the application in the relative Photos directory.

9. On the Build menu, click Build Solution.

10. In Solution Explorer, double-click MainPage.xaml.

11. Click the Toolbox tab.

12. Expand the All XAML Controls section.

13. Click the *SemanticZoom* control and drag it within the form.

14. On the Document Outline tab, select the [SemanticZoom] node and right-click the mouse button to open the context menu. Select Reset Layout and click All. The *SemanticZoom* control fills the whole parent element.

15. In XAML view, take a look at the XAML code of the *SemanticZoom* control:

```
<SemanticZoom>
        <SemanticZoom.ZoomedInView>
            <GridView ScrollViewer.IsHorizontalScrollChainingEnabled="False"
                ScrollViewer.IsVerticalScrollChainingEnabled="False"/>
        </SemanticZoom.ZoomedInView>
        <SemanticZoom.ZoomedOutView>
            <GridView ScrollViewer.IsHorizontalScrollChainingEnabled="False"
                ScrollViewer.IsVerticalScrollChainingEnabled="False"/>
        </SemanticZoom.ZoomedOutView>
</SemanticZoom>
```

The *SemanticZoom* control exposes two properties, *ZoomedInView* and *ZoomedOutView*, which represent many views of the same set of information.

16. Replace the whole source code of the MainPage.xaml page with the following code:

```
<Page
    x:Class="SemanticZoom.MainPage"
    xmlns="http://schemas.microsoft.com/winfx/2006/xaml/presentation"
    xmlns:x="http://schemas.microsoft.com/winfx/2006/xaml"
    xmlns:local="using:SemanticZoom"
    xmlns:d="http://schemas.microsoft.com/expression/blend/2008"
    xmlns:mc="http://schemas.openxmlformats.org/markup-compatibility/2006"
    mc:Ignorable="d">
    <Grid Background="{StaticResource ApplicationPageBackgroundThemeBrush}">
        <SemanticZoom x:Name="semanticZoomControl">
            <SemanticZoom.ZoomedInView>
                <GridView SelectionMode="None">
                    <GridView.ItemTemplate>
                        <DataTemplate>
                            <Grid Width="300" Height="300">
                                <Image Source="{Binding Photo}"/>
```

```
                                    <TextBlock HorizontalAlignment="Left" TextWrapping="Wrap"
                                               Text="{Binding Description}"
                                               VerticalAlignment="Top"
                                               Margin="0,256,0,0"
                                               Style="{StaticResource SubheaderTextStyle}"/>
                                </Grid>
                            </DataTemplate>
                        </GridView.ItemTemplate>
                    </GridView>
                </SemanticZoom.ZoomedInView>
                <SemanticZoom.ZoomedOutView>
                    <GridView>
                        <GridView.ItemTemplate>
                            <DataTemplate>
                                <Border Background="#FF26A0DA" Width="230" Height="230">
                                    <TextBlock Text="{Binding Key}"
                                               FontSize="30"
                                               VerticalAlignment="Bottom"
                                               Margin="10,0,0,10" />
                                </Border>
                            </DataTemplate>
                        </GridView.ItemTemplate>
                    </GridView>
                </SemanticZoom.ZoomedOutView>
            </SemanticZoom>
        </Grid>
</Page>
```

In this example, you used a *GridView* control for both views, but you could have used a *ListView* control instead. Both *GridView* controls leverage the same concepts illustrated in the "Use the *GridView* control" procedure: the *ItemsSource* property binds the collection and the *ItemTemplate* property defines the visual representation of the single item in binding. For the *GridView* control nested within the *ZoomedInView* property, you have reused the code presented in the previous procedure to define the *ItemTemplate* property.

17. In Solution Explorer, double-click MainPage.xaml.cpp.

18. Replace the following code:

```
void MainPage::OnNavigatedTo(NavigationEventArgs^ e)
{
    (void) e;        // Unused parameter
}
```

with this:

```
void MainPage::OnNavigatedTo(NavigationEventArgs^ e)
{
    (void) e;              // Unused parameter
    ds = ref new DataSource();
    dynamic_cast<GridView^>(this->semanticZoomControl->ZoomedOutView)->
                        ItemsSource = ds->Groups;
    dynamic_cast<GridView^>(this->semanticZoomControl->ZoomedInView)->
                        ItemsSource = ds->Products;
}
```

For the *ZoomedInView* property, the *ItemsSource* property of the *GridView* has been bound to the complete data collection. In the case of the *ZoomedOutView* property, the *ItemsSource* will use the *Groups* property for the same dataset to show the initials in the photo captions.

19. On the Debug menu, click Start Debugging.

The result is shown in the following image.

20. Hold down the Ctrl key while scrolling to switch between the two views offered by the *SemanticZoom* control. You can also click the minus (-) icon that appears in the lower-right corner to obtain the overview display. Clicking the display area zooms the display again.

 Note The controls of the platform have been designed to support different types of input natively; therefore, it is possible to navigate between the two views using a digital pen, a mouse, a keyboard (holding down the Ctrl key, along with the Shift key if no numeric keypad is available, and pressing the plus [+] or minus [-] key), and touch gestures (using a pinch and stretch gesture).

The result is shown in the following image.

21. Return to Visual Studio 2012. On the Debug menu, click Stop Debugging.

Designing flexible layouts

The way that the content of your user interface adapts to how an app is manipulated by a user is called a *view*. *View state* refers to the three ways a user can choose to display your Windows 8 app: full screen, snapped, and filled. The first, full screen, is the default state for all apps. When a user drags another window onto the screen, the user has the option of having that window become the current running app, snapping the new app to the side, or running it filled. Users can rotate and flip their devices, so you should ensure that your app can handle both landscape and portrait orientations.

Design flexible layouts

1. Create a new application project. To do so, open Visual Studio 2012 and select New Project from the File menu. Choose Windows Store from the list of installed templates, and then choose Blank App (XAML) from the list of available projects.

2. Name the new project **ViewState**, and then choose a location on your file system and a solution name. When you've finished, click OK.

3. In Solution Explorer, click the project name node (ViewState, in this case) and right-click to open the context menu. Then select the Add option, click Add New Item, and name the new file **DataSource.h**.

4. From the File menu, select Open | File, select the directory named Chapter 09 Demo Files, click the Code directory, open the ViewState directory and, finally, select the DataSource.h file and click the Open button.

5. Select all the content of the opened DataSource.h file, copy it onto the clipboard, and then double-click the DataSource.h node in Solution Explorer. Paste in this window the content of the clipboard. In this way, you copy the content of the DataSource.h file into a file that belongs to the project. At this point, you can close both DataSource.h files you opened in Visual Studio.

6. In Solution Explorer, double-click MainPage.xaml.h and add the line highlighted in bold to create an *include* directive for DataSource.h:

```
#pragma once

#include "MainPage.g.h"
#include "DataSource.h"
```

7. In Windows Explorer, copy the Photos folder included in the Chapter 09 Demo Files directory in the ViewState directory you created for the new Visual Studio 2012 project (it has to be the same directory containing the Assets and Common folders). This directory contains some .jpg files.

8. On the Build menu, click Build Solution.

9. In Solution Explorer, double-click MainPage.xaml. Replace all of the source code with the following:

```xml
<Page
    x:Class="ViewState.MainPage"
    xmlns="http://schemas.microsoft.com/winfx/2006/xaml/presentation"
    xmlns:x="http://schemas.microsoft.com/winfx/2006/xaml"
    xmlns:local="using:ViewState"
    xmlns:d="http://schemas.microsoft.com/expression/blend/2008"
    xmlns:mc="http://schemas.openxmlformats.org/markup-compatibility/2006"
    mc:Ignorable="d">
    <Page.Resources>
        <DataTemplate x:Key="ProductGridDataTemplate">
            <Grid Width="300" Height="300">
                <Image Source="{Binding Photo}"/>
                <TextBlock HorizontalAlignment="Left"
                        TextWrapping="Wrap"
                        Text="{Binding Description}"
                        VerticalAlignment="Top"
                        Margin="0,256,0,0"
                        Style="{StaticResource SubheaderTextStyle}"/>
            </Grid>
        </DataTemplate>
```

```xml
        <DataTemplate x:Key="ProductListDataTemplate">
            <Grid Width="400" Height="100">
                <TextBlock HorizontalAlignment="Left"
                        TextWrapping="Wrap" Text="{Binding Description}"
                        VerticalAlignment="Top"
                        Style="{StaticResource SubheaderTextStyle}"/>
                <TextBlock HorizontalAlignment="Left" TextWrapping="Wrap"
                        Text="{Binding Price}" VerticalAlignment="Top"
                        Margin="0,47,0,0" Style="{StaticResource CaptionTextStyle}"/>
            </Grid>
        </DataTemplate>
    </Page.Resources>
    <Page.DataContext>
        <local:DataSource/>
    </Page.DataContext>

    <Grid Background="{StaticResource ApplicationPageBackgroundThemeBrush}">
        <GridView x:Name="GridViewControl" ItemsSource="{Binding Products}"
                ItemTemplate="{StaticResource ProductGridDataTemplate}"/>
        <ListView x:Name="ListViewControl" ItemsSource="{Binding Products}"
                ItemTemplate="{StaticResource ProductListDataTemplate}"
                Visibility="Collapsed"/>

        <VisualStateManager.VisualStateGroups>
            <VisualStateGroup x:Name="ApplicationViewStates">
                <VisualState x:Name="FullScreenLandscape"/>
                <VisualState x:Name="FullScreenPortrait" />
                <VisualState x:Name="Filled"/>
                <VisualState x:Name="Snapped" />
            </VisualStateGroup>
        </VisualStateManager.VisualStateGroups>
    </Grid>
</Page>
```

In this listing, you can see two *DataTemplate* items already used in the former procedures "Use the *ListView* control" and "Use the *GridView* control." Inside the main *Grid* control is a *GridView* control, which will be used in both the full-screen and filled views (you will soon understand the difference between the two views) and a *ListView* control that will be displayed in the snapped view.

The *VisualStateManager* object manages states and the transitions between states for controls.

10. In Solution Explorer, double-click MainPage.xaml.h. Replace all of the source code with the following:

```cpp
// MainPage.xaml.h
// Declaration of the MainPage class.
//
```

```
#pragma once

#include "MainPage.g.h"
#include "DataSource.h"

namespace ViewState
{
    /// <summary>
    /// An empty page that can be used on its own or navigated to within a Frame.
    /// </summary>
    public ref class MainPage sealed
    {
    public:
            MainPage();

    protected:
            virtual void OnNavigatedTo(
                Windows::UI::Xaml::Navigation::NavigationEventArgs^ e)
                    override;
            void OnSizeChanged(Object^ sender,
                Windows::UI::Core::WindowSizeChangedEventArgs^ args);
    };
}
```

11. In Solution Explorer, double-click MainPage.xaml.cpp. Replace all of the source code with the following:

```
//
// MainPage.xaml.cpp
// Implementation of the MainPage class.
//

#include "pch.h"
#include "MainPage.xaml.h"

using namespace ViewState;
using namespace Platform;
using namespace Windows::Foundation;
using namespace Windows::Foundation::Collections;
using namespace Windows::UI::Xaml;
using namespace Windows::UI::Xaml::Controls;
using namespace Windows::UI::Xaml::Controls::Primitives;
using namespace Windows::UI::Xaml::Data;
using namespace Windows::UI::Xaml::Input;
using namespace Windows::UI::Xaml::Media;
using namespace Windows::UI::Xaml::Navigation;

// The Blank Page item template is documented at
// http://go.microsoft.com/fwlink/?LinkId=234238
```

```
MainPage::MainPage()
{
    InitializeComponent();
    Window::Current->SizeChanged += ref new WindowSizeChangedEventHandler( this,
                                         &MainPage::OnSizeChanged );
}


/// <summary>
/// Invoked when this page is about to be displayed in a Frame.
/// </summary>
/// <param name="e">Event data that describes how this page was reached.  The Parameter
/// property is typically used to configure the page.</param>
void MainPage::OnNavigatedTo(NavigationEventArgs^ e)
{
    (void) e;     // Unused parameter
}


void MainPage::OnSizeChanged(Object^ sender,
    Windows::UI::Core::WindowSizeChangedEventArgs^ args)
{
    switch( Windows::UI::ViewManagement::ApplicationView::Value)
    {
        case Windows::UI::ViewManagement::ApplicationViewState::FullScreenLandscape:
            VisualStateManager::GoToState( this, "FullScreenLandscape", false );
            break;
        case Windows::UI::ViewManagement::ApplicationViewState::FullScreenPortrait:
            VisualStateManager::GoToState( this, "FullScreenPortrait", false );
            break;
        case Windows::UI::ViewManagement::ApplicationViewState::Snapped:
            VisualStateManager::GoToState( this, "Snapped", false );
            break;
        case Windows::UI::ViewManagement::ApplicationViewState::Filled:
            VisualStateManager::GoToState( this, "Filled", false );
            break;

    }
}
```

In the *Window.Current.SizeChanged* event delegate, the *GoToState* method of the *VisualStateManager* is called to set the page state. The state will have the same name for the *Value* property of the *Windows.UI.ViewManagement.ApplicationView* object.

The next step consists of defining a "shape" for each state of the page.

12. In Solution Explorer, double-click MainPage.xaml. Click the Device tab.

Note If you want to keep the Device tab visible, click the Auto Hide button positioned at the right of the title bar.

13. In the View property, click the Snapped option.

    The snapped state is one of the possible application view states. Snapping an app resizes the app to 320 pixels wide, which allows it to share the screen with another app.

    Visual Studio 2012 will display the area available for that state in Design view.

14. In the Visual State property, select Enable State Recording.

    Visual Studio 2012 will enter into recording mode, marked by a red border around Design view. Any control property that is set through the Properties window will be recorded within the state (in this case, into the snapped state).

15. On the Document Outline tab, click the ListViewControl node.

    In the Properties window, expand the Appearance property and set the Visibility property to Visible.

16. On the Document Outline tab, click the GridViewControl node.

    In the Properties window, expand the Appearance property and set the Visibility property to Collapsed.

17. On the Device tab, click the Portrait option in the View property.

    Visual Studio 2012 will display the change in the orientation in Design view.

18. In the Visual State property, select Enable State Recording.

19. On the Document Outline tab, click the GridViewControl node.

    In the Properties window, expand the Layout property and set the Margin Top property to **80**.

20. On the Device tab, click Landscape in the View property.

21. In the Visual Studio 2012 toolbar, click the drop-down list by the Local Machine button to open the menu. Select the Simulator option. Click the green play icon labeled Simulator.

Visual Studio 2012 will start the Windows 8 Simulator and then run the application. In the simulator, click the Rotate Clockwise (90 Degrees) button. The result is shown in the following image.

The simulator shows the application in portrait view. Note that the margins of the *GridView* control are different from the landscape view.

22. In the simulator, click Change Resolution and select the first entry, 10.6" 1024 × 768.

Note that the scrollbar is visible, which allows the use all of the content.

Note Always be sure to try different resolutions and different orientations for your application.

23. In the simulator, click Rotate Counterclockwise (90 Degrees) to switch back to the original landscape position.

In the simulator, click Change Resolution and select the second entry, 10.6″ 1366 × 768.

Click the Windows button of the simulator to go back to the Windows 8 Start screen.

24. Launch the Weather app.

25. Place the cursor in the top-left corner of the simulator to open the thumbnail of the previous active application—that is, your application.

Drag the thumbnail to the center of the simulator and, once the snapped area is defined, release the mouse button. The result is shown in the following image.

Your application is currently in the snapped state, and the *GridView* control has stepped aside to leave its place to the *ListView* control, which is more suitable for the current state.

26. Move the delimiter of the snapped area to the right and release the mouse button at around two-thirds of the overall screen size (of the simulator). The result should resemble the following image.

The application is now in the filled state. In this example, you did not customize the user interface of this state. However, now you understand how to use the Visual State Manager to perform this task.

27. Return to Visual Studio 2012. On the Debug menu, click Stop Debugging.

28. To shut down the Windows 8 Simulator, go to the Windows 8 desktop, right-click the Simulator icon in the Windows 8 taskbar, and select Close.

Using tiles and toasts

In this section, you will learn how to modify an application tile to display the application logo on the Windows 8 Start screen from the application manifest, and then you will see how you can modify it from code create a live tile.

A tile represents the application on the Start screen, so it has to be both graphically good-looking and interesting for the user. In fact, the Start screen can be very full of tiles and you may confuse your application with another, your application may get lost in the multitude of tiles, or your application may simply be very difficult to reach if you do not carefully create your tile.

A tile can be considered an application icon. In fact, it represents the application in the ocean of apps that a user can see on the Start screen. In previous versions of Windows, the Start menu helped the user to organize applications in groups and subgroups. Think for a moment about the

Microsoft Office suite: it is composed of 10 different applications, but they are grouped together in the Microsoft Office menu item. In Windows 8, every application is listed on the Start screen uses its own tile. Users can keep applications together by creating a group of tiles, but they cannot create a tile representing a group of applications.

Users can also look for applications using Windows+Q or activating a search using the charms bar, in which case, the applications are listed using the application logos and names, not their tiles.

Figure 9-1 shows some application tiles.

FIGURE 9-1 The Windows 8 Start screen with square and rectangular tiles grouped by the user.

As you can see, there are some applications in the section on the left of the Start screen. Some of them have a wide tile (Learn with the Animals, Learn with the Fruits, and Learn with the Colors), some of them have a square tile (Internet Explorer, Learn with the Food, DevLeap, and so on), and one of them (Weather) is wide and presents the temperature of Florence, Italy. The latter is a live tile that will be explained in the following procedures.

In Chapter 3, you changed the default tile logo for your first application simply by copying some .png files to the Assets directory of the project. In the following procedures, you will learn how to define the square and the wide tile images, how to change default tile behavior, and how to change the tile from code.

Define the appearance on the Start screen

The information Windows 8 uses to deploy an application to the system is defined in the application manifest. This file defines the images that will represent the application tiles, the colors of the UI elements on the Start screen (and in the Windows Store), and some properties that are useful to change the default behavior.

In this procedure, you will learn how to change the static definition for tiles.

1. Create a new application project. To do so, open Visual Studio 2012 and select New Project from the File menu. Choose Windows Store from the list of installed templates, and then choose Blank App (XAML) from the list of available projects.

2. Name the new project **Tile_Toast**, and then choose a location on your file system and a solution name. When you've finished, click OK.

3. Copy the .png files found in the Chapter 09 Demo Files in the Logos folder to the Assets folder of the project, replacing the existing files. The files have the default names, so you do not need to modify their names in the Package.appxmanifest.

4. Right-click the Assets node in Solution Explorer and select Add | Existing Item. Select from the Assets directory all of the files. These files will be deployed with the application in the relative Assets directory.

5. Open the manifest designer by double-clicking Package.appxmanifest in Solution Explorer.

6. Change the Wide Logo definition to point to the LogoWide.png file in the Assets folder by clicking the button with the ellipses or type **Assets\LogoWide.png** in the related text box. The result is shown in the following screen shot.

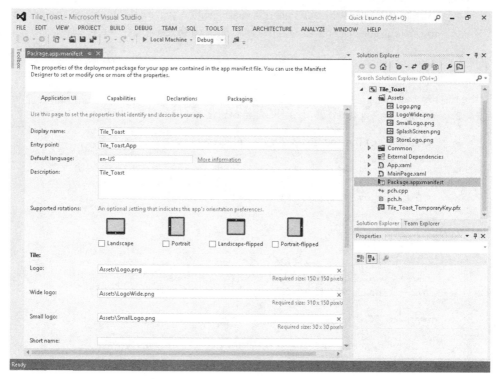

7. Right-click the project in Solution Explorer and choose Deploy.

8. Go to the Start screen and move to the right until you find the new application. Right-click the application and select Larger from the app bar. Windows will use the wide logo to represent the application tile.

9. Right-click the application again and select Smaller from the lower toolbar. The tile will return as a square.

Define a live tile

As you saw in the previous image of the Weather app, an application can modify its tile to present information to the user. In fact, tiles are considered an external view of the application that can present useful information without the user needing to open the application itself.

For instance, after you configure the native weather application to display the forecast for a particular city, it presents the most important information in the tile such as the temperature, the city, and an image of the current weather. A game application can present the latest score or the high-score record (or both) to the user in its tile.

The application you will implement in this procedure is very similar to the one you implemented in Chapter 3, with the addition of a live tile that displays the name of the person selected by the user.

1. Modify the MainPage.xaml file of the application you implemented in the previous procedure to present a list of names. Use the following code to replace the existing *Grid* control.

```xml
<Grid Background="{StaticResource ApplicationPageBackgroundThemeBrush}">
    <ListView x:Name="list" DisplayMemberPath="FullName" />
</Grid>
```

2. In Solution Explorer, double-click MainPage.xaml.h.

3. Replace all of the source code with the following:

```cpp
//
// MainPage.xaml.h
// Declaration of the MainPage class.
//

#pragma once

#include "MainPage.g.h"
using namespace Windows::Foundation::Collections;
using namespace Platform::Collections;

namespace Tile_Toast
{
    [Windows::UI::Xaml::Data::Bindable]
    public ref class Person sealed
    {
    public:
            Person() {}
            Person( Platform::String^ name ) { FullName = name; }
            property Platform::String^ FullName;
    };

    /// <summary>
    /// An empty page that can be used on its own or navigated to within a Frame.
    /// </summary>
    public ref class MainPage sealed
    {
    public:
            MainPage();

            IVector<Person^>^ GetPeople()
            {
                    Vector<Person^>^ vec = ref new Vector<Person^>();
                    vec->Append( ref new Person("Roberto Brunetti") );
                    vec->Append( ref new Person("Paolo Pialorsi") );
                    vec->Append( ref new Person("Marco Russo") );
                    vec->Append( ref new Person("Luca Regnicoli") );
                    vec->Append( ref new Person("Vanni Boncinelli") );
                    vec->Append( ref new Person("Guido Zambarda") );
                    vec->Append( ref new Person("Jessica Faustinelli") );
                    vec->Append( ref new Person("Katia Egiziano") );
                    return vec;
            };
```

```cpp
    protected:
        virtual void OnNavigatedTo(
            Windows:::NavigationEventArgs^ e) override;
    private:
        void list_SelectionChanged(
            Platform::Object^ sender,
            Windows::UI::Xaml::Controls::SelectionChangedEventArgs^ e);
    };
}
```

4. In Solution Explorer, double-click MainPage.xaml.cpp.

5. Replace all of the source code with the following:

```cpp
//
// MainPage.xaml.cpp
// Implementation of the MainPage class.
//

#include "pch.h"
#include "MainPage.xaml.h"

using namespace Tile_Toast;
using namespace Platform;
using namespace Windows::Foundation;
using namespace Windows::Foundation::Collections;
using namespace Windows::UI::Xaml;
using namespace Windows::UI::Xaml::Controls;
using namespace Windows::UI::Xaml::Controls::Primitives;
using namespace Windows::UI::Xaml::Data;
using namespace Windows::UI::Xaml::Input;
using namespace Windows::UI::Xaml::Media;
using namespace Windows::UI::Xaml::Navigation;

// The Blank Page item template is documented at
// http://go.microsoft.com/fwlink/?LinkId=234238

MainPage::MainPage()
{
    InitializeComponent();
    list->ItemsSource = this->GetPeople();
}

/// <summary>
/// Invoked when this page is about to be displayed in a Frame.
/// </summary>
/// <param name="e">Event data that describes how this page was reached.  The Parameter
/// property is typically used to configure the page.</param>
void MainPage::OnNavigatedTo(NavigationEventArgs^ e)
{
    (void) e;    // Unused parameter
}
```

6. Press F5 to test the application. It will present the list of names. Verify that you can select a name. You will use the *SelectionChanged* event handler to modify the application tile displaying the name of the person selected.

7. Go to the MainPage.xaml page and add a *SelectionChanged* event to the *ListView* control as shown in bold in the following code:

```
<ListView x:Name="list" DisplayMemberPath="FullName"
                SelectionChanged="list_SelectionChanged" />
```

8. Add the event handler in the code-behind for this event.

```
void Tile_Toast::MainPage::list_SelectionChanged(Platform::Object^ sender,
                Windows::UI::Xaml::Controls::SelectionChangedEventArgs^ e)
{
    Person^ person = safe_cast<Person^>(list->SelectedItem);
}
```

This line of code takes the item selected in the *ListView* control and assigns it to the local variable named *person*. You will use it in the next steps to create the live tile.

A tile is represented internally by an XML fragment that contains its definition. Windows 8 presents different templates to create many different visual tiles. For instance, there is a simple text-based template that you can use to display a single line of text in the tile, or you can use a more sophisticated template to display three lines of text and an image in the tile.

9. Create an XML fragment as string using the following code in the *SelectionChanged* event right after the first line:

```
String^ tileXmlString =
      "<tile>"
      + "<visual>"
        + "<binding template='TileWideText03'>"
          + "<text id='1'>" + person->FullName + "</text>"
        + "</binding>"
        + "<binding template='TileSquareText04'>"
          + "<text id='1'>" + person->FullName + "</text>"
        + "</binding>"
      + "</visual>"
    + "</tile>";
```

The code is very simple. The visual element of the tile uses the template TileWideText03 (the third template for a wide tile) to display the full name of the selected person in the first line of text. It also defines the text for the square tile to display the same name using a different template. As is now apparent, the two tiles can display completely different things. For instance, the wide tile can display the photo of the person and the square one can display only the name.

10. Add the following four lines of code after the string definition to create the XML representation of the string. Then create a new tile definition to update the current tile.

```
auto tileXml = ref new Windows::Data::Xml::Dom::XmlDocument();
```

```
tileXml->LoadXml(tileXmlString);

auto tile = ref new Windows::UI::Notifications::TileNotification( tileXml );

Windows::UI::Notifications::TileUpdateManager::CreateTileUpdaterForApplication()->
    Update(tile);
```

11. Run the code by pressing F5.

12. Select Paolo Pialorsi from the list.

13. Click the Start button to go to the Windows 8 Start screen, and scroll until you find the tile that presents the text *Paolo Pialorsi*. The result is shown in the following image.

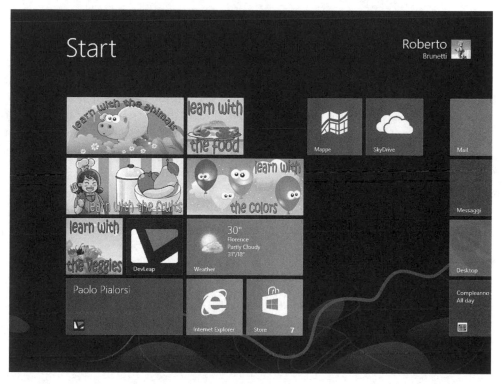

14. Right-click to open the lower toolbar and select Smaller to reveal the square tile that will present the same text.

15. Right-click to open the lower toolbar and select Turn Live Tile Off. The application will display the default square tile with the DevLeap logo.

16. Right-click another time to open the lower toolbar again and select Turn Live Tile On. The application will display the name you selected again.

With some practice, you will learn how the different tile templates work, how to change the tile foreground and background colors, and how to add images (stored in the package or downloaded directly from the web) to the tile to achieve the result of the applications shown in the previous image. At the time of this writing, the complete reference for the *TileTemplateType* enumeration is available at *http://msdn.microsoft.com/library/windows/apps/windows.ui.notifications.tiletemplatetype.*

For instance, this code creates a tile with text and an image using the simplest template for this kind of tile:

```
String^ tileXmlString =
      "<tile>"
    + "<visual>"
      + "<binding template='TileWideImageAndText01'>"
        + "<text id='1'>Tile with image</text>"
        + "<image id='1' src='ms-appx:///dir/x.png' alt='Red image'/>"
      + "</binding>"
    + "</visual>"
  + "</tile>";
```

You can also create a secondary tile for an application to display different kinds of information and to provide a "callback" to the application, passing some parameter of your choice. For example, a weather application can create a secondary tile for a different city the user chooses in the application. This way, the Start screen presents two different tiles for the same application, one displaying the information for the main city and the other showing the information for the secondary city. When the code creates the secondary tile, it can pass an argument that will be received during the application launch so that the code can present the forecast of the secondary city directly instead of on the main page.

The application can also request the system to display a badge on the application tile with some predefined glyphs and/or a number. For instance, you can enable multiselection (*SelectionMode="Multiple"*) on the *ListView* control you used in the previous examples to provide the code to display the number of selected people in the badge:

```
String^ badgeXmlString = "<badge value='" + list->SelectedItems->Size + "'/>";

auto badgeXml = ref new Windows::Data::Xml::Dom::XmlDocument();
badgeXml->LoadXml(badgeXmlString);

auto badge = ref new Windows::UI::Notifications::BadgeNotification(badgeXml);
Windows::UI::Notifications::BadgeUpdateManager::CreateBadgeUpdaterForApplication()->
    Update(badge);
```

As a sample, Microsoft provides a library that facilitates the use of the template that hides all the XML details and provides some simple classes to create tiles and badges. You can find the library in the "App tiles and badges sample" in the Windows 8 samples. You can also download it from the Windows 8 Dev Center at *http://code.msdn.microsoft.com/windowsapps/.*

With this library, the code you used to create the tile can be as simple as this:

```
auto tileContent = TileContentFactory::CreateTileWideText03();
tileContent->TextHeadingWrap->Text = person->Fullname;
```

Create and schedule a toast

An application can provide alerts to the user using toasts. A toast can be some simple text or an image, or a combination of the two. In this procedure, you will create a simple toast to remind to the user to change the selected person. Consider the simple application you wrote in the previous section as a shift workers' application that manages the shift change. When the user select the current worker, the application can remind the user to change the worker every, say, 10 seconds (likely and luckily to be less frequent in real applications).

1. Add the following lines at the end of the *SelectionChanged* event handler you created in the previous section:

```
String^ toastXmlString =
    "<toast>"
    + "<visual version='1'>"
      + "<binding template='ToastText01'>"
        + "<text id='1'>" + person->FullName + " is tired!</text>"
      + "</binding>"
    + "</visual>"
  + "</toast>";

auto toastXml = ref new Windows::Data::Xml::Dom::XmlDocument();
toastXml->LoadXml(toastXmlString);

auto calendar = ref new Windows::Globalization::Calendar();
calendar->SetToNow();
calendar->AddSeconds(10);
auto toastNotification =
    ref new Windows::UI::Notifications::ScheduledToastNotification(
        toastXml,
        calendar->GetDateTime() );

auto toastNotifier
    Windows::UI::Notifications::ToastNotificationManager::CreateToastNotifier();
toastNotifier->AddToSchedule(toastNotification);
```

The first line of code builds the toast string definition, and the two subsequent lines transform it into an XML document. Then the code creates a notification for the toast in 10 seconds, and the last two lines of code ask the *ToastNotificationManager* class to add the notification to the system toast schedule.

2. Before running the sample, you have to define the application as toast capable. To do so, open the Package.appxmanifest and set the Toast Capable option (in the Notification section) to Yes using the drop-down list.

3. Run the sample, select a name, and click the Start button to leave the application and go to the Start screen. The result that appears after approximately 10 seconds is shown in the following image.

You can also use local images (provided with the package) or images from the web, change the default sound to reflect the toast type, create a long duration toast, and receive an event in the application when the user clicks the toast. You can even change the snooze interval and maximum snooze count to tailor the toast for your purposes.

Microsoft provides a sample library for manipulating toasts. To be more precise, the library is the same one cited earlier for tiles, and it enables you to code against toasts, tiles, badges, and related features.

A toast can be sent from the cloud using the Windows Push Notification Services (WNS). The application can ask the service for a unique channel that a remote service can use to send toasts to the Windows 8 device from everywhere.

For more information on WNS, search on "Windows Notification Service" in the MSDN Developer Center to find documentation and samples.

Summary

In this chapter, you learned how to use the advanced controls of the XAML platform for a Windows 8 application (*AppBar*, *WebView*, *ListView*, *GridView*, *FlipView*, and *SemanticZoom*), as well as how to customize their appearance by using *DataTemplate* objects. You also learned how to use the *VisualStateManager* element and the *Window.Current.SizeChanged* event to support different view states, including portrait, landscape, snapped, filled, and full screen.

Additionally, you now know how to enhance the user experience using tiles, live tiles, badges, and toasts.

Quick reference

To	Do this
Add a *ListView* control to the layout	Click the Toolbox tab, expand All XAML Controls, and click the *ListView* control and drag it within the form.
Add a *GridView* control to the layout	Click the Toolbox tab, expand All XAML Controls, and click the *GridView* control and drag it within the form.
Add a *WebView* control to the layout	Click the Toolbox tab, expand All XAML Controls, and click the *WebView* control and drag it within the form.
Handle different view states and orientations	Use the *VisualStateManager* element and the *Window.Current.SizeChanged* event handler.
Run your Windows 8 app in the simulator	In the Visual Studio 2012 toolbar, click the drop-down list by the Local Machine button to open the menu and select Simulator. Click the green play icon labeled Simulator.
Create a tile	Use one of the provided templates for passing the XML definition to the WinRT classes.
Create a toast	Use one of the provided templates for passing the XML definition to the WinRT classes.

CHAPTER 10

Architecting a Windows 8 app

After completing this chapter, you will be able to

- Understand the general architecture of a Windows 8 app.

- Define the specific architecture you want for a Windows 8 app.

- Consume a remote service from a Windows 8 app.

This chapter provides some useful information about the general architecture of software solutions, with particular focus on those solutions that include a Microsoft Windows 8 app as one of the available presentation layers.

Why does this chapter reference .NET code?

This chapter presents samples in Microsoft .NET instead of native C++ code. The reason is that most of the libraries used for a complex distributed architecture are implemented in .NET and are not available as native code. Because the goal of this chapter is to show a reference architecture for a multitier application, it is strongly suggested that you use existing libraries in .NET and possibly implement the required code in .NET, especially for the server-side part. If you are writing a modern application in C++ just for the user interface, you will need to call existing services implemented in .NET. It is up to you to decide when to do the following:

- Use native Windows Runtime (WinRT) APIs.

- Wrap .NET libraries in C++, maybe by using C++/CLI instead of compiling in native code at least the plumbing code.

- Create a Windows Metadata (WinMD) library in .NET that can be called by native code written in C++. For example, you might create a WinMD library (as described in Chapter 5, "Introduction to the Windows Runtime") in C# in order to call the WCF client library, exposing an interface that will be consumed by native C++ code.

Applications architecture in general

You should implement any software solution—even a small one—starting from the overall architecture definition. In fact, every time you develop a software solution, you should consider how to organize code and logical partitioning so that you satisfy functional requirements, usability, maintainability, and performance requirements.

Over the last few decades, the software world has moved toward what are called *n-tier* solutions, which are solutions defined to satisfy maintainability, scalability, security, and the ability to consume remote services securely, safely, and quickly.

A *multitier* solution is a software project that usually targets many concurrent users. It is divided into *n* layers—generally at least two or three. Applications that use a two-tier scenario are also referred to as *client/server* software. One layer is the back-end server infrastructure, which is generally made up of a database persistence layer. The other layer, the client, includes all the required code to connect to the back-end database and display the user interface. Generally, in two-tier scenarios, the business logic and domain knowledge required for the solution are implemented within the client software. Sometimes such solutions also include database logic, such as intelligent stored procedures, triggers, and so on.

Software is *scalable* when its performance remains constant and independent regardless of the number of users. Scalable software is not necessarily fast—it simply has a fixed performance score regardless of the number of customers served, unless you expand the hardware infrastructure as the number of customers increases, without any changes to the code of the software. The very nature of a client/server solution prevents scalability—specifically, an increase in the number of users can have a huge negative impact on the back-end database layer.

Although the two-tier client/server architecture is suitable for implementing solutions that will have a relatively small number of users, this book does not cover it in detail because, aside from its scalability limitations, you should not create Windows 8 apps that directly consume content from a database. Instead, you should create Windows 8 apps that consume remote services that provide an indirect way to access data stored in a database. Moreover, remember that, when you create a Windows Store app for Windows 8, you cannot predict the number of end users who will install your app, but you definitely know that there are millions of *potential* users who have Windows 8 installed. Thus, your app could conceivably serve a huge number of users. If your app leverages a back-end database or service, you have to think about the architecture of your app, because it must be designed like an enterprise-level app so that it can provide proper performance and scalability as the number of users increases.

Over the past several years, partly for scalability reasons, architectures with at least three tiers have become more common. Many modern software solutions are available on a network and the Internet, and serve a large (and unpredictable) number of concurrent users. Three-tier solutions have a data access layer, a business layer, and a presentation layer. The data access layer (DAL) represents the set of code and data structures used to implement information persistence. The business layer (BIZ) defines business logic, business workflows, and rules that drive the behavior of the application. The presentation layer, or user interface (UI) layer, delivers the information to end users. The presentation layer in particular has become more complex because it can (and often must) be implemented in many different ways: one for each kind of consumer and/or device (for example, the web, a desktop PC with Windows, a tablet, a smartphone device, and so on). In general, you deploy the DAL and BIZ on specific and dedicated application servers, whereas the UI can be deployed on both consumer devices (desktop PC, tablet, smartphone, and so on) or delivered to browsers from specific publishing application servers (web applications on front-end web servers).

Technologies such as Simple Object Access Protocol (SOAP) services, Representational State Transfer (REST), smart clients, smartphones, and workflow services have influenced many software architects to add other layers. The now common definition of n-tier solution architecture is one in which *n* designates a value greater than or equal to three. In general, as you can see from Figure 10-1, these *n* layers are targeted to meet specific application requirements, such as security, workflow definition, management and governance, or communication.

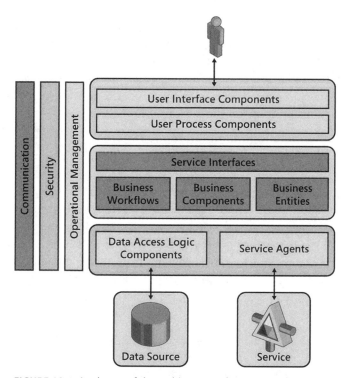

FIGURE 10-1 A schema of the architecture of an n-tier software solution.

The main reason for dividing a software solution's architecture into layers is to improve maintainability, availability, security, and deployment.

Maintainability results from the ability to change and maintain small portions (for example, single layers) of an application without needing to touch the other layers. By working this way, you reduce maintenance time and can also more accurately assess the cost of a fix or a feature change, because you can focus your attention only on the layers involved in the change. Client/server software is more costly to maintain because any code modifications must be deployed to each client, while software with a distributed architecture only sometimes requires client updates, when the changes involve the presentation layer. Moreover, in software with a distributed architecture, there will be situations where it will suffice to update the application servers, without needing updates to the presentation layer. Well-defined multitier solutions are also available to users more often because critical or highly stressed layers can be deployed in a redundant infrastructure.

From a security perspective, a layered solution can make use of different security modules, each one tightly aligned with a particular software layer to make the solution stronger. Last but not least, multitier software is usually deployed more easily because each layer can be configured and sized somewhat independently from other layers.

Architectures for Windows 8 apps

From a Windows 8 app perspective, a two-tier architecture is, generally speaking, not a good solution, because you should avoid accessing databases directly from the app. There are many good reasons that support this perspective. First of all, because of the portable and restricted .NET profile you learned about in Chapter 5, you don't have the same *System.Data.** namespaces available in a Windows 8 app that were available previously. Thus, you simply cannot use an instance of the *SqlConnection* class or an *OleDbCommand* object to consume data. Of course, you could evaluate third-party solutions to work around these limitations so you could consume databases directly from a Windows 8 app. However, by doing so, you would be implementing a solution that goes against the suggested usability guidelines provided by Microsoft.

In fact, ideally, a Windows 8 app should be able to work both online (connected to the network) or offline, by leveraging data-caching features. Moreover, it should be capable of supporting an end user while working on multiple devices (desktop PC, laptop, tablet, and so on), keeping the same configuration and context as the user moves between devices. In order to support this last scenario, Microsoft introduced the capability of sharing the user profile configuration and the user application data through the cloud and the Windows Live profile. The final goal of this approach should be to provide a user with his or her own data, regardless of device used and simply determined by the Windows Live ID.

Starting with these considerations, you can argue that a Windows 8 app that stores data locally on a single device is not a good idea, because you would be able to consume that data only on that specific device. In contrast, a Windows 8 app that consumes data from a remote site, through a SOAP or REST service, using data published in the cloud—for example, on Windows Azure—is absolutely a better option because it supports consuming and handling data from everywhere, from every device, and at any time. Moreover, having data on a unique device is highly discouraged from both a disaster recovery and a high availability viewpoint. Imagine what would happen if you save your data locally on only a single device—and that device breaks! You would lose all your data. If you instead save your data in the cloud, if a device breaks, you can simply change devices and replace your data from the cloud.

Nevertheless, there are some kinds of software solutions that require working with large numbers of data records that might need to have some local data cache for usability and performance reasons. For example, think about a sales force app, which must be able to insert customers' orders even when network connectivity is unavailable. You would probably want to have an offline copy of the products catalog, or some subset of it, as well as an offline copy of the customers that each salesperson might meet with during a specific workday. Moreover, it would probably be smart to keep a client-side copy of any reference data useful for creating a new customer or order, for example, because you should not have to download such values from the network every single time. Such data includes lists of countries, states, product categories, and so on. To address all these needs, a Windows 8 app can leverage local storage and a set of XML files consumed using the LINQ to XML API, which is available in the .NET profile for Windows 8 apps.

The security infrastructure of your app is yet another topic that can be affected by the new development model introduced by Windows 8 apps. In fact, in a standard Windows application it could suffice to leverage Windows integrated security. In contrast, a Windows 8 app installed on a mobile device would benefit from using a cross-platform authentication method, such as Windows Live ID, Facebook, or something similar. More generally, a Windows 8 app will probably need to support multiple authentication techniques and protocols. Thus, technologies such as claims-based authentication, Open Authentication (OAuth), and identity federation become essential in such architectures.

In the following sections of this chapter, you will inspect all the layers of a distributed architecture that are fundamental and specific to a Windows 8 app. For simplicity's sake, in many areas of this chapter, software architecture layers are discussed from only a logical viewpoint. Nevertheless, from a code and assembly fragmentation perspective, the examples in this chapter will merge some layers for the sake of brevity. In a real solution, you will probably need to introduce more abstraction and code fragmentation.

Implementing the data layer

The data layer is a fundamental layer of a distributed architecture. In fact, although generally speaking the data layer can be implemented easily and largely automated using Object Relational Mapping (ORM) technologies, the efficiency, scalability, and versatility of the overall software architecture depends on that data layer.

Since 2008, the official enterprise-level ORM in Microsoft .NET has been the ADO.NET Entity Framework. In .NET 4.5 and Microsoft Visual Studio 2012, you can leverage Entity Framework 5, which is a mature and complete ORM framework.

The goal of using ORM in software architectures is to convert individual data items stored in an external and physical repository into entities that work within the domain model of the software from a business perspective. Moreover, an ORM provides all the facilities to query, manage, and transfer data both to and from (retrieve and modify) external repositories. Generally speaking, in modern software, the external repository is a relational database management system (RDBMS) like Microsoft SQL Server. Nevertheless, from the ORM viewpoint, the external repository could be anything suitable.

In this section, you will create a data layer based on Entity Framework 5 useful for modeling a *Customer* domain model entity that, for the sake of simplicity, will be consumed from the generally well-known and readily available Northwind sample database.

Implement a data layer in C# with Entity Framework 5

In this procedure, you will initially create a data layer using C# and Entity Framework 5. Later, this data layer will be published by a Windows Communication Foundation (WCF) service layer and consumed by a sample Windows 8 app implemented using the common language runtime (CLR) and C#. Later in the chapter, you'll see how to publish the same data layer through an Open Data Protocol (OData) service.

1. Download the Northwind sample database from the Microsoft website (*http://www.microsoft. com/download/details.aspx?id=23654*) and install it. Double-click the SQL script under the folder SQL Server 2000 Sample Databases. The script will open in Visual Studio 2012. From there, you can execute it against your local SQL Server database, which eventually could be SQL Server Express, in case you installed it during installation of Visual Studio 2012.

2. Create a new application project. To do so, open Visual Studio 2012 and select New Project from the File menu. Choose Other Project Types, and then choose Visual Studio Solutions. Choose the Blank Solution as the target template.

3. Select version 4.5 as the Microsoft .NET Framework target version for your new project.

4. Name the new solution **NorthwindSolution**, and then choose a location on your file system. When you've finished, click OK.

5. Add a new project to the solution you have just created. Right-click the solution item in Solution Explorer and select Add | New Project. Choose Windows from the list of installed templates in Visual C# group, and then select Class Library. Keep version 4.5 as the Microsoft .NET Framework target version.

6. Name the class library project **NorthwindSolution.DataLayer**, and then choose a location on your file system. When you've finished, click OK.

7. Delete Class1.cs, which Visual Studio created in the project automatically.

8. Right-click the class library project in Solution Explorer and select Add | New Item. In the Add New Item window, select the ADO.NET Entity Data Model item template. Name the new file **NorthwindModel.edmx**.

9. You will be prompted by the Entity Data Model Wizard. In the first step, Choose Model Contents, select Generate from Database. Click Next.

10. In the second step, Choose Your Data Connection, add a New Connection and configure a connection to the Northwind database in your target SQL Server instance. Click Next.

11. In the third step, Choose Your Database Objects and Settings, expand the Tables node. Under dbo, select Customers and any other data table you want to map to an entity. To complete the exercises for this chapter, it will suffice to map the Customers table. Select Pluralize or Singularize Generated Object Names. Finally, click Finish.

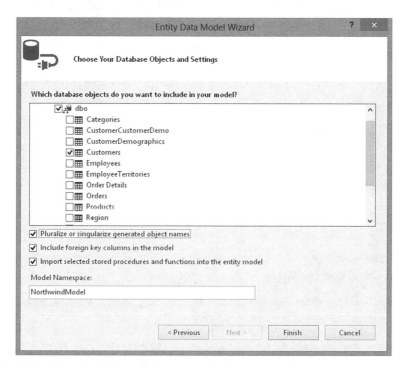

12. If Visual Studio 2012 prompts you with a security warning, trust it and click OK.

The wizard you have just followed creates an .edmx file, as well as a set of .tt (text template) code-generation files and a bunch of .cs files containing autogenerated code. The result of this procedure is a class library containing the definition of a *NorthwindEntities* class, giving you an entry point to access a collection of *Customers* defined with an autogenerated *Customer* type.

Explaining what Entity Framework is and the inner workings of its engine is beyond the scope of this book. If you are not familiar with Entity Framework, the authors recommend you read the book *Programming Microsoft LINQ in Microsoft .NET Framework 4* by Paolo Pialorsi and Marco Russo, published by Microsoft Press.

Implementing the communication layer using a SOAP service

The communication layer is another fundamental layer of a distributed architecture. Any Windows 8 app that consumes external data or interacts with external services should be based on a solid communication infrastructure.

Communication is based on various technologies and protocols. For example, you can use SOAP services transferred across HTTP channels, or you can leverage REST services that transmit either Plain Old XML (POX) messages, or Rich Site Summary (RSS) (often also called Really Simple Syndication), or JavaScript Object Notation (JSON) serialized objects. You could also use an OData service (see *www.odata.org*), which is going to become an OASIS international open standard.

Depending on your development platform, any of the previously mentioned protocols and technologies might be appropriate. For example, if you are developing a website or a Windows 8 app built with HTML5/WinJS, the best choice would probably be REST with JSON object serialization or POX/RSS. A SOAP service can be a bit more difficult to consume from JavaScript.

Alternatively, if you are developing a Windows 8 app built for the CLR (such as with C# or Visual Basic), then SOAP or OData is the best solution because the CLR and WinRT provide great automation and tooling. Using REST could work as well, but SOAP and OData are simpler to define and easier to share across multiple devices and platforms.

Implement a SOAP service to consume from C#

In this procedure, you will create a SOAP service based on WCF that publishes the data layer you defined previously that provides a list of customers to consume.

1. Open the solution *NorthwindSolution* you created in the previous exercise, when you implemented the data layer with Entity Framework 5.

2. Right-click the solution item in Solution Explorer and select Add | New Project. Choose Windows from the list of installed templates in the Visual C# group, and then select Class Library. Keep version 4.5 as the Microsoft .NET Framework target version.

3. Name the class library project **NorthwindSolution.Contracts**, and then choose a location on your file system to store the project files. When you've finished, click OK.

4. In Solution Explorer, right-click the class library project item you just created and select Add Reference. In the Assemblies group of references, select the assemblies System.ServiceModel and System.Runtime.Serialization.

5. In Solution Explorer, right-click the class library project item again, and select Add Reference. In the Solution group of references, select the NorthwindSolution.DataLayer project.

6. Remove Class1.cs and add a new interface definition item. To add the new interface definition, right-click the class library project in Solution Explorer and select Add | New Item. In the Add New Item window, select the Interface code template. Name the new file **ICustomersService.cs**.

7. Replace the initial generated interface code with the following code:

```
using NorthwindSolution.DataLayer;
using System;
using System.Collections.Generic;
using System.Linq;
using System.ServiceModel;
using System.Text;
using System.Threading.Tasks;

namespace NorthwindSolution.Contracts {
    [ServiceContract(Namespace = "http://services.devleap.com/Northwind/Customers")]
    public interface ICustomersService {
        [OperationContract(Action =
        "http://services.devleap.com/Northwind/Customers/GetCustomer")]
        Customer GetCustomer(String customerId);

        [OperationContract(Action =
        "http://services.devleap.com/Northwind/Customers/ListCustomers")]
        List<Customer> ListCustomers();
    }
}
```

In the previous procedure about leveraging Entity Framework 5 in the data layer, you defined the *Customer* type.

The *ServiceContract* and *OperationContract* attributes declare that the interface defines a new service interface, whereas the methods are the operations of the service interface.

> **Note** If you are not familiar with WCF, the authors recommend reading *Learning WCF* by Michele Leroux Bustamante, published by O'Reilly, or *Windows Communication Foundation 4 Step by Step* by John Sharp, published by Microsoft Press.

8. Add another new class library project to the solution in the same way you did in steps 2 through 5. Name this new project **NorthwindSolution.Services**.

9. In Solution Explorer, right-click the class library project item you have just created and select Add Reference. In the Solution group of references, add the NorthwindSolution.Contracts project.

10. In Solution Explorer, right-click the NorthwindSolution.Services project item you just created and select Manage NuGet Packages.

11. In the Manage NuGet Packages dialog box, select EntityFramework (version 5.0.0) under the group NuGet Official Package Source in the Online group. Click Install, and then, after installation has completed successfully, click Close.

12. In Solution Explorer, right-click the Class1.cs file defined in the project you just created and select Rename. Rename the file **CustomersService.cs**. When prompted by Visual Studio, confirm that you also want to rename the class. Open the CustomersService.cs file and replace its code with the following:

```
using NorthwindSolution.DataLayer;
using NorthwindSolution.Contracts;
using System;
using System.Collections.Generic;
using System.Linq;
using System.Text;
using System.Threading.Tasks;

namespace NorthwindSolution.Services {
    public class CustomersService : ICustomersService {

        public Customer GetCustomer(string customerId) {
            NorthwindEntities nw = new NorthwindEntities();
            return (nw.Customers.FirstOrDefault(c => c.CustomerID == customerId));
        }

        public List<Customer> ListCustomers() {
            NorthwindEntities nw = new NorthwindEntities();
            return (nw.Customers.ToList());
        }
    }
}
```

Again, the *Customer* type is the same one you defined in the previous procedure about leveraging Entity Framework 5 in the data layer. As you can see, the service implementation simply invokes the data layer on the back end.

Note In a real solution, you will probably have a business layer in the middle, between the data layer and the service definition, that implements custom business logic, security, validation, and other aspects needed in modern software architectures. To keep it simple, this example has a short circuit between the service implementation and the underlying data layer.

13. Right-click the solution item in Solution Explorer and select Add | New Web Project. Choose ASP.NET Empty Web Site from the list of installed templates in the Visual C# group. Keep version 4.5 as the Microsoft .NET Framework target version.

14. Name the website project **NorthwindSolution.WebHost**, and then choose a location on your file system. When you've finished, click OK. If Visual Studio 2012 asks if you want to create the target folder, click Yes.

15. In Solution Explorer, right-click the website project item you just created and select Add Reference. In the Assemblies group of references, select the assemblies System.ServiceModel and System.Runtime.Serialization.

16. In Solution Explorer, right-click the website project item you just created and select Add Reference. In the Solution group of references, select NorthwindSolution.DataLayer, NorthwindSolution.Contracts, and NorthwindSolution.Services.

17. In Solution Explorer, right-click the website project item again, and select Manage NuGet Packages. In the subsequent window, select EntityFramework (version 5.0.0) under the group NuGet Official Package Source in the Online group. Select Install | Close.

18. Right-click the website project in Solution Explorer and select Add | Add New Item. In the Add New Item window, select the WCF Service code template. Name the new file **CustomersService.svc**.

19. Remove the files created under the App_Code folder of the website project, keeping only the CustomersService.svc file.

> **Note** It is better to separate contracts, implementations, and endpoints into different assemblies, rather than mixing all of them into a single website project. Thus, you will remove the code autogenerated by Visual Studio 2012 to create a well-layered and organized solution.

20. Double-click CustomersService.svc to open the file and replace its code with the following:

```
<%@ ServiceHost Language="C#" Debug="true"
      Service="NorthwindSolution.Services.CustomersService" %>
```

The *CodeBehind* attribute has been removed because the code of the service in this exercise is not behind the .svc file but is compiled in the *NorthwindSolution.Services* assembly. The value of the *Service* attribute has been changed, providing the full name of the *CustomersService* class you created in step 12.

21. Rebuild the entire solution (Ctrl+Shift+B) and then right-click CustomersService.svc in Solution Explorer. Select View in Browser. You will see, in your default browser, the welcome page of the WCF service you've just created. The sample page is shown in the following image.

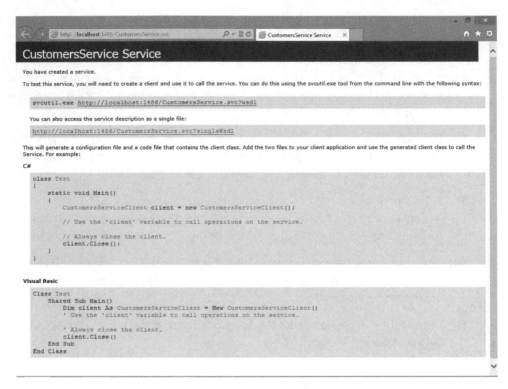

Later in this chapter, you will consume this service from a Windows 8 app.

Implementing the communication layer using an OData service

In this section, you will learn how to implement a simple OData service, which is functionally equivalent to the SOAP service you created in the previous procedure. You should consider that an OData service still uses WCF in its infrastructure, simply leveraging a specific set of communication contracts and behaviors.

Implement an OData service to consume from C#

In this procedure, you will create an OData service for publishing the previously defined data layer.

1. Open the solution *NorthwindSolution* you created in the previous exercise, when you implemented the data layer with Entity Framework 5.

2. Right-click the website project NorthwindSolution.WebHost in Solution Explorer and select Add | Add New Item. In the Add New Item window, select the WCF Data Service code template. Name the new file **CustomersDataService.svc**.

3. Under the App_Code folder of the website project, open CustomersDataService.cs and replace the class declaration with the following line of code:

```
public class CustomersDataService :
    DataService<NorthwindSolution.DataLayer.NorthwindEntities>
```

The *DataService<T>* base class that the *CustomersDataService* type inherits from is part of the .NET Framework and provides all the basic infrastructure to publish an OData service based on a generic type *T*, which has to be a class publishing one or more collections of entities implementing a specific interface named *IQueryable*. The *NorthwindEntities* class created while defining the data layer adheres to these requirements and can be used to publish the collection of entities of type *Customer* directly.

4. Replace the entire code for the *CustomerDataService* class with the following code:

```
public class CustomersDataService :
    DataService<NorthwindSolution.DataLayer.NorthwindEntities> {
    public static void InitializeService(DataServiceConfiguration config) {
        config.SetEntitySetAccessRule("Customers", EntitySetRights.AllRead);
        config.DataServiceBehavior.MaxProtocolVersion = DataServiceProtocolVersion.V3;
    }
}
```

The preceding bold code shows what to change in the body of the *InitializeService* method. The first line of code inside the *InitializeService* method declares that the *Customer* entity provided by the *NorthwindEntities* model will be read-only accessible by everybody. Table 10-1 lists all the available values for the *EntitySetRights* enumeration. The second line of code, still in *InitializeService*, defines that the OData service will be capable of talking with external consumers using version 1, 2, or 3 of the protocol.

TABLE 10-1 List of permissions available for configuring entity set rights

Value	Description
None	Denial of all rights to access data
ReadSingle	Authorization to read single data items
ReadMultiple	Authorization to read sets of data
AllRead	Authorization to read any data
WriteAppend	Authorization to create new data items in data sets
WriteReplace	Authorization to replace data
WriteDelete	Authorization to delete data items from data sets
WriteMerge	Authorization to merge data
AllWrite	Authorization to write any data
All	Authorization to create, read, update, and delete data

5. Open the web.config file of the website project and configure the connection string to the SQL Server database under the covers of the *NorthwindEntities* model. You can copy the connection string configuration from the App.config file available in the *NorthwindSolution.DataLayer* project. Copy the following code from the App.config file and paste it in the web.config file:

```
<connectionStrings>
    <add name="NorthwindEntities" connectionString="metadata=res://*/NorthwindModel.
            csdl|res://*/NorthwindModel.ssdl|res://*/NorthwindModel.msl;provider=
            System.Data.SqlClient;provider connection string=&quot;datasource=.;initial
            catalog=Northwind;integrated security=True;MultipleActiveResultSets=True;
            App=EntityFramework&quot;" providerName="System.Data.EntityClient" />
</connectionStrings>
```

6. Rebuild the entire solution (Ctrl+Shift+B) and then right-click CustomersDataService.svc in Solution Explorer. Select View in Browser. As in the previous procedure, in your default browser you will see the welcome page of the OData service you've just created. In this case, the welcome page will be an XML document declaring the entities published by the service. The XML document will look like the following code excerpt:

```
<?xml version="1.0" encoding="utf-8"?>
<service xml:base="http://localhost:1486/CustomersDataService.svc/"
      xmlns="http://www.w3.org/2007/app" xmlns:atom="http://www.w3.org/2005/Atom">
  <workspace>
    <atom:title>Default</atom:title>
    <collection href="Customers">
      <atom:title>Customers</atom:title>
    </collection>
  </workspace>
</service>
```

7. Try to navigate to the service URL *http://localhost:1486/CustomersDataService.svc/* by adding **Customers** at the end of the URL. The URL to navigate in this example is *http://localhost:1486/CustomersDataService.svc/Customers*. The result is shown in the following screen shot. As you can see, the result looks like an RSS feed.

8. To look at the XML under the covers, you need to change the default configuration for Microsoft Internet Explorer. Open Internet Explorer and select Tools | Internet Options. Click the Content tab of the Internet Options window. Click Settings under Feed and Web Slices. Clear the Turn on Feed Reading View option when you are prompted. For further details, see the following image.

9. Click OK, and then click OK again. Now request the page again from the previously specified URL. You should see something like the following image.

As you can see, the result is an RSS feed with an entry item for each *Customer* entity in the collection of *Customers* published by the OData service. If you want to access a specific customer instance, you can use a direct access URL by providing the *CustomerID* as a selection key in the URL. In the XML shown in the browser, you can see that every entry element has an *id* child element that contains a

URL. Copy the URL for any customer entry into the address bar of your browser and the request will return XML that defines that single customer instance. The result should look something like the following XML:

```
<?xml version="1.0" encoding="utf-8" ?>
<entry xml:base="http://localhost:1486/CustomersDataService.svc/"
    xmlns="http://www.w3.org/2005/Atom" xmlns:d="http://schemas.microsoft.com/ado/2007/08/
    dataservices" xmlns:m="http://schemas.microsoft.com/ado/2007/08/dataservices/metadata">
 <id>http://localhost:1486/CustomersDataService.svc/Customers('ALFKI')</id>
 <category  term="NorthwindModel.Customer"
     scheme="http://schemas.microsoft.com/ado/2007/08/dataservices/scheme" />
 <link  rel="edit" title="Customer" href="Customers('ALFKI')" />
 <title />
 <updated>2012-09-02T17:20:50Z</updated>
 <author>
   <name />
 </author>
 <content type="application/xml">
 <m:properties>
    <d:CustomerID>ALFKI</d:CustomerID>
    <d:CompanyName>Alfreds Futterkiste</d:CompanyName>
    <d:ContactName>Maria Anders</d:ContactName>
    <d:ContactTitle>Sales Representative</d:ContactTitle>
    <d:Address>Obere Str. 57</d:Address>
    <d:City>Berlin</d:City>
    <d:Region  m:null="true" />
    <d:PostalCode>12209</d:PostalCode>
    <d:Country>Germany</d:Country>
    <d:Phone>030-0074321</d:Phone>
    <d:Fax>030-0076545</d:Fax>
 </m:properties>
 </content>
</entry>
```

Under the *m:properties* element, you can see the list of data properties for the current customer. In the next section, you will learn how to consume this data from a Windows 8 app.

Consuming data from a Windows 8 app

Now you are ready to consume the already implemented services from a Windows 8 app. First, you need to create the app by completing the following procedure.

Implement a Windows 8 app to consume the SOAP service

1. Open the solution *NorthwindSolution* you created in the previous exercise, when you implemented the data layer with Entity Framework 5.

2. Right-click the solution item in Solution Explorer and select Add | New Project. Choose Windows Store from the list of installed templates in the Visual C# group, and then select Grid App (XAML), keeping version 4.5 as the Microsoft .NET Framework target version.

3. Name the class library project **NorthwindSolution.SOAPClientApp**, and then choose a location on your file system. When you've finished, click OK.

4. In Solution Explorer, right-click the NorthwindSolution.SOAPClientApp project item you just created and select Add Service Reference. In the Add Service Reference window, insert the URL of the CustomersService.svc service file you created earlier in the procedure "Implement a SOAP service to consume from C#." In this case, the URL is *http://localhost:1486/CustomersService.svc*, but in your example the port number could be different. Click Go. You will see the definition of *CustomersService*. In the lower side of the window, provide a value of **CustomersServiceReference** for the Namespace property and click OK.

5. Double-click the Package.appxmanifest file of the new app. Click the Packaging tab and provide a suitable value for the Package Name property. For example, you might use the value **NorthwindSoapApp**.

6. Right-click the NorthwindSolution.SOAPClientApp project and select Debug | Start New Instance. The app will start and you will see a grid of fake items, grouped into multiple fake groups. Close the app by pressing Alt+F4 or stopping the debugger in Visual Studio 2012.

7. Expand the DataModel folder of the *NorthwindSolution.SOAPClientApp* project and rename the SampleDataSource.cs file to **NorthwindDataSource.cs**. Next, you'll rename *SampleDataSource* to **NorthwindDataSource**, both in code and text. To complete that task, right-click the class name and select Refactor | Rename. Type the new name and select Search in Strings. When you get to the preview window, click Apply.

   This code file contains all the client-side logic to manage the behind-the-scenes data model of a Windows 8 app. The *SampleDataSource* class represents the entry point for the data source. The *SampleDataCommon* type is the base class for every data item. The *SampleDataItem* type defines a single data item. Lastly, the *SampleDataGroup* type declares the groups of items.

8. Using the same approach as described in step 7, rename the *SampleDataItem* type to **CustomerDataItem**, the *SampleDataCommon* type to **NorthwindDataCommon**, and the *SampleDataGroup* type to **CustomersDataGroup**.

9. Insert the following code, just after the default constructor of the *NorthwindDataSource* type.

```
private String[] shadowedFaces = new String[] {
    "shadow-black-face",
    "shadow-blue-face",
    "shadow-orange-face",
    "shadow-red-face",
};

private async void populateDataSource() {
    CustomersServiceReference.CustomersServiceClient nw =
        new CustomersServiceReference.CustomersServiceClient();

    var customers = await nw.ListCustomersAsync();
```

```
String fakeCustomerContent = "Lorem ipsum dolor sit amet, consectetur adipiscing
        elit. Vivamus tempor scelerisque lorem in vehicula. Aliquam tincidunt, lacus
        ut sagittis tristique, turpis massa volutpat augue, eu rutrum ligula ante a
        ante";
String previousCountry = String.Empty;
CustomersDataGroup group = null;

// Create a random number generator
Random rnd = new Random(DateTime.Now.Second);

foreach (var c in customers.OrderBy(c => c.Country)) {
    // Check if I need to create a new group
    if (previousCountry != c.Country) {

        // Add the previous group
        if (group != null) this.AllGroups.Add(group);

        // Create the new group
        group = new CustomersDataGroup(c.Country,
            c.Country,
            String.Format("Customers from: {0}", c.Country),
            "Assets/LightGray.png",
            String.Empty);
    }

    // Add the current customer to the current group
    group.Items.Add(new CustomerDataItem(c.CustomerID,
        c.ContactName,
        c.CompanyName,
        String.Format("Assets/{0}.png", shadowedFaces[rnd.Next() % 4]),
        String.Format("{0} {1} working at {2}", c.ContactTitle,
            c.ContactName, c.CompanyName),
        fakeCustomerContent,
        group));

    // Set the previous country
    previousCountry = c.Country;
    }
}
```

This new code downloads the list of customers asynchronously from the external SOAP service and puts them into a collection of *CustomerDataItem*s, grouped by *Country*, where groups will be based on the *CustomersDataGroup* type. To better understand the asynchronous behavior, review Chapter 8, "Asynchronous patterns."

10. Replace the default constructor code of the *NorthwindDataSource* type with the following:

```
public NorthwindDataSource() {
    populateDataSource();
}
```

11. Add the following files (available in the sample code for this book in the Ch10 folder) into the Assets folder of your Windows 8 app project: shadow-black-face.png, shadow-blue-face.png, shadow-orange-face.png, and shadow-red-face.png.

12. Rebuild the entire solution (Ctrl+Shift+B) and then execute the app.

Now you can play with your new Windows 8 app, navigating backward and forward through the countries and customers, and consuming data from the SOAP external service.

Moreover, you can create a similar app that consumes an OData service instead, which you'll do in the next procedure.

Implement a Windows 8 app to consume the OData service

 Note To consume an OData service from a Windows 8 app, you need to download and install the OData Client Tools for Windows Store Apps from *http://msdn.microsoft.com/jj658961*.

1. Open the solution *NorthwindSolution* you created in the previous exercise, when you implemented the data layer with Entity Framework 5.

2. Right-click the solution item in Solution Explorer and select Add | New Project. Choose Windows Store from the list of installed templates in Visual C# group, and then select Grid App (XAML). Keep version 4.5 as the Microsoft .NET Framework target version.

3. Name the class library project **NorthwindSolution.ODataClientApp**, and then choose a location on your file system. When you've finished, click OK.

4. In Solution Explorer, right-click the NorthwindSolution.ODataClientApp project you just created and select Add Service Reference. In the Add Service Reference window, insert the URL of the CustomersDataService.svc service file you previously created in the procedure "Implement an OData service to consume from C#." In this case, the URL is *http://localhost:1486/ CustomersDataService.svc*, but in your example the port number could be different. Click Go. You will see the definition of *CustomersDataService*. In the lower side of the window, provide a value of **CustomersDataServiceReference** for the Namespace property and click OK. Note that the previously mentioned installation of the OData Client Tools for Windows Store Apps is mandatory in order to complete this step.

5. Double-click the Package.appxmanifest file of the app project. Click the Packaging tab and provide a suitable value for the Package Name property. For example, you might use the value **NorthwindODataApp**.

6. Right-click the NorthwindSolution.ODataClientApp project and select Debug | Start New Instance. The app will start and you will see a grid of fake items, grouped into multiple fake groups. Close the app by pressing Alt+F4 or stopping the debugger in Visual Studio 2012.

   Expand the DataModel folder of the *NorthwindSolution.ODataClientApp* project and rename the SampleDataSource.cs file as **NorthwindDataSource.cs**. Next, rename the *SampleDataSource* type to **NorthwindDataSource**, both in code and text. To complete that task, right-click the class name and select Refactor | Rename. Provide the new name and select Search in Strings. On the preview window, click Apply.

This code file contains all the client-side logic to manage the data model behind the scenes of the Windows 8 app. The *SampleDataSource* class represents the entry point for the data source. The *SampleDataCommon* type is the base class for every data item. The *SampleDataItem* type defines a single data item. Lastly, the *SampleDataGroup* type declares the groups of items.

7. As you did in step 6, rename the *SampleDataItem* type to **CustomerDataItem**, the *SampleDataCommon* type to **NorthwindDataCommon**, and the *SampleDataGroup* type to **CustomersDataGroup**.

8. Insert the following code, just after the default constructor of the *NorthwindDataSource* type.

```
private String[] shadowedFaces = new String[] {
    "shadow-black-face",
    "shadow-blue-face",
    "shadow-orange-face",
    "shadow-red-face",
};

private DataServiceCollection<Customer> customers = null;

private void populateDataSource() {
    CustomersDataServiceReference.NorthwindEntities nw =
        new CustomersDataServiceReference.NorthwindEntities(
            new Uri("http://localhost:1486/CustomersDataService.svc/"));

    customers = new DataServiceCollection<Customer>(nw);
    customers.LoadCompleted += customers_LoadCompleted;
    customers.LoadAsync(
        from c in nw.Customers
        orderby c.Country
        select c);
}

async void customers_LoadCompleted(object sender, LoadCompletedEventArgs e) {

    if (e.Error != null) {
        MessageDialog errorDialog = new MessageDialog(
            e.Error.Message, "An error occurred!");
        await errorDialog.ShowAsync();
    }
    String fakeCustomerContent = "Lorem ipsum dolor sit amet, consectetur adipiscing
            elit. Vivamus tempor scelerisque lorem in vehicula. Aliquam tincidunt, lacus
            ut sagittis tristique, turpis massa volutpat augue, eu rutrum ligula ante a
            ante";
    String previousCountry = String.Empty;
    CustomersDataGroup group = null;

    // Create a random number generator
    Random rnd = new Random(DateTime.Now.Second);

    foreach (Customer c in customers) {
```

```
        // Check if I need to create a new group
        if (previousCountry != c.Country) {
            // Add the previous group
            if (group != null) this.AllGroups.Add(group);

            // Create the new group
            group = new CustomersDataGroup(c.Country,
                c.Country,
                String.Format("Customers from: {0}", c.Country),
                "Assets/LightGray.png",
                String.Empty);
        }

        // Add the current customer to the current group
        group.Items.Add(new CustomerDataItem(c.CustomerID,
            c.ContactName,
            c.CompanyName,
            String.Format("Assets/{0}.png", shadowedFaces[rnd.Next() % 4]),
            String.Format("{0} {1} working at {2}", c.ContactTitle,
                c.ContactName, c.CompanyName),
            fakeCustomerContent,
            group));

        // Set the previous country
        previousCountry = c.Country;
    }
}
```

9. This new code downloads the list of customers asynchronously from the external OData
    service. Take note of the variable of type *DataServiceCollection<T>*, which will hold the results
    of the query executed by the external OData service. Also notice the error handling in the
    customers_LoadCompleted method implementation. If any communication exception occurs,
    the app will display a dialog box containing the error message that occurred through a
    MessageDialog type instance.

10. Replace the default constructor code of the *NorthwindDataSource* type with the following
    code:

```
public NorthwindDataSource() {
    populateDataSource();
}
```

11. Add the following files (available in the sample code for this book in the Ch10 folder) into the
    Assets folder of the Windows 8 app project: shadow-black-face.png, shadow-blue-face.png,
    shadow-orange-face.png, shadow red-face.png.

12. Rebuild the entire solution (Ctrl+Shift+B) and then execute the app. The result will be almost
    identical to the one shown in the screen shot near the end of the previous procedure.

Implementing an app storage/cache

In the previous sections, you saw how to publish and consume data from a Windows 8 app. However, as stated at the beginning of this chapter, there are many times when you also need to manage temporary data and look up and reference data. Also, many situations require working while offline, using some kind of offline cache. For example, imagine that you want to cache the entire list of customers locally, so that users can navigate through them even when offline. In a real solution, you should carefully consider caching such data because a list of customers could become very large and consume many resources. In a real solution, it might be best to cache only active customers or customers who are a target for the current user. Nevertheless, because this is just an example, and for simplicity's sake, in this section you will cache the entire customer list.

First, you need to understand the tools available to cache data locally in a Windows 8 app. WinRT provides a *Windows.Storage* WinMD library and a corresponding namespace that contains a bunch of types for managing local, remote, and temporary storage. All these storage types work the same way and share the same behavior by implementing the same basic types. For example, if you want to save a setting locally from a Windows 8 app, you can use code like the following:

```
Windows.Storage.ApplicationData.Current
    .LocalSettings.Values["LastExecutionDateTime"] = DateTime.Now.ToString();
```

Under the covers, this simple line of code saves a local copy of a variable with the name *LastExecutionDateTime* and a value corresponding to the current date and time.

To read a value you saved previously in this way, you use code like this:

```
Object lastExecutionDateTimeValue;
if (Windows.Storage.ApplicationData.Current
    .LocalSettings.Values.TryGetValue("LastExecutionDateTime",
        out lastExecutionDateTimeValue)) {
            String lastExecutionDateTime = lastExecutionDateTimeValue.ToString();
}
```

Notice that the name of each setting is limited to 255 characters. Each setting value can be up to 8 KB in size, and each composite setting can be up to 64 KB in size.

Moreover, if you want to save the same settings on remote storage, based on a roaming profile linked to the Windows Live ID account of the current user, you can replace the *LocalSettings* property of the current *ApplicationData* class with the *RoamingSettings* property. Again, the following code excerpt shows how to save a value into the user's roaming profile, which can be shared across multiple machines based on the user's Live ID account:

```
Windows.Storage.ApplicationData.Current
    .RoamingSettings.Values["LastExecutionDateTime"] = DateTime.Now.ToString();
```

This code retrieves the value from the roaming profile:

```
Object lastExecutionDateTimeValue;
if (Windows.Storage.ApplicationData.Current
    .RoamingSettings.Values.TryGetValue("LastExecutionDateTime",
        out lastExecutionDateTimeValue)) {
                String lastExecutionDateTime = lastExecutionDateTimeValue.ToString();
}
```

Note that the *RoamingSettings* storage has the same size and property naming limitations as the *LocalSettings* storage.

Due to the size limitations when saving values, you cannot rely on this feature to persist a large set of data. However, the *ApplicationData* class also provides access to a virtual file system, which is almost like the isolated storage available in prior versions of Windows.

In fact, the *ApplicationData* class provides a *LocalFolder* property that retrieves the root folder of the local app data store. Conveniently, it now also provides a *RoamingFolder* property, which corresponds to the root folder of a roaming app data store. To create a file in these folders, you simply need to leverage the available WinRT API. In fact, both the *LocalFolder* and *RoamingFolder* properties are implementations of the *StorageFolder* type. Through this type, you can open, create, update, rename, or delete a file or a subfolder, with up to 32 nesting levels for folders.

For example, the following excerpt shows the code behind the click event of a button that creates an XML file with an empty element inside:

```
private async void WriteLocalStorageFile_Click(object sender, RoutedEventArgs e) {
    var file = await Windows.Storage.ApplicationData.Current
        .LocalFolder.CreateFileAsync("SampleFile.xml",
        Windows.Storage.CreationCollisionOption.ReplaceExisting);

    using (var stream = await file.OpenStreamForWriteAsync()) {
        XElement x = new XElement("EmptyLocalXmlFile");
        x.Save(stream);
        await stream.FlushAsync();
    }
}
```

The following code example shows how to retrieve the file stored by the preceding code and how to read its contents:

```
private async void ReadLocalStorageFile_Click(object sender, RoutedEventArgs e) {
    var file = await Windows.Storage.ApplicationData.Current
        .LocalFolder.GetFileAsync("SampleFile.xml");

    using (var stream = await file.OpenStreamForReadAsync()) {
        XElement x = XElement.Load(stream);
        OutputText.Text = x.ToString();
    }
}
```

Roaming storage has a storage quota restriction of 100 KB for each app, as you can see by checking the *ApplicationData.RoamingStorageQuota* property. If your roaming data exceeds that quota, it won't roam until its size is less than the quota again. Also notice that roaming application data is not intended for simultaneous use by applications on more than one device at a time. If a concurrency conflict occurs, the system always favors the value that was written last.

One last option you have is to use the *TemporaryFolder* property, which is again available through *ApplicationData* and behaves exactly like the *LocalFolder* and *RoamingFolder* properties because it inherits from the same type (*StorageFolder*). However, WinRT can delete the content of the *TemporaryFolder* property at any time, so you should not use it to store critical data.

Lastly, consider that the storage options available for a Windows 8 app are tied to the lifetime of the app. Therefore, if you remove an app, its local, roaming, and temporary data will also be removed. Therefore, if you want to keep contents and files independent of any particular app's lifetime, you should rely on the user's libraries (Documents, Pictures, and so on) or Microsoft SkyDrive.

Cache data in a Windows 8 app

1. Open the solution *NorthwindSolution* you used in the previous exercises.

2. Open the *NorthwindSolution.SOAPClientApp* project and edit the code of the NorthwindDataSource.cs file, under the DataModel folder.

3. At the very top of the file, add the following *using* statements:

```
using Windows.Networking.Connectivity;
using System.IO;
using System.Runtime.Serialization;
```

4. Replace the first two lines of code of the *populateDataSource* method implementation with the following code:

```
private async void populateDataSource() {
    ObservableCollection<CustomersServiceReference.Customer> customers = null;

    ConnectionProfile internetProfile =
        NetworkInformation.GetInternetConnectionProfile();


    // In case there is no internet connectivity
    if (internetProfile == null || internetProfile.GetNetworkConnectivityLevel() ==
        NetworkConnectivityLevel.None) {

        // Load the customers from an XML file saved in the local app storage
        var customersXmlFile = await Windows.Storage.ApplicationData.Current
            .LocalFolder.GetFileAsync("Customers.xml");
```

```
        using (var stream = await customersXmlFile.OpenStreamForReadAsync()) {
            DataContractSerializer dcs = new DataContractSerializer(typeof(
                ObservableCollection<CustomersServiceReference.Customer>));
            customers = dcs.ReadObject(stream) as
                ObservableCollection<CustomersServiceReference.Customer>;
        }
    }
    else {

        // Otherwise load the customers from the remote SOAP service
        CustomersServiceReference.CustomersServiceClient nw =
            new CustomersServiceReference.CustomersServiceClient();

        customers = await nw.ListCustomersAsync();

        // Save the customers into an XML file
        var customersXmlFile = await Windows.Storage.ApplicationData.Current
            .LocalFolder.CreateFileAsync("Customers.xml",
                Windows.Storage.CreationCollisionOption.ReplaceExisting);

        using (var stream = await customersXmlFile.OpenStreamForWriteAsync()) {
            DataContractSerializer dcs = new DataContractSerializer(typeof(
                ObservableCollection<CustomersServiceReference.Customer>));
            dcs.WriteObject(stream, customers);
        }
    }

    // Code omitted for the sake of brevity ...
}
```

5. As you can see, the code checks whether there is an Internet connection available and if it is active by using the *NetworkInformation* type. When there is connectivity, the code invokes the remote SOAP service. Otherwise, if there's no Internet connectivity, it will try to use an XML file saved in the local app storage, if present. For the sake of simplicity, the code illustrated in this exercise does not handle any type of exception and does not check whether the file exists prior to accessing it.

6. Rebuild the entire solution (Ctrl+Shift+B), and then execute the project *NorthwindSolution. SOAPClientApp*, first with network connectivity enabled and then with network connectivity disabled. To check the behavior of the local app storage cache, insert a breakpoint at the very beginning of the *populateDataSource* method.

SOAP security infrastructure

One last fundamental layer to implement in a solid and reliable architecture is the security infrastructure. You should manage both authentication and authorization tasks through this layer. The authorization topic is beyond the scope of this chapter because the authorization infrastructure should be implemented on the service/server side. However, authentication is a key topic for the app you are implementing. In fact, regardless of the authorization policies you will apply on the service side, your app's users will have to authenticate while using the app.

Let's start by considering the SOAP service. Depending on the target deployment and the target users of your Windows 8 app, you have multiple authentication options. For example, if your app targets users of a Windows 8 domain, you could leverage integrated Windows authentication for free. You simply need to change the binding configuration when publishing the SOAP service.

From a WCF perspective, the binding is the set of transport, encoding, security, and infrastructural layers involved in the communication pipeline that receives or sends messages across the wire. By default, a WCF service published through an ASP.NET website over HTTP will use a binding called *basicHttpBinding*, which leverages a set of configurations compliant with the Web Services Interoperability Organization (WS-I) Basic Profile specification.

By default, *basicHttpBinding* relies on transport-level security, which means HTTPS, to satisfy confidentiality and integrity requirements. Optionally, you can also leverage HTTP authentication (Basic, Digest, NTLM, Windows, and Certificate) at the transport level. Another available option while working with *basicHttpBinding* is to configure the *TransportWithMessageCredentials* configuration, which means using HTTPS for confidentiality and integrity together with a WS-Security authentication SOAP header for handling the client's authentication. In that case, authentication can be based on a set of user names and passwords. Exploring all the available security configurations available on the service side is beyond the scope of this book. Only the most useful and most frequently used authentication options, from a Windows 8 app perspective, are covered here. For further details about all the available bindings and security options available while developing a WCF service, you can read the article "Windows Communication Foundation Security" on MSDN: *http://msdn.microsoft.com/ms732362.aspx*.

From a service-side viewpoint, you could also leverage many other bindings, even those that are more secure and affordable and still HTTP based, such as *wsHttpBinding*, *wsFederationHttpBinding*, and so on. Nevertheless, the WinRT client profile allows you to use only *basicHttpBinding* as the HTTP-based binding. Alternatively, you can publish your service using the *netTcpBinding* binding over a custom WCF-specific TCP protocol. However, in that case, you would need to open communication between your Windows 8 app and the service layer across TCP ports that are not guaranteed to be open on every network and through every firewall.

To configure the binding of the service to support authentication, you simply need to change the web.config file of the website publishing the service. You may also need to refresh the service reference on the consumer side, depending on the configuration changes you make.

Enable *basicHttpBinding* with *TransportWithMessageCredentials*

1. Open the solution *NorthwindSolution* you used in the previous exercises.

2. Open the *NorthwindSolution.WebHost* website project and edit the content of the web.config file by adding the following XML excerpt as a child of the *system.serviceModel* element.

```
<bindings>
  <basicHttpBinding>
    <binding>
      <security mode="TransportWithMessageCredential">
        <message clientCredentialType="UserName" />
      </security>
    </binding>
  </basicHttpBinding>
</bindings>
```

3. This custom configuration instructs WCF to enforce transport-level security (HTTPS) with the user name and password transferred within a SOAP header, for the default binding based on *basicHttpBinding*.

4. Click the NorthwindSolution.WebHost website project and change the value of SSL Enabled to a value of True in the project property grid. In fact, you cannot publish a WCF service declaring that you want transport-level security unless you effectively publish it through HTTPS.

5. Right-click CustomersService.svc in Solution Explorer and select View in Browser. You will see, in your default browser, the welcome page of the WCF service. By clicking the link to the Web Services Description Language (WSDL) file, you will see that the WSDL of the service is now more complex than before. The augmented complexity is derived from the presence of a bunch of new XML elements describing the WS-SecurityPolicy aspects.

Consume the SOAP service with user name and password authentication

1. Open the solution *NorthwindSolution* you used in the previous exercises.

2. Open the *NorthwindSolution.SOAPClientApp* project and right-click CustomersServiceReference, available under the Service References folder. Select Update Service Reference. Through this action, Visual Studio 2012 will reload the WSDL and update the autogenerated code of the service consumer.

3. Open the DataModel folder of the *NorthwindSolution.SOAPClientApp* project and edit the NorthwindDataSource.cs file by adding the following lines of code in the *populateDataSource* method, just after the code that creates a new instance of the *CustomerServiceClient* class:

```
CustomersServiceReference.CustomersServiceClient nw =
    new CustomersServiceReference.CustomersServiceClient();

nw.ClientCredentials.UserName.UserName = "Paolo.Pialorsi";
nw.ClientCredentials.UserName.Password = "Pass@word1!";
```

As you can see, the code simply configures the user name and the password that will be used by the SOAP client to authenticate against the service. In your testing environment, you will need to provide the user name and the password of an existing user, defined either in the local development machine or in the Active Directory domain. Of course, in a real software solution, you should ask for the user name and password through a specific user interface instead of storing them in the code of the app.

4. Rebuild the entire solution (Ctrl+Shift+B) and then execute the project *NorthwindSolution. SOAPClientApp*. You will see an exception because IIS Express used under the covers of the website project is using a self-issued SSL certificate, which is not trusted by your Windows 8 app. You can experience the issue by using Internet Explorer to browse the URL of the service, using the SSL endpoint. By default, IIS Express uses the 44300 port to publish over SSL. In order to fix this issue, you will need to publish your service under IIS—using a trusted SSL certificate—or you could replace the self-issued certificate used by IIS Express with a trusted certificate. The final option you have is to trust the self-publisher used by IIS Express to emit the self-issued certificate.

5. Launch the Microsoft Management Console (MMC) tool by pressing Windows+Q and typing **MMC** in the search box. Right-click the mmc.exe application resulting from the search and select Run as Administrator. Click Yes in response to the security question. Under the File menu of the MMC console, select the menu item Add/Remove Snap-in. In the dialog box, select Certificates on the left and click Add. In the next step of the wizard, select Computer Account | Local Computer. Click Finish and then click OK.

6. Under the Personal Certificates folder you will find a certificate named localhost. Double-click it. On the Certification Path tab, check that this is the certificate self-issued by IIS Express. Click OK.

7. Right-click the localhost certificate and select All Tasks | Export. In the wizard, select to not export the private key. Then, elect to export a DER certificate file with a .cer extension. In the last step, provide a file name for the exported file. Click Next and then Finish.

8. Now select the Trusted Root Certification Authorities certificates folder. Right-click it and select Import. Click Next and provide the file name and path you just used for saving the localhost certificate. Choose to place the certificate in the Trusted Root Certification Authorities store. Click Next and then click Finish.

9. Use Internet Explorer to browse to the service URL published under SSL. You will see that the service URL is trusted by the browser.

10. Place a breakpoint in the *ListCustomers* method of the service implementation, which is inside the CustomersService.cs file in the *NorthwindSolution.Services* class library project. Restart your client app in debug mode, debugging the web host project. To debug the host project,

open the Debug menu in Visual Studio 2012 and select Attach to Process to attach the IISExpress.exe process. As soon as you invoke the service, the debugger will hit the breakpoint. By pressing Shift+F9 you will be able to inspect the contents of the *System.Threading.Thread. CurrentPrincipal* property. You will see that the *Identity.Name* property of *CurrentPrincipal* will assume a value equal to the user name you provided for authentication.

In the next procedure, you will provide the current user name and authentication method to the calling client app by using a fake customer with a *ContactName* equal to the *Identity.Name* of the calling *CurrentPrincipal*, and a *CompanyName* property with a value corresponding to the *AuthenticationType* used while securing the communication.

Validate and check the customer authentication through the SOAP service

1. Open the code of the CustomersService.cs file, defined in the *NorthwindSolution.Services* class library project.

2. Replace the code of the *ListCustomers* method with the following code:

```
public List<Customer> ListCustomers() {
    NorthwindEntities nw = new NorthwindEntities();

    List<Customer> result = nw.Customers.ToList();
    if (System.Threading.Thread.CurrentPrincipal != null &&
        System.Threading.Thread.CurrentPrincipal.Identity != null) {
        result.Add(new Customer {
            Country = "A Fake Country",
            CustomerID = "FAKE",
            ContactName = System.Threading.Thread.CurrentPrincipal.Identity.Name,
            CompanyName =
                System.Threading.Thread.CurrentPrincipal.Identity.AuthenticationType,
        });
    }
    return (result);
}
```

The code highlighted in bold inserts a fake customer at the very top of the list of customers, ordered by country. The fake customer will hold some useful information, like the currently calling user name and the authentication method used to authenticate the caller.

3. Rebuild the entire solution (Ctrl+Shift+B), and then execute *NorthwindSolution.SOAPClientApp*. The following screen shot shows a new and fake customer at the very top of the customers list.

The user name and password credentials provided by the client application can be validated, not only against a Windows directory service, but also using a custom user name and password validator. For example, you could use a custom database with a table of users and passwords, or you could even use the standard ASP.NET membership API and a classic ASPNETDB to authenticate users.

OData security infrastructure

In this last section, you will see how to enforce authentication while calling an OData service.

From a security viewpoint, an OData service is just another service channel published over HTTP/HTTPS, as is a SOAP channel. Thus, one option to secure an OData channel is to leverage the standard HTTP/HTTPS authentication techniques. For example, you could configure the web host application to use HTTP Windows Authentication. To do that in your development environment, you simply need to change the configuration of the web host application. Click the project in Solution Explorer and change the Windows Authentication option from Disabled to Enabled in the project property grid. Furthermore, you also need to disable Anonymous Authentication in order to force clients to provide credentials while consuming your services. Figure 10-2 shows a screen shot of the proper configuration for your service host.

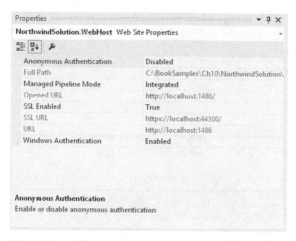

FIGURE 10-2 The property grid panel for configuring the IIS Express bindings of the current web service app.

From a Windows 8 app consumer perspective, you will only need to configure the *Credentials* property to a suitable set of credentials, which can be the current user credentials taken from the *CredentialCache* object of .NET or a specific set of credentials defined using a dedicated instance of the *System.Net.NetworkCredential* type. In the following lines of code, you can see both options:

```
nw.Credentials = System.Net.CredentialCache.DefaultCredentials;

nw.Credentials = new System.Net.NetworkCredentials(
    "Paolo.Pialorsi", "Pass@word1!", "WIN8DEV1");
```

As shown in the previous examples, you will need to change the credentials and the machine or domain name with those in your own environment. Nevertheless, in the world of Windows 8 apps, you probably will not always have an Active Directory available for users' authentication. For instance, think about a Windows 8 app that you are offering to the world. It probably would be a better choice to allow users to authenticate using their Live ID, Facebook, or Twitter account. All these identity management systems provide support for the OAuth (*www.oauth.net*) specification.

Windows 8 apps support authentication through OAuth, or any other web-based authentication technique, leveraging the *WebAuthenticationBroker* class. This class renders a dialog box that displays the web sign-in page of the authentication platform you choose to use.

Imagine that you want your Windows 8 app to authenticate users through their Facebook accounts. The following code excerpt shows how to implement a button click event that prompts users for their Facebook account information:

```
private async void ShowLoginPage_Click(object sender, RoutedEventArgs e) {
    try {
        String FacebookURL = "https://www.facebook.com/dialog/oauth?client_id=" +
            FacebookClientID.Text + "&redirect_uri=" +
            Uri.EscapeUriString(FacebookCallbackUrl.Text) +
            "&scope=" + FacebookPermissions.Text +
            "&display=popup&response_type=token";
```

```
        System.Uri StartUri = new Uri(FacebookURL);
        System.Uri EndUri = new Uri(FacebookCallbackUrl.Text);

        WebAuthenticationResult WebAuthenticationResult =
            await WebAuthenticationBroker.AuthenticateAsync(
                WebAuthenticationOptions.None,
                StartUri,
                EndUri);

        if (WebAuthenticationResult.ResponseStatus == WebAuthenticationStatus.Success) {
            OutputToken(WebAuthenticationResult.ResponseData.ToString());
        }
        else if (WebAuthenticationResult.ResponseStatus == WebAuthenticationStatus.ErrorHttp) {
            OutputToken("HTTP Error returned by AuthenticateAsync() : " +
                WebAuthenticationResult.ResponseErrorDetail.ToString());
        }
        else {
            OutputToken("Error returned by AuthenticateAsync() : " +
                WebAuthenticationResult.ResponseStatus.ToString());
        }
    }
    catch (Exception ex) {
        MessageDialog errorDialog = new MessageDialog(
            e.Error.Message, "An error occurred!");
        await errorDialog.ShowAsync();
    }
}
```

As you can see, the code creates a URL string (the *FacebookURL* variable) corresponding to the OAuth authentication URL of Facebook. The URL must include some query string parameters, which are used to declare the *ClientID* of the Facebook app that will be associated with your Windows 8 app, as well as a callback URL that routes customers back after a valid authentication and the list of permissions required by the app.

You can find more details about the OAuth support provided by Facebook at *http://developers. facebook.com/docs/reference/dialogs/oauth/*. You can also create a *ClientID* and configure the callback URL by going to *https://developers.facebook.com/apps*. After authenticating with your Facebook account, create a new app integration. Note that the Facebook side of this story is beyond the scope of this chapter.

Additionally, the code invokes the static method *AuthenticateAsync* of the *WebAuthenticationBroker* class to start the authentication process. Figure 10-3 shows the output containing the prompt for the user.

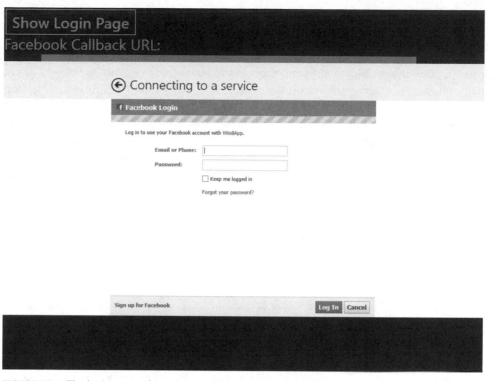

FIGURE 10-3 The login page of Facebook within the dialog box created by the *WebAuthenticationBroker* class.

As soon as the user provides a valid set of credentials, the identity management system (Facebook in this example) will ask the user for consent—allowing the Windows 8 app to access the user's profile information. Depending on the type of integration you need, you will have the capability to request information such as published posts, email, friends, or pictures.

The result of the authentication process will be a variable of type *WebAuthenticationResult* that contains a property named *WebAuthenticationStatus*, which can assume one of the following values:

- **ErrorHttp** An HTTP error occurred.

- **Success** The authentication process completed correctly.

- **UserCancel** The end user cancelled the authentication process.

If an exception occurs, you will find details in the *ResponseErrorDetail* property of the *WebAuthenticationResult* instance. For a successful login, you will find the result in the *ResponseData* property.

For Facebook authentication, you will get back a URL, which is the callback URL you originally provided, with an access token (*access_token*) parameter appended to the end of the URL, together with an expiration timeout (*expires_in*) for that token. Here's an example of the resulting URL: *http://www. devleap.com/#access_token=AAADp1Ykd5hwBAM3r0VDE9ZC9wuj9BnUdvfBdHwxz84YZCx5X8mw0v8 XwfxlJFUMv4ZAi3mls5ZARRbwpvQ67FyzrDSUcFwl5d7rnhQzpugZDZD&expires_in=6624.*

Of course, the actual URL could be different. Within your code, you should extract the value of the *access_token* parameter and use it to talk with Facebook proprietary APIs—for example, the Facebook Graph API. A thorough exploration of the Facebook APIs is beyond the scope of this chapter.

However, using the *WebAuthenticationBroker* class to authenticate against any other authentication platform, such as Microsoft Windows Azure Access Control Service (ACS), *is* within the scope of this chapter. In fact, ACS is a Windows Azure service that provides an easy way of authenticating users who need to access your web applications and services without forcing you to factor complex authentication logic into your code. You can use ACS to manage identity authentication for any of your services, including SOAP or OData. Furthermore, ACS can redirect the authentication process to any external and widely adopted identity provider such as Windows Live ID, Facebook, Google, and so forth.

Because ACS supports OAuth 2.0, you can use it to authenticate access to your services, in almost the same way you used it in the previous example while authenticating against Facebook.

Summary

In this chapter, you learned some basic information about contemporary software architectures and how they apply to a Windows 8 app. Moreover, you saw how to implement a very basic data layer based on ADO.NET Entity Framework 5. You published that data layer through both a SOAP service and an OData service. Then you consumed those services with a Windows 8 app that leveraged local storage to cache data locally. Lastly, you learned how to make secure calls to a service—whether SOAP based or OData based—using an OAuth authentication platform such as Facebook or Microsoft Windows Azure ACS.

Quick reference

To	Do this
Consume data from a Windows 8 app	Create a service reference to a SOAP service or to an OData service.
Publish a data set via OData	Create a web application and define a WCF Data Service item, publishing, for example, a model created with ADO.NET Entity Framework 5.
Cache some local data in a Windows 8 app	Use the *Windows.Storage* namespace of WinRT, leveraging the local app storage.
Share some settings/preferences across multiple devices for a single Windows Live ID account	Use the *Windows.Storage* namespace of WinRT, leveraging the roaming app storage.
Authenticate against an external web-based sign-in platform such as Facebook or ACS	Use the *WebAuthenticationBroker* class.

Index

Symbols

* character, 212
#include statement, 151, 276

A

Account picture provider extension, 24
ACK (Windows App Certification Kit), 111
ActivatableClassId key, 159
activating applications
    OnSearchActivated method, 122–124
    overview, 122
ActivationKind enumeration, 95, 118
Add-AppxDevPakage.bat file, 109
Akzidenz-Grotesk font, 32
All keyword, 100
AllowCropping property, 176
ALMEvents application, 117, 124, 126
Alt+F4 shortcut, 72
Alt+Tab shortcut
    using in Windows 8, 90
    new implementation of, 48
Always on to command, 26
Animation Library, Microsoft, 58
animations, 58
AppBar control, 265–268
app bars, Windows 8, 3, 8–10
App class, 162, 194, 266
App_Code folder, 317
App.config file, 320
Appearance property group, 215, 291
ApplicationData class, 330, 331
applications
    activating
        OnSearchActivated method, 122–124
        overview, 122

launching
    creating using C++, 114
    Kind property, 118
    OnLaunched event, 115–118
    previous execution state, 119–121
manifest, 104–106
packages, 107–110
registration for WinRT, 157–159
resuming
    debugging in Visual Studio, 132–135
    overview, 131–132
    refreshing data, 132–135
suspending
    debugging in Visual Studio, 132–135
    overview, 125
    requesting more suspension time, 129–130
    Suspending event, 127–128
    time limit for responding to suspension
        event, 128–129
    verifying suspension, 125–127
    Windows Store and, 110–114
Application UI tab, Manifest Designer, 105
ApplicationView class, 290
app variable, 189
App.xaml.cpp file, 91, 114, 122, 162, 266
App.xaml file, 69
App.xaml.h file, 91, 114
.appxsym file, 109
.appxupload file, 108
architecture
    app storage/cache
        caching data in Windows 8 app, 332–333
        overview, 330–332
    communication layer using OData service
        implementing, 318–323
        overview, 318

About the authors

LUCA REGNICOLI is a consultant, trainer, and author who has specialized in user interface technologies for .NET applications since 2003. He developed the presentation tier of many enterprise applications in Windows Presentation Foundation, Silverlight, and Windows Phone. Luca is a cofounder of DevLeap, a company focused on providing high-value content and consulting services to professional developers. He is the author of a book in Italian language about ASP.NET. He has also been a regular speaker at major conferences since 2001.

PAOLO PIALORSI is a consultant, trainer, and author who specializes in developing distributed application architectures and Microsoft SharePoint enterprise solutions. He is the author of about 10 books, including *Programming Microsoft LINQ in Microsoft .NET Framework 4* and *Microsoft SharePoint 2010 Developer Reference*. Paolo is a cofounder of DevLeap, a company focused on providing content and consulting to professional developers. He is also a popular speaker at industry conferences.

ROBERTO BRUNETTI is a consultant, trainer, and author with experience in enterprise applications since 1997. Roberto is a cofounder of DevLeap—together with Paolo Pialorsi, Marco Russo, and Luca Regnicoli—a company focused on providing high-value content and consulting services to professional developers. He is the author of a few books: one about ASP.NET, published in 2003, another about Windows Azure Beta, and the last one on Windows Azure published by Microsoft Press in 2011. He has also been a regular speaker at major conferences since 1996 and he works closely with Microsoft in events and training courses.

How To Download Your eBook

Thank you for purchasing this Microsoft Press® title. Your companion PDF eBook is ready to download from O'Reilly Media, official distributor of Microsoft Press titles.

To download your eBook, go to
http://go.microsoft.com/FWLink/?Linkid=224345
and follow the instructions.

Please note: You will be asked to create a free online account and enter the access code below.

Your access code:

NBTVBDG

Build Windows® 8 Apps with Microsoft® Visual
C++® Step by Step

Your PDF eBook allows you to:

- Search the full text
- Print
- Copy and paste

Best yet, you will be notified about free updates to your eBook.

If you ever lose your eBook file, you can download it again just by logging in to your account.

Need help? Please contact:
mspbooksupport@oreilly.com
or call 800-889-8969.

What do you think of this book?

We want to hear from you!

To participate in a brief online survey, please visit:

microsoft.com/learning/booksurvey

Tell us how well this book meets your needs—what works effectively, and what we can do better. Your feedback will help us continually improve our books and learning resources for you.

Thank you in advance for your input!